PVM: Parallel Virtual Machine

Paris Yiapanis

Scientific and Engineering Computation
Janusz Kowalik, Editor

Data-Parallel Programming on MIMD Computers
by Philip J. Hatcher and Michael J. Quinn, 1991

Unstructured Scientific Computation on Scalable Multiprocessors
edited by Piyush Mehrotra, Joel Saltz, and Robert Voigt, 1991

Parallel Computational Fluid Dynamics: Implementations and Results
edited by Horst D. Simon, 1992

Enterprise Integration Modeling: Proceedings of the First International Conference
edited by Charles J. Petrie, Jr., 1992

The High Performance Fortran Handbook
by Charles H. Koelbel, David B. Loveman, Robert S. Schreiber, Guy L. Steele Jr., and
Mary E. Zosel, 1994

Using MPI: Portable Parallel Programming with the Message-Passing Interface
by William Gropp, Ewing Lusk, and Anthony Skjellum, 1994

*PVM: Parallel Virtual Machine – A Users' Guide and Tutorial for Networked Parallel
Computing*
by Al Geist, Adam Beguelin, Jack Dongarra, Weicheng Jiang, Robert Manchek, and
Vaidy Sunderam, 1994

PVM: Parallel Virtual Machine
A Users' Guide and Tutorial for Networked Parallel Computing

Al Geist
Adam Beguelin
Jack Dongarra
Weicheng Jiang
Robert Manchek
Vaidy Sunderam

The MIT Press
Cambridge, Massachusetts
London, England

This book was set in LaTeX by the authors and was printed and bound in the United States of America.

Library of Congress Cataloging-in-Publication Data

PVM : parallel virtual machine — a users' guide and tutorial for networked parallel computing / Al Geist ... [et al].
    p.   cm. — (Scientific and engineering computation)
  Includes bibliographical references and index.
  ISBN 0-262-57108-0 (pbk. : acid-free paper)
  1. Parallel computers. 2. Computer networks. I. Geist, Al. II. Series.
QA76.58.P85   1994
005.2—dc20   94-23404
                                            CIP

This book is also available in postscript and html forms over the Internet.
To retrieve the postscript file you can use one of the following methods:

- anonymous ftp
    ```
    ftp netlib2.cs.utk.edu
    cd pvm3/book
    get pvm-book.ps
    quit
    ```

- from any machine on the Internet type:
    ```
    rcp anon@netlib2.cs.utk.edu:pvm3/book/pvm-book.ps pvm-book.ps
    ```

- sending email to `netlib@ornl.gov` and in the message type:
    ```
    send pvm-book.ps from pvm3/book
    ```

- use Xnetlib and click "library", click "pvm3", click "book", click "pvm3/pvm-book.ps", click "download", click "Get Files Now". (Xnetlib is an X-window interface to the netlib software based on a client-server model. The software can be found in netlib, "send index from xnetlib").

To view the html file use the URL:

- `http://www.netlib.org/pvm3/book/pvm-book.html`

Contents

Series Foreword

The world of modern computing potentially offers many helpful methods and tools to scientists and engineers, but the fast pace of change in computer hardware, software, and algorithms often makes practical use of the newest computing technology difficult. The Scientific and Engineering Computation series focuses on rapid advances in computing technologies and attempts to facilitate transferring these technologies to applications in science and engineering. It will include books on theories, methods, and original applications in such areas as parallelism, large-scale simulations, time-critical computing, computer-aided design and engineering, use of computers in manufacturing, visualization of scientific data, and human-machine interface technology.

The series will help scientists and engineers to understand the current world of advanced computation and to anticipate future developments that will impact their computing environments and open up new capabilities and modes of computation.

This volume presents a software package for developing parallel programs executable on networked Unix computers. The tool called Parallel Virtual Machine (PVM) allows a heterogeneous collection of workstations and supercomputers to function as a single high-performance parallel machine. PVM is portable and runs on a wide variety of modern platforms. It has been well accepted by the global computing community and used successfully for solving large-scale problems in science, industry, and business.

Janusz S. Kowalik

Preface

In this book we describe the Parallel Virtual Machine (PVM) system and how to develop programs using PVM. PVM is a software system that permits a heterogeneous collection of Unix computers networked together to be viewed by a user's program as a single parallel computer. PVM is the mainstay of the Heterogeneous Network Computing research project, a collaborative venture between Oak Ridge National Laboratory, the University of Tennessee, Emory University, and Carnegie Mellon University.

The PVM system has evolved in the past several years into a viable technology for distributed and parallel processing in a variety of disciplines. PVM supports a straightforward but functionally complete message-passing model.

PVM is designed to link computing resources and provide users with a parallel platform for running their computer applications, irrespective of the number of different computers they use and where the computers are located. When PVM is correctly installed, it is capable of harnessing the combined resources of typically heterogeneous networked computing platforms to deliver high levels of performance and functionality.

In this book, we describe the architecture of the PVM system and discuss its computing model; the programming interface it supports; auxiliary facilities for process groups; the use of PVM on highly parallel systems such as the Intel Paragon, Cray T3D, and Thinking Machines CM-5; and some of the internal implementation techniques employed. Performance issues, dealing primarily with communication overheads, are analyzed, and recent findings as well as enhancements are presented. To demonstrate the viability of PVM for large-scale scientific supercomputing, we also provide some example programs.

This book is not a textbook; rather, it is meant to provide a fast entrance to the world of heterogeneous network computing. We intend this book to be used by two groups of readers: students and researchers working with networks of computers. As such, we hope this book can serve both as a reference and as a supplement to a teaching text on aspects of network computing.

This guide will familiarize readers with the basics of PVM and the concepts used in programming on a network. The information provided here will help with the following PVM tasks:

- Writing a program in PVM
- Building PVM on a system
- Starting PVM on a set of machines
- Debugging a PVM application

A Bit of History

The PVM project began in the summer of 1989 at Oak Ridge National Laboratory. The prototype system, PVM 1.0, was constructed by Vaidy Sunderam and Al Geist; this version of the system was used internally at the Lab and was not released to the outside. Version 2 of PVM was written at the University of Tennessee and released in March 1991. During the following year, PVM began to be used in many scientific applications. After user feedback and a number of changes (PVM 2.1 - 2.4), a complete rewrite was undertaken, and version 3 was completed in February 1993. It is PVM version 3.3 that we describe in this book (and refer to simply as PVM). The PVM software has been distributed freely and is being used in computational applications around the world.

Who Should Read This Book?

To successfully use this book, one should be experienced with common programming techniques and understand some basic parallel processing concepts. In particular, this guide assumes that the user knows how to write, execute, and debug Fortran or C programs and is familiar with Unix.

Typographical Conventions

We use the following conventions in this book:

- Terms used for the first time, variables, and book titles are in *italic type*. For example: For further information on *PVM daemon* see the description in *PVM: Parallel Virtual Machine – A Users' Guide and Tutorial for Networked Parallel Computing*.

- Text that the user types is in `Courier bold font`. For example: `$ pvm`

The Map

This guide is divided into three major parts; it includes nine chapters, a glossary, two appendixes and a bibliography.

- Part I – Basics (Chapters 1–6). This part provides the facts, as well as some interpretation of the underlying system. It describes the overall concepts, system, and techniques for making PVM work for applications.

  - Introduction to PVM – introduction to network computing and PVM; terms and concepts, including an overview of the system

– Overview of PVM

  * C, C++, and Fortran

  * basic principles

  * "hello.c" example

  * other systems (e.g., MPI)

– PVM Tutorial

  * setting up PVM

  * running an existing program

  * console

  * XPVM

– Programming

  * basic programming techniques

  * data decomposition / partitioning

  * function decomposition

  * putting PVM in existing code

– User Interface

  * functions

  * hostfile

– Program Examples

  * PVM programs

- Part 2 – Details (Chapters 7–9). This part describes the internals of PVM.

– How PVM Works

  * Unix hooks to PVM interfaces

  * multiprocessors - shared and distributed memory

– Advanced Topics

  * portability

  * debugging

  * tracing

  * XPVM details

– Troubleshooting; interesting tidbits and information on PVM, including frequently asked questions.

- Part 3 – The Remains. This part provides some useful information on the use of the PVM interface.

  – Glossary of Terms: gives a short description for terms used in the PVM context.

  – Appendix A, History of PVM versions: list of all the versions of PVM that have been released from the first one in February 1991 through July 1994. Along with each version we include a brief synopsis of the improvements made in version 3.

  – Appendix B, Man Pages: provides an alphabetical listing of all the PVM 3 routines. Each routine is described in detail for both C and Fortran use. There are examples and diagnostics for each routine.

  – Quick Reference Card for PVM: provides the name and calling sequence for the PVM routines in both C and Fortran. (If this card is missing from the text a replacement can be downloaded over the network by ftp'ing to `netlib2.cs.utk.edu`; `cd pvm3/book`; `get refcard.ps`.)

  – Bibliography

Comments and Questions

PVM is an ongoing research project. As such, we provide limited support. We welcome feedback on this book and other aspects of the system to help in enhancing PVM. Please send comments and questions to `pvm@msr.epm.ornl.gov`. by e-mail. While we would like to respond to all the electronic mail received, this may not be always possible. We therefore recommend also posting messages to the newsgroup `comp.parallel.pvm`. This unmoderated newsgroup was established on the Internet in May 1993 to provide a forum for discussing issues related to the use of PVM. Questions (from beginner to the very experienced), advice, exchange of public-domain extensions to PVM, and bug reports can be posted to the newsgroup.

Acknowledgments

We gratefully acknowledge the valuable assistance of many people who have contributed to the PVM project. In particular, we thank Peter Rigsbee and Neil Lincoln for their help and insightful comments. We thank the PVM group at the University of Tennessee and Oak Ridge National Laboratory—Carolyn Aebischer, Martin Do, June Donato, Jim Kohl, Keith Moore, Phil Papadopoulos, and Honbo Zhou—for their assistance with the development of various pieces and components of PVM. In addition we express appreciation to all those who helped in the preparation of this work, in particular to Clint

Whaley and Robert Seccomb for help on the examples, Ken Hawick for contributions to the glossary, and Gail Pieper for helping with the task of editing the manuscript.

A number of computer vendors have encouraged and provided valuable suggestions during the development of PVM. We thank Cray Research Inc., IBM, Convex Computer, Silicon Graphics, Sequent Computer, and Sun Microsystems for their assistance in porting the software to their platforms.

This work would not have been possible without the support of the Office of Scientific Computing, U.S. Department of Energy, under Contract DE-AC05-84OR21400; the National Science Foundation Science and Technology Center Cooperative Agreement No. CCR-8809615; and the Science Alliance, a state-supported program at the University of Tennessee.

PVM: Parallel Virtual Machine

1 Introduction

Parallel processing, the method of having many small tasks solve one large problem, has emerged as a key enabling technology in modern computing. The past several years have witnessed an ever-increasing acceptance and adoption of parallel processing, both for high-performance scientific computing and for more "general-purpose" applications, was a result of the demand for higher performance, lower cost, and sustained productivity. The acceptance has been facilitated by two major developments: massively parallel processors (MPPs) and the widespread use of distributed computing.

MPPs are now the most powerful computers in the world. These machines combine a few hundred to a few thousand CPUs in a single large cabinet connected to hundreds of gigabytes of memory. MPPs offer enormous computational power and are used to solve computational Grand Challenge problems such as global climate modeling and drug design. As simulations become more realistic, the computational power required to produce them grows rapidly. Thus, researchers on the cutting edge turn to MPPs and parallel processing in order to get the most computational power possible.

The second major development affecting scientific problem solving is *distributed computing*. Distributed computing is a process whereby a set of computers connected by a network are used collectively to solve a single large problem. As more and more organizations have high-speed local area networks interconnecting many general-purpose workstations, the combined computational resources may exceed the power of a single high-performance computer. In some cases, several MPPs have been combined using distributed computing to produce unequaled computational power.

The most important factor in distributed computing is cost. Large MPPs typically cost more than $10 million. In contrast, users see very little cost in running their problems on a local set of existing computers. It is uncommon for distributed-computing users to realize the raw computational power of a large MPP, but they are able to solve problems several times larger than they could using one of their local computers.

Common between distributed computing and MPP is the notion of message passing. In all parallel processing, data must be exchanged between cooperating tasks. Several paradigms have been tried including shared memory, parallelizing compilers, and message passing. The message-passing model has become the paradigm of choice, from the perspective of the number and variety of multiprocessors that support it, as well as in terms of applications, languages, and software systems that use it.

The Parallel Virtual Machine (PVM) system described in this book uses the message-passing model to allow programmers to exploit distributed computing across a wide variety of computer types, including MPPs. A key concept in PVM is that it makes a collection of computers appear as one large *virtual* machine, hence its name.

1.1   Heterogeneous Network Computing

In an MPP, every processor is exactly like every other in capability, resources, software, and communication speed. Not so on a network. The computers available on a network may be made by different vendors or have different compilers. Indeed, when a programmer wishes to exploit a collection of networked computers, he may have to contend with several different types of heterogeneity:

- architecture,
- data format,
- computational speed,
- machine load, and
- network load.

The set of computers available can include a wide range of architecture types such as 386/486 PC class machines, high-performance workstations, shared-memory multiprocessors, vector supercomputers, and even large MPPs. Each architecture type has its own optimal programming method. In addition, a user can be faced with a hierarchy of programming decisions. The parallel virtual machine may itself be composed of parallel computers. Even when the architectures are only serial workstations, there is still the problem of incompatible binary formats and the need to compile a parallel task on each different machine.

Data formats on different computers are often incompatible. This incompatibility is an important point in distributed computing because data sent from one computer may be unreadable on the receiving computer. Message-passing packages developed for heterogeneous environments must make sure all the computers understand the exchanged data. Unfortunately, the early message-passing systems developed for specific MPPs are not amenable to distributed computing because they do not include enough information in the message to encode or decode it for any other computer.

Even if the set of computers are all workstations with the same data format, there is still heterogeneity due to different computational speeds. As an simple example, consider the problem of running parallel tasks on a virtual machine that is composed of one supercomputer and one workstation. The programmer must be careful that the supercomputer doesn't sit idle waiting for the next data from the workstation before continuing. The problem of computational speeds can be very subtle. The virtual machine can be composed of a set of identical workstations. But since networked computers can have several other users on them running a variety of jobs, the machine load can vary dramatically.

The result is that the effective computational power across identical workstations can vary by an order of magnitude.

Like machine load, the time it takes to send a message over the network can vary depending on the network load imposed by all the other network users, who may not even be using any of the computers in the virtual machine. This sending time becomes important when a task is sitting idle waiting for a message, and it is even more important when the parallel algorithm is sensitive to message arrival time. Thus, in distributed computing, heterogeneity can appear dynamically in even simple setups.

Despite these numerous difficulties caused by heterogeneity, distributed computing offers many advantages:

- By using existing hardware, the cost of this computing can be very low.

- Performance can be optimized by assigning each individual task to the most appropriate architecture.

- One can exploit the heterogeneous nature of a computation. Heterogeneous network computing is not just a local area network connecting workstations together. For example, it provides access to different data bases or to special processors for those parts of an application that can run only on a certain platform.

- The virtual computer resources can grow in stages and take advantage of the latest computational and network technologies.

- Program development can be enhanced by using a familiar environment. Programmers can use editors, compilers, and debuggers that are available on individual machines.

- The individual computers and workstations are usually stable, and substantial expertise in their use is readily available.

- User-level or program-level fault tolerance can be implemented with little effort either in the application or in the underlying operating system.

- Distributed computing can facilitate collaborative work.

All these factors translate into reduced development and debugging time, reduced contention for resources, reduced costs, and possibly more effective implementations of an application. It is these benefits that PVM seeks to exploit. From the beginning, the PVM software package was designed to make programming for a heterogeneous collection of machines straightforward.

1.2 Trends in Distributed Computing

Stand-alone workstations delivering several tens of millions of operations per second are commonplace, and continuing increases in power are predicted. When these computer systems are interconnected by an appropriate high-speed network, their combined computational power can be applied to solve a variety of computationally intensive applications. Indeed, network computing may even provide supercomputer-level computational power. Further, under the right circumstances, the network-based approach can be effective in coupling several similar multiprocessors, resulting in a configuration that might be economically and technically difficult to achieve with supercomputer hardware.

To be effective, distributed computing requires high communication speeds. In the past fifteen years or so, network speeds have increased by several orders of magnitude (see Figure 1.1).

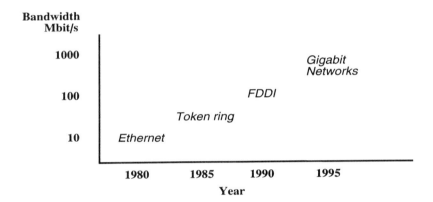

Figure 1.1
Networking speeds

Among the most notable advances in computer networking technology are the following:

- Ethernet – the name given to the popular local area packet-switched network technology invented by Xerox PARC. The Ethernet is a 10 Mbit/s broadcast bus technology with distributed access control.

- FDDI – the Fiber Distributed Data Interface. FDDI is a 100-Mbit/sec token-passing ring that uses optical fiber for transmission between stations and has dual counter-rotating rings to provide redundant data paths for reliability.

- HiPPI – the high-performance parallel interface. HiPPI is a copper-based data communications standard capable of transferring data at 800 Mbit/sec over 32 parallel lines or 1.6 Gbit/sec over 64 parallel lines. Most commercially available high-performance computers offer a HIPPI interface. It is a point-to-point channel that does not support multidrop configurations.

- SONET – Synchronous Optical Network. SONET is a series of optical signals that are multiples of a basic signal rate of 51.84 Mbit/sec called OC-1. The OC-3 (155.52 Mbit/sec) and OC-12 (622.08 Mbit/sec) have been designated as the customer access rates in future B-ISDN networks, and signal rates of OC-192 (9.952 Gbit/sec) are defined.
- ATM – Asynchronous Transfer Mode. ATM is the technique for transport, multiplexing, and switching that provides a high degree of flexibility required by B-ISDN. ATM is a connection-oriented protocol employing fixed-size packets with a 5-byte header and 48 bytes of information.

These advances in high-speed networking promise high throughput with low latency and make it possible to utilize distributed computing for years to come. Consequently, increasing numbers of universities, government and industrial laboratories, and financial firms are turning to distributed computing to solve their computational problems. The objective of PVM is to enable these institutions to use distributed computing *efficiently*.

1.3 PVM Overview

The PVM software provides a unified framework within which parallel programs can be developed in an efficient and straightforward manner using existing hardware. PVM enables a collection of heterogeneous computer systems to be viewed as a single parallel virtual machine. PVM transparently handles all message routing, data conversion, and task scheduling across a network of incompatible computer architectures.

The PVM computing model is simple yet very general, and accommodates a wide variety of application program structures. The programming interface is deliberately straightforward, thus permitting simple program structures to be implemented in an intuitive manner. The user writes his application as a collection of cooperating *tasks*. Tasks access PVM resources through a library of standard interface routines. These routines allow the initiation and termination of tasks across the network as well as communication and synchronization between tasks. The PVM message-passing primitives are oriented towards heterogeneous operation, involving strongly typed constructs for buffering and transmission. Communication constructs include those for sending and receiving data structures as well as high-level primitives such as broadcast, barrier synchronization, and global sum.

PVM tasks may possess arbitrary control and dependency structures. In other words, at any point in the execution of a concurrent application, any task in existence may start or stop other tasks or add or delete computers from the virtual machine. Any process may communicate and/or synchronize with any other. Any specific control and dependency structure may be implemented under the PVM system by appropriate use of PVM constructs and host language control-flow statements.

Owing to its ubiquitous nature (specifically, the virtual machine concept) and also because of its simple but complete programming interface, the PVM system has gained widespread acceptance in the high-performance scientific computing community.

1.4   Other Packages

Several research groups have developed software packages that like PVM assist programmers in using distributed computing. Among the most well known efforts are P4 [1], Express [6], MPI [7], and Linda [3]. Various other systems with similar capabilities are also in existence; a reasonably comprehensive listing may be found in [17].

1.4.1   The p4 System

P4 [1] is a library of macros and subroutines developed at Argonne National Laboratory for programming a variety of parallel machines. The p4 system supports both the shared-memory model (based on monitors) and the distributed-memory model (using message-passing). For the shared-memory model of parallel computation, p4 provides a set of useful monitors as well as a set of primitives from which monitors can be constructed. For the distributed-memory model, p4 provides typed send and receive operations and creation of processes according to a text file describing group and process structure.

Process management in the p4 system is based on a configuration file that specifies the host pool, the object file to be executed on each machine, the number of processes to be started on each host (intended primarily for multiprocessor systems), and other auxiliary information. An example of a configuration file is

```
# start one slave on each of sun2 and sun3
local 0
sun2  1  /home/mylogin/p4pgms/sr_test
sun3  1  /home/mylogin/p4pgms/sr_test
```

Two issues are noteworthy in regard to the process management mechanism in p4. First, there is the notion a "master" process and "slave" processes, and multilevel hierarchies may be formed to implement what is termed a *cluster* model of computation. Second, the primary mode of process creation is static, via the configuration file; dynamic process creation is possible only by a statically created process that must invoke a special o4 function that spawns a new process on the local machine. Despite these restrictions, a variety of application paradigms may be implemented in the p4 system in a fairly straightforward manner.

Message passing in the p4 system is achieved through the use of traditional `send` and `recv` primitives, parameterized almost exactly as other message-passing systems. Several variants are provided for semantics, such as heterogeneous exchange and blocking or nonblocking transfer. A significant proportion of the burden of buffer allocation and management, however, is left to the user. Apart from basic message passing, p4 also offers a variety of global operations, including broadcast, global maxima and minima, and barrier synchronization.

1.4.2 Express

In contrast to the other parallel processing systems described in this section, Express [6] toolkit is a collection of tools that individually address various aspects of concurrent computation. The toolkit is developed and marketed commercially by ParaSoft Corporation, a company that was started by some members of the Caltech concurrent computation project.

The philosophy behind computing with Express is based on beginning with a sequential version of an application and following a recommended development life cycle culminating in a parallel version that is tuned for optimality. Typical development cycles begin with the use of VTOOL, a graphical program that allows the progress of sequential algorithms to be displayed in a dynamic manner. Updates and references to individual data structures can be displayed to explicitly demonstrate algorithm structure and provide the detailed knowledge necessary for parallelization. Related to this program is FTOOL, which provides in-depth analysis of a program including variable use analysis, flow structure, and feedback regarding potential parallelization. FTOOL operates on both sequential and parallel versions of an application. A third tool called ASPAR is then used; this is an automated parallelizer that converts sequential C and Fortran programs for parallel or distributed execution using the Express programming models.

The core of the Express system is a set of libraries for communication, I/O, and parallel graphics. The communication primitives are akin to those found in other message-passing systems and include a variety of global operations and data distribution primitives. Extended I/O routines enable parallel input and output, and a similar set of routines are provided for graphical displays from multiple concurrent processes. Express also contains the NDB tool, a parallel debugger that uses commands based on the popular "dbx" interface.

1.4.3 MPI

The Message Passing Interface (MPI) [7] standard, whose specification was completed in April 1994, is the outcome of a community effort to try to define both the syntax

and semantics of a core of message-passing library routines that would be useful to a
wide range of users and efficiently implementable on a wide range of MPPs. The main
advantage of establishing a message-passing standard is portability. One of the goals of
developing MPI is to provide MPP vendors with a clearly defined base set of routines that
they can implement efficiently or, in some cases, provide hardware support for, thereby
enhancing scalability.

MPI is not intended to be a complete and self-contained software infrastructure that
can be used for distributed computing. MPI does not include necessities such as process
management (the ability to start tasks), (virtual) machine configuration, and support
for input and output. As a result, it is anticipated that MPI will be realized as a
communications interface layer that will be built upon native facilities of the underlying
hardware platform, with the exception of certain data transfer operations that might be
implemented at a level close to hardware. This scenario permits the provision of PVM's
being ported to MPI to exploit any communication performance a vendor supplies.

1.4.4   The Linda System

Linda [3] is a concurrent programming model that has evolved from a Yale University research project. The primary concept in Linda is that of a "tuple-space", an abstraction
via which cooperating processes communicate. This central theme of Linda has been
proposed as an alternative paradigm to the two traditional methods of parallel processing: that based on shared memory, and that based on message passing. The tuple-space
concept is essentially an abstraction of distributed shared memory, with one important
difference (tuple-spaces are associative), and several minor distinctions (destructive and
nondestructive reads and different coherency semantics are possible). Applications use
the Linda model by embedding explicitly, within cooperating sequential programs, constructs that manipulate (insert/retrieve tuples) the tuple space.

From the application point of view Linda is a set of programming language extensions for facilitating parallel programming. It provides a shared-memory abstraction for
process communication without requiring the underlying hardware to physically share
memory.

The Linda system usually refers to a specific implementation of software that supports
the Linda programming model. System software is provided that establishes and maintains tuple spaces and is used in conjunction with libraries that appropriately interpret
and execute Linda primitives. Depending on the environment (shared-memory multiprocessors, message-passing parallel computers, networks of workstations, etc.), the tuple
space mechanism is implemented using different techniques and with varying degrees of
efficiency. Recently, a new *system* scheme has been proposed, at least nominally related
to the Linda project. This scheme, termed "Pirhana" [9], proposes a proactive approach

to concurrent computing: computational resources (viewed as active agents) seize computational tasks from a well-known location based on availability and suitability. This scheme may be implemented on multiple platforms and manifested as a "Pirhana system" or "Linda-Pirhana system."

2 The PVM System

PVM (Parallel Virtual Machine) is a byproduct of an ongoing heterogeneous network computing research project involving the authors and their institutions. The general goals of this project are to investigate issues in, and develop solutions for, heterogeneous concurrent computing. PVM is an integrated set of software tools and libraries that emulates a general-purpose, flexible, heterogeneous concurrent computing framework on interconnected computers of varied architecture. The overall objective of the PVM system is to to enable such a collection of computers to be used cooperatively for concurrent or parallel computation. Detailed descriptions and discussions of the concepts, logistics, and methodologies involved in this network-based computing process are contained in the remainder of the book. Briefly, the principles upon which PVM is based include the following:

- User-configured host pool: The application's computational tasks execute on a set of machines that are selected by the user for a given run of the PVM program. Both single-CPU machines and hardware multiprocessors (including shared-memory and distributed-memory computers) may be part of the host pool. The host pool may be altered by adding and deleting machines during operation (an important feature for fault tolerance).

- Translucent access to hardware: Application programs either may view the hardware environment as an attributeless collection of virtual processing elements or may choose to exploit the capabilities of specific machines in the host pool by positioning certain computational tasks on the most appropriate computers.

- Process-based computation: The unit of parallelism in PVM is a task (often but not always a Unix process), an independent sequential thread of control that alternates between communication and computation. No process-to-processor mapping is implied or enforced by PVM; in particular, multiple tasks may execute on a single processor.

- Explicit message-passing model: Collections of computational tasks, each performing a part of an application's workload using data-, functional-, or hybrid decomposition, cooperate by explicitly sending and receiving messages to one another. Message size is limited only by the amount of available memory.

- Heterogeneity support: The PVM system supports heterogeneity in terms of machines, networks, and applications. With regard to message passing, PVM permits messages containing more than one datatype to be exchanged between machines having different data representations.

- Multiprocessor support: PVM uses the native message-passing facilities on multiprocessors to take advantage of the underlying hardware. Vendors often supply their own optimized PVM for their systems, which can still communicate with the public PVM version.

The PVM system is composed of two parts. The first part is a daemon, called *pvmd3* and sometimes abbreviated *pvmd*, that resides on all the computers making up the virtual machine. (An example of a daemon program is the mail program that runs in the background and handles all the incoming and outgoing electronic mail on a computer.) Pvmd3 is designed so any user with a valid login can install this daemon on a machine. When a user wishes to run a PVM application, he first creates a virtual machine by starting up PVM. (Chapter 3 details how this is done.) The PVM application can then be started from a Unix prompt on any of the hosts. Multiple users can configure overlapping virtual machines, and each user can execute several PVM applications simultaneously.

The second part of the system is a library of PVM interface routines. It contains a functionally complete repertoire of primitives that are needed for cooperation between tasks of an application. This library contains user-callable routines for message passing, spawning processes, coordinating tasks, and modifying the virtual machine.

The PVM computing model is based on the notion that an application consists of several tasks. Each task is responsible for a part of the application's computational workload. Sometimes an application is parallelized along its functions; that is, each task performs a different function, for example, input, problem setup, solution, output, and display. This process is often called functional parallelism. A more common method of parallelizing an application is called data parallelism. In this method all the tasks are the same, but each one only knows and solves a small part of the data. This is also referred to as the SPMD (single-program multiple-data) model of computing. PVM supports either or a mixture of these methods. Depending on their functions, tasks may execute in parallel and may need to synchronize or exchange data, although this is not always the case. An exemplary diagram of the PVM computing model is shown in Figure 2.1. and an architectural view of the PVM system, highlighting the heterogeneity of the computing platforms supported by PVM, is shown in Figure 2.2.

The PVM system currently supports C, C++, and Fortran languages. This set of language interfaces have been included based on the observation that the predominant majority of target applications are written in C and Fortran, with an emerging trend in experimenting with object-based languages and methodologies.

The C and C++ language bindings for the PVM user interface library are implemented as functions, following the general conventions used by most C systems, including Unix-like operating systems. To elaborate, function arguments are a combination of value parameters and pointers as appropriate, and function result values indicate the outcome of the call. In addition, macro definitions are used for system constants, and global

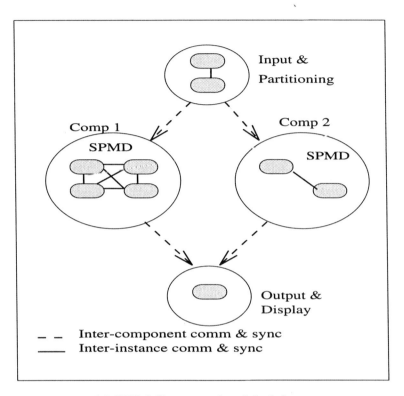

(a) PVM Computation Model

Figure 2.1
PVM system overview

variables such as `errno` and `pvm_errno` are the mechanism for discriminating between multiple possible outcomes. Application programs written in C and C++ access PVM library functions by linking against an archival library (`libpvm3.a`) that is part of the standard distribution.

Fortran language bindings are implemented as subroutines rather than as functions. This approach was taken because some compilers on the supported architectures would not reliably interface Fortran functions with C functions. One immediate implication of this is that an additional argument is introduced into each PVM library call for status results to be returned to the invoking program. Also, library routines for the placement and retrieval of typed data in message buffers are unified, with an additional parameter indicating the datatype. Apart from these differences (and the standard naming prefixes — *pvm_* for C, and *pvmf* for Fortran), a one-to-one correspondence exists between the two

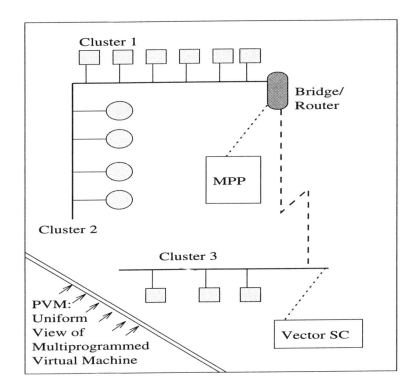

(b) PVM Architectural Overview

Figure 2.2
PVM system overview

language bindings. Fortran interfaces to PVM are implemented as library stubs that in turn invoke the corresponding C routines, after casting and/or dereferencing arguments as appropriate. Thus, Fortran applications are required to link against the stubs library (`libfpvm3.a`) as well as the C library.

All PVM tasks are identified by an integer *task identifier* (TID) . Messages are sent to and received from tids. Since tids must be unique across the entire virtual machine, they are supplied by the local pvmd and are not user chosen. Although PVM encodes information into each TID (see Chapter 7 for details) the user is expected to treat the tids as opaque integer identifiers. PVM contains several routines that return TID values so that the user application can identify other tasks in the system.

There are applications where it is natural to think of a *group of tasks* . And there are cases where a user would like to identify his tasks by the numbers $0 - (p - 1)$, where p is the number of tasks. PVM includes the concept of user named groups. When a task joins a group, it is assigned a unique "instance" number in that group. Instance numbers start at 0 and count up. In keeping with the PVM philosophy, the group functions are designed to be very general and transparent to the user. For example, any PVM task can join or leave any group at any time without having to inform any other task in the affected groups. Also, groups can overlap, and tasks can broadcast messages to groups of which they are not a member. Details of the available group functions are given in Chapter 5. To use any of the group functions, a program must be linked with libgpvm3.a.

The general paradigm for application programming with PVM is as follows. A user writes one or more sequential programs in C, C++, or Fortran 77 that contain embedded calls to the PVM library. Each program corresponds to a task making up the application. These programs are compiled for each architecture in the host pool, and the resulting object files are placed at a location accessible from machines in the host pool. To execute an application, a user typically starts one copy of one task (usually the "master" or "initiating" task) by hand from a machine within the host pool. This process subsequently starts other PVM tasks, eventually resulting in a collection of active tasks that then compute locally and exchange messages with each other to solve the problem. Note that while the above is a typical scenario, as many tasks as appropriate may be started manually. As mentioned earlier, tasks interact through explicit message passing, identifying each other with a system-assigned, opaque TID.

Shown in Figure 2.3 is the body of the PVM program *hello*, a simple example that illustrates the basic concepts of PVM programming. This program is intended to be invoked manually; after printing its task id (obtained with pvm_mytid()), it initiates a copy of another program called *hello_other* using the pvm_spawn() function. A successful spawn causes the program to execute a blocking receive using pvm_recv. After receiving the message, the program prints the message sent by its counterpart, as well its task id; the buffer is extracted from the message using pvm_upkstr. The final pvm_exit call dissociates the program from the PVM system.

Figure 2.4 is a listing of the "slave" or spawned program; its first PVM action is to obtain the task id of the "master" using the pvm_parent call. This program then obtains its hostname and transmits it to the master using the three-call sequence — pvm_initsend to initialize the send buffer; pvm_pkstr to place a string, in a strongly typed and architecture-independent manner, into the send buffer; and pvm_send to transmit it to the destination process specified by *ptid*, "tagging" the message with the number 1.

```
#include "pvm3.h"

main()
{
int cc, tid, msgtag;
char buf[100];

printf("i'm t%x\n", pvm_mytid());

cc = pvm_spawn("hello_other", (char**)0, 0, "", 1, &tid);

if (cc == 1) {
        msgtag = 1;
pvm_recv(tid, msgtag);
pvm_upkstr(buf);
printf("from t%x: %s\n", tid, buf);
} else
printf("can't start hello_other\n");

pvm_exit();
}
```

Figure 2.3
PVM program *hello.c*

```
#include "pvm3.h"

main()
{
int ptid, msgtag;
char buf[100];

ptid = pvm_parent();

strcpy(buf, "hello, world from ");
gethostname(buf + strlen(buf), 64);
    msgtag = 1;
pvm_initsend(PvmDataDefault);
pvm_pkstr(buf);
pvm_send(ptid, msgtag);

pvm_exit();
}
```

Figure 2.4
PVM program *hello_other.c*

3 Using PVM

This chapter describes how to set up the PVM software package, how to configure a simple virtual machine, and how to compile and run the example programs supplied with PVM. The chapter is written as a tutorial, so the reader can follow along with the book beside the terminal. The first part of the chapter describes the straightforward use of PVM and the most common errors and problems in set up and running. The latter part of the chapter describes some of the more advanced options available to customize the reader's PVM environment.

3.1 How to Obtain the PVM Software

The latest version of the PVM source code and documentation is always available through *netlib*. Netlib is a software distribution service set up on the Internet that contains a wide range of computer software. Software can be retrieved from netlib by ftp, WWW, xnetlib, or email.

PVM files can be obtained by anonymous ftp to `netlib2.cs.utk.edu`. Look in directory pvm3. The file `index` describes the files in this directory and its subdirectories.

Using a world wide web tool like Xmosaic the PVM files are accessed by using the address `http://www.netlib.org/pvm3/index.html`.

Xnetlib is a X-Window interface that allows a user to browse or query netlib for available software and to automatically transfer the selected software to the user's computer. To get xnetlib send email to `netlib@ornl.gov` with the message `send xnetlib.shar from xnetlib` or anonymous ftp from `cs.utk.edu pub/xnetlib`.

The PVM software can be requested by email. To receive this software send email to `netlib@ornl.gov` with the message: `send index from pvm3`. An automatic mail handler will return a list of available files and further instructions by email. The advantage of this method is that anyone with email access to Internet can obtain the software.

The PVM software is distributed as a uuencoded, compressed, tar file. To unpack the distribution the file must be uudecoded, uncompressed, and tar xvf filename. This will create a directory called pvm3 wherever it is untarred. The PVM documentation is distributed as postscript files and includes a User's Guide, reference manual, and quick reference card.

3.2 Setup to Use PVM

One of the reasons for PVM's popularity is that it is simple to set up and use. PVM does not require special privileges to be installed. Anyone with a valid login on the hosts can do so. In addition, only one person at an organization needs to get and install PVM for everyone at that organization to use it.

PVM uses two environment variables when starting and running. Each PVM user needs to set these two variables to use PVM. The first variable is PVM_ROOT, which is set to the location of the installed pvm3 directory. The second variable is PVM_ARCH, which tells PVM the architecture of this host and thus what executables to pick from the PVM_ROOT directory.

The easiest method is to set these two variables in your .cshrc file. We assume you are using *csh* as you follow along this tutorial. Here is an example for setting PVM_ROOT:

```
setenv PVM_ROOT $HOME/pvm3
```

It is recommended that the user set PVM_ARCH by concatenating to the file .cshrc, the content of file $PVM_ROOT/lib/cshrc.stub. The stub should be placed after PATH and PVM_ROOT are defined. This stub automatically determines the PVM_ARCH for this host and is particularly useful when the user shares a common file system (such as NFS) across several different architectures.

Table 1 lists the PVM_ARCH names and their corresponding architecture types that are supported in PVM 3.3.

The PVM source comes with directories and makefiles for most architectures you are likely to have. Chapter 8 describes how to port the PVM source to an unsupported architecture. Building for each architecture type is done automatically by logging on to a host, going into the PVM_ROOT directory, and typing make. The makefile will automatically determine which architecture it is being executed on, create appropriate subdirectories, and build pvm, pvmd3, libpvm3.a, and libfpvm3.a, pvmgs, and libgpvm3.a. It places all these files in $PVM_ROOT/lib/PVM_ARCH, with the exception of pvmgs which is placed in $PVM_ROOT/bin/PVM_ARCH.

3.3 Setup Summary

- Set PVM_ROOT and PVM_ARCH in your .cshrc file
- Build PVM for each architecture type
- Create a .rhosts file on each host listing all the hosts you wish to use
- Create a $HOME/.xpvm_hosts file listing all the hosts you wish to use prepended by an "&".

PVM_ARCH	Machine	Notes
AFX8	Alliant FX/8	
ALPHA	DEC Alpha	DEC OSF-1
BAL	Sequent Balance	DYNIX
BFLY	BBN Butterfly TC2000	
BSD386	80386/486 PC runnning Unix	BSDI, 386BSD, NetBSD
CM2	Thinking Machines CM2	Sun front-end
CM5	Thinking Machines CM5	Uses native messages
CNVX	Convex C-series	IEEE f.p.
CNVXN	Convex C-series	native f.p.
CRAY	C-90, YMP, T3D port available	UNICOS
CRAY2	Cray-2	
CRAYSMP	Cray S-MP	
DGAV	Data General Aviion	
E88K	Encore 88000	
HP300	HP-9000 model 300	HPUX
HPPA	HP-9000 PA-RISC	
I860	Intel iPSC/860	Uses native messages
IPSC2	Intel iPSC/2 386 host	SysV, Uses native messages
KSR1	Kendall Square KSR-1	OSF-1, uses shared memory
LINUX	80386/486 PC running Unix	LINUX
MASPAR	Maspar	DEC front-end
MIPS	MIPS 4680	
NEXT	NeXT	
PGON	Intel Paragon	Uses native messages
PMAX	DECstation 3100, 5100	Ultrix
RS6K	IBM/RS6000	AIX 3.2
RT	IBM RT	
SGI	Silicon Graphics IRIS	IRIX 4.x
SGI5	Silicon Graphics IRIS	IRIX 5.x
SGIMP	SGI multiprocessor	Uses shared memory
SUN3	Sun 3	SunOS 4.2
SUN4	Sun 4, SPARCstation	SunOS 4.2
SUN4SOL2	Sun 4, SPARCstation	Solaris 2.x
SUNMP	SPARC multiprocessor	Solaris 2.x, uses shared memory
SYMM	Sequent Symmetry	
TITN	Stardent Titan	
U370	IBM 370	AIX
UVAX	DEC MicroVAX	

Table 3.1
PVM_ARCH names used in PVM 3

3.4   Starting PVM

Before we go over the steps to compile and run parallel PVM programs, you should be sure you can start up PVM and configure a virtual machine. On any host on which PVM has been installed you can type

```
% pvm
```

and you should get back a PVM console prompt signifying that PVM is now running on this host. You can add hosts to your virtual machine by typing at the console prompt

```
pvm> add hostname
```

And you can delete hosts (except the one you are on) from your virtual machine by typing

```
pvm> delete hostname
```

If you get the message "Can't Start pvmd," then check the common startup problems section and try again.

To see what the present virtual machine looks like, you can type

```
pvm> conf
```

To see what PVM tasks are running on the virtual machine, you type

```
pvm> ps -a
```

Of course you don't have any tasks running yet; that's in the next section. If you type "quit" at the console prompt, the console will quit but your virtual machine and tasks will continue to run. At any Unix prompt on any host in the virtual machine, you can type

```
% pvm
```

and you will get the message "pvm already running" and the console prompt. When you are finished with the virtual machine, you should type

```
pvm> halt
```

This command kills any PVM tasks, shuts down the virtual machine, and exits the console. This is the recommended method to stop PVM because it makes sure that the virtual machine shuts down cleanly.

You should practice starting and stopping and adding hosts to PVM until you are comfortable with the PVM console. A full description of the PVM console and its many command options is given at the end of this chapter.

If you don't want to type in a bunch of host names each time, there is a hostfile option. You can list the hostnames in a file one per line and then type

```
% pvm hostfile
```

PVM will then add all the listed hosts simultaneously before the console prompt appears. Several options can be specified on a per-host basis in the hostfile. These are described at the end of this chapter for the user who wishes to customize his virtual machine for a particular application or environment.

There are other ways to start up PVM. The functions of the console and a performance monitor have been combined in a graphical user interface called XPVM, which is available precompiled on netlib (see Chapter 8 for XPVM details). If XPVM has been installed at your site, then it can be used to start PVM. To start PVM with this X window interface, type

```
% xpvm
```

The menu button labled "hosts" will pull down a list of hosts you can add. If you click on a hostname, it is added and an icon of the machine appears in an animation of the virtual machine. A host is deleted if you click on a hostname that is already in the virtual machine (see Figure 3.1). On startup XPVM reads the file $HOME/.xpvm_hosts, which is a list of hosts to display in this menu. Hosts without leading "&" are added all at once at startup.

The quit and halt buttons work just like the PVM console. If you quit XPVM and then restart it, XPVM will automatically display what the running virtual machine looks like. Practice starting and stopping and adding hosts with XPVM. If there are errors, they should appear in the window where you started XPVM.

3.5 Common Startup Problems

If PVM has a problem starting up, it will print an error message either to the screen
or in the log file /tmp/pvml.<uid>. This section describes the most common startup
problems and how to solve them. Chapter 9 contains a more complete troubleshooting
guide.

If the message says

```
[t80040000] Can't start pvmd
```

first check that your .rhosts file on the remote host contains the name of the host from
which you are starting PVM. An external check that your .rhosts file is set correctly is
to type

```
% rsh remote_host ls
```

If your .rhosts is set up correctly, then you will see a listing of your files on the remote
host.

Other reasons to get this message include not having PVM installed on a host or not
having PVM_ROOT set correctly on some host. You can check these by typing

```
% rsh remote_host $PVM_ROOT/lib/pvmd
```

Some Unix shells, for example ksh, do not set environment variables on remote hosts
when using rsh. In PVM 3.3 there are two work arounds for such shells. First, if you set
the environment variable, PVM_DPATH, on the master host to pvm3/lib/pvmd, then
this will override the default dx path. The second method is to tell PVM explicitly were
to find the remote pvmd executable by using the dx= option in the hostfile.

If PVM is manually killed, or stopped abnormally (e.g., by a system crash), then check
for the existence of the file /tmp/pvmd.<uid>. This file is used for authentication and
should exist only while PVM is running. If this file is left behind, it prevents PVM from
starting. Simply delete this file.

If the message says

```
[t80040000] Login incorrect
```

it probably means that no account is on the remote machine with your login name. If
your login name is different on the remote machine, then you must use the lo= option
in the hostfile (see Section 3.7).

If you get any other strange messages, then check your .cshrc file. It is important
that you not have any I/O in the .cshrc file because this will interfere with the startup
of PVM. If you wish to print out information (such as who or uptime) when you log in,
you should do it in your .login script, not when you're running a csh command script.

3.6   Running PVM Programs

In this section you'll learn how to compile and run PVM programs. Later chapters of
this book describe how to write parallel PVM programs. In this section we will work
with the example programs supplied with the PVM software. These example programs
make useful templates on which to base your own PVM programs.

The first step is to copy the example programs into your own area:

```
% cp -r $PVM_ROOT/examples $HOME/pvm3/examples
% cd $HOME/pvm3/examples
```

The examples directory contains a *Makefile.aimk* and *Readme* file that describe how
to build the examples. PVM supplies an architecture-independent make, `aimk`, that
automatically determines PVM_ARCH and links any operating system specific libraries
to your application. `aimk` was automatically added to your $PATH when you placed the
`cshrc.stub` in your `.cshrc` file. Using `aimk` allows you to leave the source code and
makefile unchanged as you compile across different architectures.

The master/slave programming model is the most popular model used in distributed
computing. (In the general parallel programming arena, the SPMD model is more popular.) To compile the master/slave C example, type

```
% aimk master slave
```

If you prefer to work with Fortran, compile the Fortran version with

```
% aimk fmaster fslave
```

Depending on the location of PVM_ROOT, the `INCLUDE` statement at the top of the
Fortran examples may need to be changed. If PVM_ROOT is not HOME/pvm3, then
change the include to point to `$PVM_ROOT/include/fpvm3.h`. Note that PVM_ROOT is
not expanded inside the Fortran, so you must insert the actual path.

The makefile moves the executables to `$HOME/pvm3/bin/PVM_ARCH`, which is the default
location PVM will look for them on all hosts. If your file system is not common across
all your PVM hosts, then you will have to build or copy (depending on the architectures)
these executables on all your PVM hosts.

Now, from one window, start PVM and configure some hosts. These examples are
designed to run on any number of hosts, including one. In another window `cd` to
`$HOME/pvm3/bin/PVM_ARCH` and type

```
% master
```

The program will ask how many tasks. The number of tasks does not have to match the number of hosts in these examples. Try several combinations.

The first example illustrates the ability to run a PVM program from a Unix prompt on any host in the virtual machine. This is just like the way you would run a serial `a.out` program on a workstation. In the next example, which is also a master/slave model called `hitc`, you will see how to spawn PVM jobs from the PVM console and also from XPVM.

`hitc` illustrates dynamic load balancing using the pool-of-tasks paradigm. In the pool of tasks paradigm, the master program manages a large queue of tasks, always sending idle slave programs more work to do until the queue is empty. This paradigm is effective in situations where the hosts have very different computational powers, because the least loaded or more powerful hosts do more of the work and all the hosts stay busy until the end of the problem. To compile `hitc`, type

```
% aimk hitc hitc_slave
```

Since `hitc` does not require any user input, it can be spawned directly from the PVM console. Start up the PVM console and add a few hosts. At the PVM console prompt type

```
pvm> spawn -> hitc
```

The "->" spawn option causes all the print statements in `hitc` and in the slaves to appear in the console window. This feature can be useful when debugging your first few PVM programs. You may wish to experiment with this option by placing print statements in hitc.f and hitc_slave.f and recompiling.

`hitc` can be used to illustrate XPVM's real-time animation capabilities. Start up XPVM and build a virtual machine with four hosts. Click on the "tasks" button and select "spawn" from the menu. Type "hitc" where XPVM asks for the command, and click on "start". You will see the host icons light up as the machines become busy. You will see the hitc_slave tasks get spawned and see all the messages that travel between the tasks in the *Space Time* display. Several other views are selectable from the XPVM "views" menu. The "task output" view is equivalent to the "->" option in the PVM console. It causes the standard output from all tasks to appear in the window that pops up.

There is one restriction on programs that are spawned from XPVM (and the PVM console). The programs must not contain any interactive input, such as asking for how many slaves to start up or how big a problem to solve. This type of information can be read from a file or put on the command line as arguments, but there is nothing in place to get user input from the keyboard to a potentially remote task.

3.7   PVM Console Details

The PVM console, called **pvm**, is a stand-alone PVM task that allows the user to inter-actively start, query, and modify the virtual machine. The console may be started and stopped multiple times on any of the hosts in the virtual machine without affecting PVM or any applications that may be running.

When started, **pvm** determines whether PVM is already running; if it is not, **pvm** automatically executes pvmd on this host, passing pvmd the command line options and hostfile. Thus PVM need not be running to start the console.

```
pvm [-n<hostname>] [hostfile]
```

The -n option is useful for specifying an alternative name for the master pvmd (in case hostname doesn't match the IP address you want). Once PVM is started, the console prints the prompt

```
pvm>
```

and accepts commands from standard input. The available commands are

add followed by one or more host names, adds these hosts to the virtual machine.

alias defines or lists command aliases.

conf lists the configuration of the virtual machine including hostname, pvmd task ID, architecture type, and a relative speed rating.

delete followed by one or more host names, deletes these hosts from the virtual machine. PVM processes still running on these hosts are lost.

echo echo arguments.

halt kills all PVM processes including console, and then shuts down PVM. All daemons exit.

help can be used to get information about any of the interactive commands. Help may be followed by a command name that lists options and flags available for this command.

id prints the console task id.

jobs lists running jobs.

kill can be used to terminate any PVM process.

mstat shows the status of specified hosts.

ps -a lists all processes currently on the virtual machine, their locations, their task id's, and their parents' task id's.

pstat shows the status of a single PVM process.

quit exits the console, leaving dæmons and PVM jobs running.

reset kills all PVM processes except consoles, and resets all the internal PVM tables and message queues. The dæmons are left in an idle state.

setenv displays or sets environment variables.

sig followed by a signal number and TID, sends the signal to the task.

spawn starts a PVM application. Options include the following:

-count number of tasks; default is 1.

-host spawn on host; default is any.

-ARCH spawn of hosts of type ARCH.

-? enable debugging.

-> redirect task output to console.

->file redirect task output to file.

->>file redirect task output append to file.

-@ trace job, display output on console

-@file trace job, output to file

trace sets or displays the trace event mask.

unalias undefines command alias.

version prints version of PVM being used.

The console reads `$HOME/.pvmrc` before reading commands from the tty, so you can do things like

```
alias ? help
alias h help
alias j jobs
setenv PVM_EXPORT DISPLAY
# print my id
echo new pvm shell
id
```

PVM supports the use of multiple consoles. It is possible to run a console on any host in an existing virtual machine and even multiple consoles on the same machine. It is also possible to start up a console in the middle of a PVM application and check on its progress.

3.8   Host File Options

As we stated earlier, only one person at a site needs to install PVM, but each PVM user can have his own hostfile, which describes his own personal virtual machine.

The *hostfile* defines the initial configuration of hosts that PVM combines into a virtual machine. It also contains information about hosts that you may wish to add to the configuration later.

The hostfile in its simplest form is just a list of hostnames one to a line. Blank lines are ignored, and lines that begin with a # are comment lines. This allows you to document the hostfile and also provides a handy way to modify the initial configuration by commenting out various hostnames (see Figure 3.2).

Several options can be specified on each line after the hostname. The options are separated by white space.

lo= userid allows you to specify an alternative login name for this host; otherwise, your login name on the start-up machine is used.

so=pw will cause PVM to prompt you for a password on this host. This is useful in the cases where you have a different userid and password on a remote system. PVM uses rsh by default to start up remote pvmd's, but when pw is specified, PVM will use rexec() instead.

dx= location of pvmd allows you to specify a location other than the default for this host. This is useful if you want to use your own personal copy of pvmd,

ep= paths to user executables allows you to specify a series of paths to search down to find the requested files to spawn on this host. Multiple paths are separated by a colon. If ep= is not specified, then PVM looks in `$HOME/pvm3/bin/PVM_ARCH` for the application tasks.

sp= value specifies the relative computational speed of the host compared with other hosts in the configuration. The range of possible values is 1 to 1000000 with 1000 as the default.

bx= location of debugger specifies which debugger script to invoke on this host if debugging is requested in the spawn routine.
Note: The environment variable PVM_DEBUGGER can also be set. The default debugger is `pvm3/lib/debugger`.

wd= working_directory specifies a working directory in which all spawned tasks on this host will execute. The default is `$HOME`.

ip= hostname specifies an alternate name to resolve to the host IP address.

so=ms specifies that a slave pvmd will be started manually on this host. This is useful if rsh and rexec network services are disabled but IP connectivity exists. When using this option you will see in the tty of the pvmd3

```
[t80040000] ready   Fri Aug 27 18:47:47 1993
*** Manual startup ***
Login to "honk" and type:
pvm3/lib/pvmd -S -d0 -nhonk 1 80a9ca95:0cb6 4096 2 80a95c43:0000
Type response:
```

On honk, after typing the given line, you should see

```
ddpro<2312> arch<ALPHA> ip<80a95c43:0a8e> mtu<4096>
```

which you should relay back to the master pvmd. At that point, you will see

```
Thanks
```

and the two pvmds should be able to communicate.

If you want to set any of the above options as defaults for a series of hosts, you can place these options on a single line with a * for the hostname field. The defaults will be in effect for all the following hosts until they are overridden by another set-defaults line.

Hosts that you don't want in the initial configuration but may add later can be specified in the hostfile by beginning those lines with an &. An example hostfile displaying most of these options is shown in Figure 3.3.

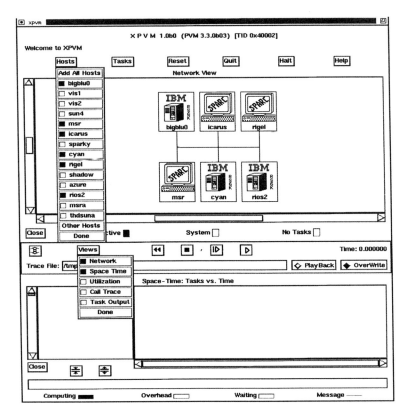

Figure 3.1
XPVM system adding hosts

```
# configuration used for my run
sparky
azure.epm.ornl.gov
thud.cs.utk.edu
sun4
```

Figure 3.2
Simple hostfile listing virtual machine configuration

```
# Comment lines start with # (blank lines ignored)
gstws
ipsc dx=/usr/geist/pvm3/lib/I860/pvmd3
ibm1.scri.fsu.edu lo=gst so=pw

# set default options for following hosts with *
* ep=$sun/problem1:~/nla/mathlib
sparky
#azure.epm.ornl.gov
midnight.epm.ornl.gov

# replace default options with new values
* lo=gageist so=pw ep=problem1
thud.cs.utk.edu
speedy.cs.utk.edu

# machines for adding later are specified with &
# these only need listing if options are required
&sun4   ep=problem1
&castor dx=/usr/local/bin/pvmd3
&dasher.cs.utk.edu lo=gageist
&elvis  dx=~/pvm3/lib/SUN4/pvmd3
```

Figure 3.3
PVM hostfile illustrating customizing options

4 Basic Programming Techniques

Developing applications for the PVM system—in a general sense, at least—follows the traditional paradigm for programming distributed-memory multiprocessors such as the nCUBE or the Intel family of multiprocessors. The basic techniques are similar both for the logistical aspects of programming and for algorithm development. Significant differences exist, however, in terms of (a) task management, especially issues concerning dynamic process creation, naming, and addressing; (b) initialization phases prior to actual computation; (c) granularity choices; and (d) heterogeneity. In this chapter, we discuss the programming process for PVM and identify factors that may impact functionality and performance.

4.1 Common Parallel Programming Paradigms

Parallel computing using a system such as PVM may be approached from three fundamental viewpoints, based on the organization of the computing tasks. Within each, different workload allocation strategies are possible and will be discussed later in this chapter. The first and most common model for PVM applications can be termed "crowd" computing : a collection of closely related processes, typically executing the same code, perform computations on different portions of the workload, usually involving the periodic exchange of intermediate results. This paradigm can be further subdivided into two categories:

- The master-slave (or host-node) model in which a separate "control" program termed the master is responsible for process spawning, initialization, collection and display of results, and perhaps timing of functions. The slave programs perform the actual computation involved; they either are allocated their workloads by the master (statically or dynamically) or perform the allocations themselves.

- The node-only model where multiple instances of a single program execute, with one process (typically the one initiated manually) taking over the noncomputational responsibilities in addition to contributing to the computation itself.

The second model supported by PVM is termed a "tree" computation. In this scenario, processes are spawned (usually dynamically as the computation progresses) in a tree-like manner, thereby establishing a tree-like, parent-child relationship (as opposed to crowd computations where a star-like relationship exists). This paradigm, although less commonly used, is an extremely natural fit to applications where the total workload is not known *a priori*, for example, in branch-and-bound algorithms, alpha-beta search, and recursive "divide-and-conquer" algorithms.

The third model, which we term "hybrid," can be thought of as a combination of the tree model and crowd model. Essentially, this paradigm possesses an arbitrary spawning structure: that is, at any point during application execution, the process relationship structure may resemble an arbitrary and changing graph.

We note that these three classifications are made on the basis of process relationships, though they frequently also correspond to communication topologies. Nevertheless, in all three, it is possible for any process to interact and synchronize with any other. Further, as may be expected, the choice of model is application dependent and should be selected to best match the natural structure of the parallelized program.

4.1.1   Crowd Computations

Crowd computations typically involve three phases. The first is the initialization of the process group; in the case of node-only computations, dissemination of group information and problem parameters, as well as workload allocation, is typically done within this phase. The second phase is computation. The third phase is collection results and display of output; during this phase, the process group is disbanded or terminated.

The master-slave model is illustrated below, using the well-known Mandelbrot set computation which is representative of the class of problems termed "embarrassingly" parallel. The computation itself involves applying a recursive function to a collection of points in the complex plane until the function values either reach a specific value or begin to diverge. Depending upon this condition, a graphical representation of each point in the plane is constructed. Essentially, since the function outcome depends only on the starting value of the point (and is independent of other points), the problem can be partitioned into completely independent portions, the algorithm applied to each, and partial results combined using simple combination schemes. However, this model permits dynamic load balancing, thereby allowing the processing elements to share the workload unevenly. In this and subsequent examples within this chapter, we only show a skeletal form of the algorithms, and also take syntactic liberties with the PVM routines in the interest of clarity. The control structure of the master-slave class of applications is shown in Figure 4.1.

```
{Master Mandelbrot algorithm.}

{Initial placement}
for i := 0 to NumWorkers - 1
pvm_spawn(<worker name>)     {Start up worker i}
pvm_send(<worker tid>,999) {Send task to worker i}
```

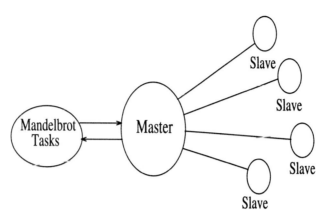

Figure 4.1
Master-slave paradigm

```
endfor

{Receive-send}
while (WorkToDo)
pvm_recv(888)            {Receive result}

pvm_send(<available worker tid>,999)
{Send next task to available worker}

display result
endwhile

{Gather remaining results.}
for i := 0 to NumWorkers - 1
pvm_recv(888)                  {Receive result}
pvm_kill(<worker tid i>)       {Terminate worker i}
display result
endfor
```

```
{Worker Mandelbrot algorithm.}

while (true)
pvm_recv(999)                          {Receive task}
result := MandelbrotCalculations(task) {Compute result}
pvm_send(<master tid>,888)         {Send result to master}
endwhile
```

The master-slave example described above involves no communication among the slaves. Most crowd computations of any complexity do need to communicate among the computational processes; we illustrate the structure of such applications using a node-only example for matrix multiply using Cannon's algorithm [2] (programming details for a similar algorithm are given in another chapter). The matrix-multiply example, shown pictorially in Figure 4.2 multiplies matrix subblocks locally, and uses row-wise multicast of matrix A subblocks in conjunction with column-wise shifts of matrix B subblocks.

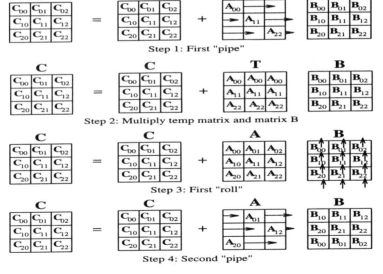

Figure 4.2
General crowd computation

```
{Matrix Multiplication Using Pipe-Multiply-Roll Algorithm}

{Processor 0 starts up other processes}
if (<my processor number> = 0) then
    for i := 1 to MeshDimension*MeshDimension
        pvm_spawn(<component name>, . .)
    endfor
endif

forall processors Pij, 0 <= i,j < MeshDimension
    for k := 0 to MeshDimension-1
        {Pipe.}
        if myrow = (mycolumn+k) mod MeshDimension
            {Send A to all Pxy, x = myrow, y <> mycolumn}
            pvm_mcast((Pxy, x = myrow, y <> mycolumn),999)
        else
            pvm_recv(999)    {Receive A}
        endif

        {Multiply.  Running totals maintained in C.}
        Multiply(A,B,C)

        {Roll.}
        {Send B to Pxy, x = myrow-1, y = mycolumn}
        pvm_send((Pxy, x = myrow-1, y = mycolumn),888)
        pvm_recv(888)        {Receive B}
    endfor
endfor
```

4.1.2 Tree Computations

As mentioned earlier, tree computations typically exhibit a tree-like process control structure which also conforms to the communication pattern in many instances. To illustrate this model, we consider a parallel sorting algorithm that works as follows. One process (the manually started process in PVM) possesses (inputs or generates) the list to be sorted. It then spawns a second process and sends it half the list. At this point, there are two processes each of which spawns a process and sends them one-half of their already halved lists. This continues until a tree of appropriate depth is constructed. Each process then independently sorts its portion of the list, and a merge phase follows where sorted sublists are transmitted upwards along the tree edges, with intermediate merges being done at each node. This algorithm is illustrative of a tree computation in which the workload is known in advance; a diagram depicting the process is given in Figure 4.3; an algorithmic outline is given below.

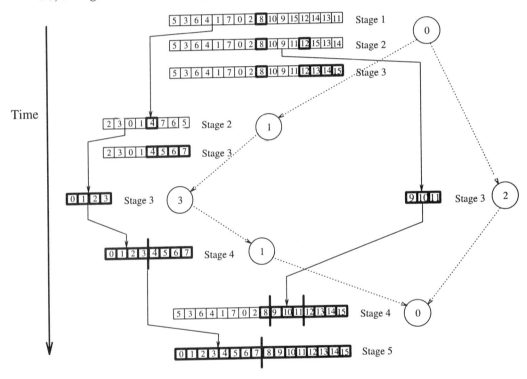

Split-Sort-Merge Algorithm on Four-Node Hypercube

Figure 4.3
Tree-computation example

```
{ Spawn and partition list based on a broadcast tree pattern. }
for i := 1 to N, such that 2^N = NumProcs
forall processors P such that P < 2^i
pvm_spawn(...) {process id P XOR 2^i}
```

```
if P < 2^(i-1) then
midpt: = PartitionList(list);
{Send list[0..midpt] to P XOR 2^i}
pvm_send((P XOR 2^i),999)
list := list[midpt+1..MAXSIZE]
else
pvm_recv(999)      {receive the list}
endif
endfor
endfor


{ Sort remaining list. }
Quicksort(list[midpt+1..MAXSIZE])


{ Gather/merge sorted sub-lists. }
for i := N downto 1, such that 2^N = NumProcs
forall processors P such that P < 2^i
if P > 2^(i-1) then
pvm_send((P XOR 2^i),888)
{Send list to P XOR 2^i}
else
pvm_recv(888)      {receive temp list}
merge templist into list
endif
endfor
endfor
```

4.2   Workload Allocation

In the preceding section, we discussed the common parallel programming paradigms with
respect to process structure, and we outlined representative examples in the context of
the PVM system. In this section we address the issue of workload allocation, subsequent
to establishing process structure, and describe some common paradigms that are used
in distributed-memory parallel computing. Two general methodologies are commonly
used. The first, termed *data decomposition* or partitioning, assumes that the overall
problem involves applying computational operations or transformations on one or more

data structures and, further, that these data structures may be divided and operated upon. The second, called *function decomposition*, divides the work based on different operations or functions. In a sense, the PVM computing model supports both function decomposition (fundamentally different tasks perform different operations) and data decomposition (identical tasks operate on different portions of the data).

4.2.1 Data Decomposition

As a simple example of data decomposition, consider the addition of two vectors, A[1..N] and B[1..N], to produce the result vector, C[1..N]. If we assume that P processes are working on this problem, data partitioning involves the allocation of N/P elements of each vector to each process, which computes the corresponding N/P elements of the resulting vector. This data partitioning may be done either "statically," where each process knows *a priori* (at least in terms of the variables N and P) its share of the workload, or "dynamically," where a control process (e.g., the master process) allocates subunits of the workload to processes as and when they become free. The principal difference between these two approaches is "scheduling." With static scheduling, individual process workloads are fixed; with dynamic scheduling, they vary as the computation progresses. In most multiprocessor environments, static scheduling is effective for problems such as the vector addition example; however, in the general PVM environment, static scheduling is not necessarily beneficial. The reason is that PVM environments based on networked clusters are susceptible to external influences; therefore, a statically scheduled, data-partitioned problem might encounter one or more processes that complete their portion of the workload much faster or much slower than the others. This situation could also arise when the machines in a PVM system are heterogeneous, possessing varying CPU speeds and different memory and other system attributes.

In a real execution of even this trivial vector addition problem, an issue that cannot be ignored is input and output. In other words, how do the processes described above receive their workloads, and what do they do with the result vectors? The answer to these questions depends on the application and the circumstances of a particular run, but in general:

1. Individual processes generate their own data internally, for example, using random numbers or statically known values. This is possible only in very special situations or for program testing purposes.

2. Individual processes independently input their data subsets from external devices. This method is meaningful in many cases, but possible only when parallel I/O facilities are supported.

3. A controlling process sends individual data subsets to each process. This is the most com-

mon scenario, especially when parallel I/O facilities do not exist. Further, this method is also appropriate when input data subsets are derived from a previous computation within the same application.

The third method of allocating individual workloads is also consistent with dynamic scheduling in applications where interprocess interactions during computations are rare or nonexistent. However, nontrivial algorithms generally require intermediate exchanges of data values, and therefore only the initial assignment of data partitions can be accomplished by these schemes. For example, consider the data partitioning method depicted in Figure 4.2. In order to multiply two matrices A and B, a group of processes is first spawned, using the master-slave or node-only paradigm. This set of processes is considered to form a mesh; the matrices to be multiplied are divided into subblocks, also forming a mesh. Each subblock of the A and B matrices is placed on the corresponding process, by utilizing one of the data decomposition and workload allocation strategies listed above. During computation, subblocks need to be forwarded or exchanged between processes, thereby transforming the original allocation map, as shown in the figure. At the end of the computation, however, result matrix subblocks are situated on the individual processes, in conformance with their respective positions on the process grid, and consistent with a data partitioned map of the resulting matrix C. The foregoing discussion illustrates the basics of data decomposition. In a later chapter, example programs highlighting details of this approach will be presented.

4.2.2 Function Decomposition

Parallelism in distributed-memory environments such as PVM may also be achieved by partitioning the overall workload in terms of different operations. The most obvious example of this form of decomposition is with respect to the three stages of typical program execution, namely, input, processing, and result output. In function decomposition, such an application may consist of three separate and distinct programs, each one dedicated to one of the three phases. Parallelism is obtained by concurrently executing the three programs and by establishing a "pipeline" (continuous or quantized) between them. Note, however, that in such a scenario, data parallelism may also exist within each phase. An example is shown in Figure 2.1, where distinct functions are realized as PVM components, with multiple instances within each component implementing portions of different data partitioned algorithms.

Although the concept of function decomposition is illustrated by the trivial example above, the term is generally used to signify partitioning and workload allocation by function *within* the computational phase. Typically, application computations contain several different subalgorithms—sometimes on the same data (the MPSD or multiple-program single-data scenario), sometimes in a pipelined sequence of transformations, and sometimes exhibiting an unstructured pattern of exchanges. We illustrate the general functional decomposition paradigm by considering the hypothetical simulation of an aircraft consisting of multiple interrelated and interacting, functionally decomposed subalgorithms. A diagram providing an overview of this example is shown in Figure 4.4 (and will also be used in a later chapter dealing with graphical PVM programming).

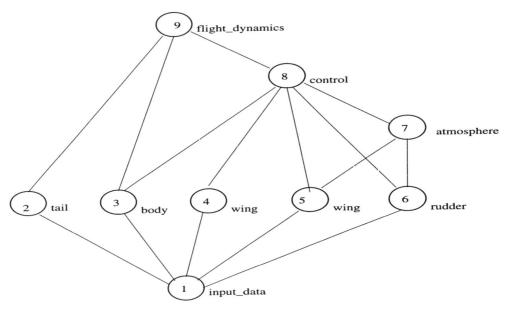

Figure 4.4
Function decomposition example

In the figure, each node or circle in the "graph" represents a functionally decomposed piece of the application. The input function distributes the particular problem parameters to the different functions 2 through 6, after spawning processes corresponding to distinct programs implementing each of the application subalgorithms. The same data may be sent to multiple functions (e.g., as in the case of the two *wing* functions), or data appropriate for the given function alone may be delivered. After performing some amount of computations these functions deliver intermediate or final results to functions 7, 8, and 9 that may have been spawned at the beginning of the computation or as results become available. The diagram indicates the primary concept of decomposing applications by function, as well as control and data dependency relationships. Parallelism is achieved in two respects—by the concurrent and independent execution of modules as in functions 2 through 6, and by the simultaneous, pipelined, execution of modules in a dependency chain, as, for example, in functions 1, 6, 8, and 9.

4.3 Porting Existing Applications to PVM

In order to utilize the PVM system, applications must evolve through two stages. The first concerns development of the distributed-memory parallel version of the application algorithm(s); this phase is common to the PVM system as well as to other distributed-memory multiprocessors. The actual parallelization decisions fall into two major categories – those related to structure, and those related to efficiency. For structural decisions in parallelizing applications, the major decisions to be made include the choice of model to be used (i.e., crowd computation vs. tree computation and data decomposition vs. function decomposition). Decisions with respect to efficiency when parallelizing for distributed-memory environments are generally oriented toward minimizing the frequency and volume of communications. It is typically in this latter respect that the parallelization process differs for PVM and hardware multiprocessors; for PVM environments based on networks, large granularity generally leads to better performance. With this qualification, the parallelization process is very similar for PVM and for other distributed-memory environments, including hardware multiprocessors.

The parallelization of applications may be done *ab initio*, from existing sequential versions, or from existing parallel versions. In the first two cases, the stages involved are to select an appropriate algorithm for each of the subtasks in the application, usually from published descriptions or by inventing a parallel algorithm, and to then code these algorithms in the language of choice (C, C++, or Fortran 77 for PVM) and interface them with each other as well as with process management and other constructs. Parallelization from existing sequential programs also follows certain general guidelines, primary among which are to decompose loops, beginning with outermost loops and working inward. In this process, the main concern is to detect dependencies and to partition loops such that the dependencies are preserved while allowing for concurrency. This parallelization process is described in numerous textbooks and papers on parallel computing, although few textbooks discuss the practical and specific aspects of transforming a sequential program to a parallel one.

Existing parallel programs may be based upon either the shared-memory or distributed-memory paradigms. Converting existing shared-memory programs to PVM is similar to converting from sequential code, when the shared-memory versions are based upon vector or loop-level parallelism. In the case of explicit shared memory programs, the primary task is to locate synchronization points and replace these with message passing. In order to convert existing distributed-memory parallel code to PVM, the main task is to convert from one set of concurrency constructs to another. Typically, existing distributed memory parallel programs are written either for hardware multiprocessors or other networked environments such as p4 or Express. In both cases, the major changes required are with regard to process management. For example, in the Intel family of DMMPs, it is common for processes to be started from an interactive shell command line. Such a paradigm should be replaced for PVM by either a master program or a node program that takes responsibility for process spawning. With regard to interaction, there is, fortunately, a great deal of commonality between the message-passing calls in various programming environments. The major differences between PVM and other systems in this context are with regard to (a) process management and process addressing schemes; (b) virtual machine configuration/reconfiguration and its impact on executing applications; (c) heterogeneity in messages as well as the aspect of heterogeneity that deals with different architectures and data representations; and (d) certain unique and specialized features such as signaling, and task scheduling methods.

5 PVM User Interface

In this chapter we give a brief description of the routines in the PVM 3 user library. This chapter is organized by the functions of the routines. For example, in the section on *Message Passing* is a discussion of all the routines for sending and receiving data from one PVM task to another and a description of PVM's message passing options. The calling syntax of the C and Fortran PVM routines are highlighted by boxes in each section.

An alphabetical listing of all the routines is given in Appendix B. Appendix B contains a detailed description of each routine, including a description of each argument in each routine, the possible error codes a routine may return, and the possible reasons for the error. Each listing also includes examples of both C and Fortran use.

In PVM 3 all PVM tasks are identified by an integer supplied by the local pvmd. In the following descriptions this task identifier is called TID. It is similar to the process ID (PID) used in the Unix system and is assumed to be opaque to the user, in that the value of the TID has no special significance to him. In fact, PVM encodes information into the TID for its own internal use. Details of this encoding can be found in Chapter 7.

All the PVM routines are written in C. C++ applications can link to the PVM library. Fortran applications can call these routines through a Fortran 77 interface supplied with the PVM 3 source. This interface translates arguments, which are passed by reference in Fortran, to their values if needed by the underlying C routines. The interface also takes into account Fortran character string representations and the various naming conventions that different Fortran compilers use to call C functions.

The PVM communication model assumes that any task can send a message to any other PVM task and that there is no limit to the size or number of such messages. While all hosts have physical memory limitations that limits potential buffer space, the communication model does not restrict itself to a particular machine's limitations and assumes sufficient memory is available. The PVM communication model provides asynchronous blocking send, asynchronous blocking receive, and nonblocking receive functions. In our terminology, a blocking send returns as soon as the send buffer is free for reuse, and an asynchronous send does not depend on the receiver calling a matching receive before the send can return. There are options in PVM 3 that request that data be transferred directly from task to task. In this case, if the message is large, the sender may block until the receiver has called a matching receive.

A nonblocking receive immediately returns with either the data or a flag that the data has not arrived, while a blocking receive returns only when the data is in the receive buffer. In addition to these point-to-point communication functions, the model supports multicast to a set of tasks and broadcast to a user-defined group of tasks. There are also functions to perform global max, global sum, etc., across a user-defined group of tasks. Wildcards can be specified in the receive for the source and label, allowing either or both of these contexts to be ignored. A routine can be called to return information about received messages.

The PVM model guarantees that message order is preserved. If task 1 sends message A to task 2, then task 1 sends message B to task 2, message A will arrive at task 2 before message B. Moreover, if both messages arrive before task 2 does a receive, then a wildcard receive will always return message A.

Message buffers are allocated dynamically. Therefore, the maximum message size that can be sent or received is limited only by the amount of available memory on a given host. There is only limited flow control built into PVM 3.3. PVM may give the user a *can't get memory* error when the sum of incoming messages exceeds the available memory, but PVM does not tell other tasks to stop sending to this host.

5.1   Process Control

```
int tid = pvm_mytid( void )
call pvmfmytid( tid )
```

The routine pvm_mytid() returns the TID of this process and can be called multiple times. It enrolls this process into PVM if this is the first PVM call. Any PVM system call (not just pvm_mytid) will enroll a task in PVM if the task is not enrolled before the call, but it is common practice to call pvm_mytid first to perform the enrolling.

```
int info = pvm_exit( void )
call pvmfexit( info )
```

The routine pvm_exit() tells the local pvmd that this process is leaving PVM. This routine does not kill the process, which can continue to perform tasks just like any other UNIX process. Users typically call pvm_exit right before exiting their C programs and right before STOP in their Fortran programs.

```
int numt = pvm_spawn(  char *task, char **argv, int flag,
                       char *where, int ntask, int *tids )
call pvmfspawn( task, flag, where, ntask, tids, numt )
```

The routine pvm_spawn() starts up `ntask` copies of an executable file `task` on the virtual machine. `argv` is a pointer to an array of arguments to `task` with the end of the array specified by NULL. If task takes no arguments, then `argv` is NULL. The `flag` argument is used to specify options, and is a sum of:

Value	Option	Meaning
0	PvmTaskDefault	PVM chooses where to spawn processes.
1	PvmTaskHost	`where` argument is a particular host to spawn on.
2	PvmTaskArch	`where` argument is a PVM_ARCH to spawn on.
4	PvmTaskDebug	starts tasks under a debugger.
8	PvmTaskTrace	trace data is generated.
16	PvmMppFront	starts tasks on MPP front-end.
32	PvmHostCompl	complements host set in `where`.

These names are predefined in **pvm3/include/pvm3.h**. In Fortran all the names are predefined in parameter statements which can be found in the *include* file **pvm3/include/fpvm3.h**.

PvmTaskTrace is a new feature in PVM 3.3. It causes spawned tasks to generate trace events. PvmTasktrace is used by XPVM (see Chapter 8). Otherwise, the user must specify where the trace events are sent in pvm_setopt().

On return, `numt` is set to the number of tasks successfully spawned or an error code if no tasks could be started. If tasks were started, then pvm_spawn() returns a vector of the spawned tasks' `tids`; and if some tasks could not be started, the corresponding error codes are placed in the last $ntask - numt$ positions of the vector.

The pvm_spawn() call can also start tasks on multiprocessors. In the case of the Intel iPSC/860 the following restrictions apply. Each spawn call gets a subcube of size `ntask` and loads the program `task` on all of these nodes. The iPSC/860 OS has an allocation limit of 10 subcubes across all users, so it is better to start a block of tasks on an iPSC/860 with a single pvm_spawn() call rather than several calls. Two different blocks of tasks spawned separately on the iPSC/860 can still communicate with each other as well as any other PVM tasks even though they are in separate subcubes. The iPSC/860

OS has a restriction that messages going from the nodes to the outside world be less than 256 Kbytes.

```
int info = pvm_kill( int tid )
call pvmfkill( tid, info )
```

The routine pvm_kill() kills some other PVM task identified by TID. This routine is not designed to kill the calling task, which should be accomplished by calling pvm_exit() followed by exit().

```
int info = pvm_catchout( FILE *ff )
call pvmfcatchout( onoff )
```

The default is to have PVM write the *stderr* and *stdout* of spawned tasks to the log file /tmp/pvml.<uid>. The routine pvm_catchout causes the calling task to catch output from tasks subsequently spawned. Characters printed on *stdout* or *stderr* in children tasks are collected by the pvmds and sent in control messages to the parent task, which tags each line and appends it to the specified file (in C) or standard output (in Fortran). Each of the prints is prepended with information about which task generated the print, and the end of the print is marked to help separate outputs coming from several tasks at once.

If pvm_exit is called by the parent while output collection is in effect, it will block until all tasks sending it output have exited, in order to print all their output. To avoid this, one can turn off the output collection by calling pvm_catchout(0) before calling pvm_exit.

New capabilities in PVM 3.3 include the ability to register special PVM tasks to handle the jobs of adding new hosts, mapping tasks to hosts, and starting new tasks. This creates an interface for advanced batch schedulers (examples include Condor [11], DQS [10], and LSF [5]) to plug into PVM and run PVM jobs in batch mode. These register routines also create an interface for debugger writers to develop sophisticated debuggers for PVM.

The routine names are pvm_reg_rm(), pvm_reg_hoster(), and pvm_reg_tasker(). These are advanced functions not meant for the average PVM user and thus are not presented in detail here. Specifics can be found in Appendix B.

5.2   Information

```
int tid = pvm_parent( void )
call pvmfparent( tid )
```

The routine pvm_parent() returns the TID of the process that spawned this task or the value of PvmNoParent if not created by pvm_spawn().

```
int dtid = pvm_tidtohost( int tid )
call pvmftidtohost( tid, dtid )
```

The routine pvm_tidtohost() returns the TID dtid of the daemon running on the same host as TID. This routine is useful for determining on which host a given task is running. More general information about the entire virtual machine, including the textual name of the configured hosts, can be obtained by using the following functions:

```
int info = pvm_config(  int *nhost, int *narch,
                        struct pvmhostinfo **hostp )
call pvmfconfig( nhost, narch, dtid, name, arch, speed, info)
```

The routine pvm_config() returns information about the virtual machine including the number of hosts, nhost, and the number of different data formats, narch. hostp is a pointer to a user declaried array of pvmhostinfo structures. The array should be of size at least nhost. On return, each pvmhostinfo structure contains the pvmd TID, host name, name of the architecture, and relative CPU speed for that host in the configuration.

The Fortran function returns information about one host per call and cycles through all the hosts. Thus, if pvmfconfig is called nhost times, the entire virtual machine will be represented. The Fortran interface works by saving a copy of the hostp array and returning one entry per call. All the hosts must be cycled through before a new hostp array is obtained. Thus, if the virtual machine is changing during these calls, then the change will appear in the nhost and narch parameters, but not in the host information. Presently, there is no way to reset pvmfconfig() and force it to restart the cycle when it is in the middle.

```
int info = pvm_tasks(     int which, int *ntask,
                          struct pvmtaskinfo **taskp )
call pvmftasks(            which, ntask, tid, ptid, dtid,
                          flag, aout, info )
```

The routine pvm_tasks() returns information about the PVM tasks running on the
virtual machine. The integer which specifies which tasks to return information about.
The present options are (0), which means all tasks, a pvmd TID (dtid), which means
tasks running on that host, or a TID, which means just the given task.

The number of tasks is returned in ntask. taskp is a pointer to an array of pvmtaskinfo
structures. The array is of size ntask. Each pvmtaskinfo structure contains the TID,
pvmd TID, parent TID, a status flag, and the spawned file name. (PVM doesn't know
the file name of manually started tasks and so leaves these blank.) The Fortran function
returns information about one task per call and cycles through all the tasks. Thus, if
where = 0, and pvmftasks is called ntask times, all tasks will be represented. The Fortran
implementation assumes that the task pool is not changing while it cycles through the
tasks. If the pool changes, these changes will not appear until the next cycle of ntask
calls begins.

Examples of the use of pvm_config and pvm_tasks can be found in the source to the
PVM console, which is just a PVM task itself. Examples of the use of the Fortran
versions of these routines can be found in the source pvm3/examples/testall.f.

5.3   Dynamic Configuration

```
int info = pvm_addhosts( char **hosts, int nhost, int *infos)
int info = pvm_delhosts( char **hosts, int nhost, int *infos)
call pvmfaddhost( host, info )
call pvmfdelhost( host, info )
```

The C routines add or delete a set of hosts in the virtual machine. The Fortran
routines add or delete a single host in the virtual machine. In the Fortran routine info
is returned as 1 or a status code. In the C version info is returned as the number of
hosts successfully added. The argument infos is an array of length nhost that contains
the status code for each individual host being added or deleted. This allows the user to
check whether only one of a set of hosts caused a problem rather than trying to add or
delete the entire set of hosts again.

These routines are sometimes used to set up a virtual machine, but more often they are used to increase the flexibility and fault tolerance of a large application. These routines allow an application to increase the available computing power (adding hosts) if it determines the problem is getting harder to solve. One example of this would be a CAD/CAM program where, during the computation, the finite-element grid is refined, dramatically increasing the size of the problem. Another use would be to increase the fault tolerance of an application by having it detect the failure of a host and adding in a replacement.

5.4   Signaling

```
int info = pvm_sendsig( int tid, int signum )
call pvmfsendsig( tid, signum, info )
int info = pvm_notify( int what, int msgtag, int cnt, int tids )
call pvmfnotify( what, msgtag, cnt, tids, info )
```

The routine pvm_sendsig() sends a signal signum to another PVM task identified by TID. The routine pvm_notify requests PVM to notify the caller on detecting certain events. The present options are as follows:

PvmTaskExit - notify if a task exits.

PvmHostDelete - notify if a host is deleted (or fails).

PvmHostAdd - notify if a host is added.

In response to a notify request, some number of messages (see Appendix B) are sent by PVM back to the calling task. The messages are tagged with the user supplied msgtag. The tids array specifies who to monitor when using TaskExit or HostDelete. The array contains nothing when using HostAdd. If required, the routines pvm_config and pvm_tasks can be used to obtain task and pvmd tids.

If the host on which task A is running fails, and task B has asked to be notified if task A exits, then task B will be notified even though the exit was caused indirectly by the host failure.

5.5 Setting and Getting Options

```
int oldval = pvm_setopt( int what, int val )
int val = pvm_getopt( int what )
call pvmfsetopt( what, val, oldval )
call pvmfgetopt( what, val )
```

The routine pvm_setopt is a general-purpose function that allows the user to set or get
options in the PVM system. In PVM 3, pvm_setopt can be used to set several options,
including automatic error message printing, debugging level, and communication routing
method for all subsequent PVM calls. pvm_setopt returns the previous value of set in
oldval. The PVM 3.3 what can have the following values:

Option Value		Meaning
PvmRoute	1	routing policy
PvmDebugMask	2	debugmask
PvmAutoErr	3	auto error reporting
PvmOutputTid	4	stdout destination for children
PvmOutputCode	5	output msgtag
PvmTraceTid	6	trace destination for children
PvmTraceCode	7	trace msgtag
PvmFragSize	8	message fragment size
PvmResvTids	9	allow messages to reserved tags and tids
PvmSelfOutputTid	10	stdout destination for self
PvmSelfOutputCode	11	output msgtag
PvmSelfTraceTid	12	trace destination for self
PvmSelfTraceCode	13	trace msgtag

See Appendix B for allowable values for these options. Future expansions to this list are
planned.

The most popular use of pvm_setopt is to enable direct route communication between
PVM tasks. As a general rule of thumb, PVM communication bandwidth over a network
doubles by calling

```
pvm_setopt( PvmRoute, PvmRouteDirect );
```

The drawback is that this faster communication method is not scalable under Unix;

hence, it may not work if the application involves over 60 tasks that communicate randomly with each other. If it doesn't work, PVM automatically switches back to the default communication method. It can be called multiple times during an application to selectively set up direct task-to-task communication links, but typical use is to call it once after the initial call to pvm_mytid().

5.6   Message Passing

Sending a message comprises three steps in PVM. First, a send buffer must be initialized by a call to pvm_initsend() or pvm_mkbuf(). Second, the message must be "packed" into this buffer using any number and combination of pvm_pk*() routines. (In Fortran all message packing is done with the pvmfpack() subroutine.) Third, the completed message is sent to another process by calling the pvm_send() routine or multicast with the pvm_mcast() routine.

A message is received by calling either a blocking or nonblocking receive routine and then "unpacking" each of the packed items from the receive buffer. The receive routines can be set to accept *any* message, or any message from a specified source, or any message with a specified message tag, or only messages with a given message tag from a given source. There is also a probe function that returns whether a message has arrived, but does not actually receive it.

If required, other receive contexts can be handled by PVM 3. The routine pvm_recvf() allows users to define their own receive contexts that will be used by the subsequent PVM receive routines.

5.6.1   Message Buffers

```
int bufid = pvm_initsend( int encoding )
call pvmfinitsend( encoding, bufid )
```

If the user is using only a single send buffer (and this is the typical case) then pvm_initsend() is the only required buffer routine. It is called before packing a new message into the buffer. The routine pvm_initsend clears the send buffer and creates a new one for packing a new message. The encoding scheme used for this packing is set by encoding. The new buffer identifier is returned in bufid.

The encoding options are as follows:

PvmDataDefault – XDR encoding is used by default because PVM cannot know whether the user is going to add a heterogeneous machine before this message is sent. If the user knows that the next message will be sent only to a machine that understands the native format, then he can use *PvmDataRaw* encoding and save on encoding costs.

PvmDataRaw – no encoding is done. Messages are sent in their original format. If the receiving process cannot read this format, it will return an error during unpacking.

PvmDataInPlace – data left in place to save on packing costs. Buffer contains only sizes and pointers to the items to be sent. When pvm_send() is called, the items are copied directly out of the user's memory. This option decreases the number of times the message is copied at the expense of requiring the user to not modify the items between the time they are packed and the time they are sent. One use of this option would be to call pack once and modify and send certain items (arrays) multiple times during an application. An example would be passing of boundary regions in a discretized PDE implementation.

The following message buffer routines are required only if the user wishes to manage multiple message buffers inside an application. Multiple message buffers are not required for most message passing between processes. In PVM 3 there is one *active* send buffer and one *active* receive buffer per process at any given moment. The developer may create any number of message buffers and switch between them for the packing and sending of data. The packing, sending, receiving, and unpacking routines affect only the *active* buffers.

```
int bufid = pvm_mkbuf( int encoding )
call pvmfmkbuf( encoding, bufid )
```

The routine pvm_mkbuf creates a new empty send buffer and specifies the encoding method used for packing messages. It returns a buffer identifier `bufid`.

```
int info = pvm_freebuf( int bufid )
call pvmffreebuf( bufid, info )
```

The routine pvm_freebuf() disposes of the buffer with identifier `bufid`. This should be done after a message has been sent and is no longer needed. Call pvm_mkbuf() to create a buffer for a new message if required. Neither of these calls is required when using pvm_initsend(), which performs these functions for the user.

```
int bufid = pvm_getsbuf( void )
call pvmfgetsbuf( bufid )
int bufid = pvm_getrbuf( void )
call pvmfgetrbuf( bufid )
```

pvm_getsbuf() returns the active send buffer identifier. pvm_getrbuf() returns the active receive buffer identifier.

```
int oldbuf = pvm_setsbuf( int bufid )
call pvmfsetrbuf( bufid, oldbuf )
int oldbuf = pvm_setrbuf( int bufid )
call pvmfsetrbuf( bufid, oldbuf )
```

These routines set the active send (or receive) buffer to bufid, save the state of the previous buffer, and return the previous active buffer identifier oldbuf.

If bufid is set to 0 in pvm_setsbuf() or pvm_setrbuf(), then the present buffer is saved and there is no active buffer. This feature can be used to save the present state of an application's messages so that a math library or graphical interface which also uses PVM messages will not interfere with the state of the application's buffers. After they complete, the application's buffers can be reset to active.

It is possible to forward messages without repacking them by using the message buffer routines. This is illustrated by the following fragment.

```
bufid = pvm_recv( src, tag );
oldid = pvm_setsbuf( bufid );
info  = pvm_send( dst, tag );
info  = pvm_freebuf( oldid );
```

5.6.2   Packing Data

Each of the following C routines packs an array of the given data type into the active send buffer. They can be called multiple times to pack data into a single message. Thus, a message can contain several arrays each with a different data type. C structures must be passed by packing their individual elements. There is no limit to the complexity of the packed messages, but an application should unpack the messages exactly as they were packed. Although this is not strictly required, it is a safe programming practice.

The arguments for each of the routines are a pointer to the first item to be packed, nitem which is the total number of items to pack from this array, and stride which is the stride to use when packing. A stride of 1 means a contiguous vector is packed, a

stride of 2 means every other item is packed, and so on. An exception is pvm_pkstr()
which by definition packs a NULL terminated character string and thus does not need
`nitem` or `stride` arguments.

```
int info = pvm_pkbyte(   char   *cp, int nitem, int stride )
int info = pvm_pkcplx(   float  *xp, int nitem, int stride )
int info = pvm_pkdcplx(  double *zp, int nitem, int stride )
int info = pvm_pkdouble( double *dp, int nitem, int stride )
int info = pvm_pkfloat(  float  *fp, int nitem, int stride )
int info = pvm_pkint(    int    *np, int nitem, int stride )
int info = pvm_pklong(   long   *np, int nitem, int stride )
int info = pvm_pkshort(  short  *np, int nitem, int stride )
int info = pvm_pkstr(    char   *cp )
int info = pvm_packf( const char *fmt, ... )
```

PVM also supplies a packing routine that uses a printf-like format expression to specify
what data to pack and how to pack it into the send buffer. All variables are passed as
addresses if count and stride are specified; otherwise, variables are assumed to be values.
A description of the format syntax is given in Appendix B.

A single Fortran subroutine handles all the packing functions of the above C routines.

```
call pvmfpack( what, xp, nitem, stride, info )
```

The argument xp is the first item of the array to be packed. Note that in Fortran the
number of characters in a string to be packed must be specified in `nitem`. The integer
`what` specifies the type of data to be packed. The supported options are as follows:

STRING	0	REAL4	4
BYTE1	1	COMPLEX8	5
INTEGER2	2	REAL8	6
INTEGER4	3	COMPLEX16	7

These names have been predefined in parameter statements in the include file
`pvm3/include/fpvm3.h`. Some vendors may extend this list to include 64-bit architectures in their PVM implementations. We will be adding INTEGER8, REAL16, etc.,
as soon as XDR support for these data types is available.

5.6.3   Sending and Receiving Data

```
int info = pvm_send( int tid, int msgtag )
call pvmfsend( tid, msgtag, info )
int info = pvm_mcast( int *tids, int ntask, int msgtag )
call pvmfmcast( ntask, tids, msgtag, info )
```

The routine pvm_send() labels the message with an integer identifier `msgtag` and sends it immediately to the process `TID`.

The routine pvm_mcast() labels the message with an integer identifier `msgtag` and broadcasts the message to all tasks specified in the integer array `tids` (except itself). The `tids` array is of length `ntask`.

```
int info = pvm_psend(   int tid, int msgtag,
                        void *vp, int cnt, int type )
call pvmfpsend( tid, msgtag, xp, cnt, type, info )
```

The routine pvm_psend() packs and sends an array of the specified datatype to the task identified by `TID`. The defined datatypes for Fortran are the same as for pvmfpack(). In C the `type` argument can be any of the following:

PVM_STR	PVM_FLOAT
PVM_BYTE	PVM_CPLX
PVM_SHORT	PVM_DOUBLE
PVM_INT	PVM_DCPLX
PVM_LONG	PVM_UINT
PVM_USHORT	PVM_ULONG

PVM contains several methods of receiving messages at a task. There is no function matching in PVM, for example, that a pvm_psend must be matched with a pvm_precv. Any of the following routines can be called for any incoming message no matter how it was sent (or multicast).

```
int bufid = pvm_recv( int tid, int msgtag )
call pvmfrecv( tid, msgtag, bufid )
```

This blocking receive routine will wait until a message with label `msgtag` has arrived from `TID`. A value of -1 in `msgtag` or `TID` matches anything (wildcard). It then places the message in a new active receive buffer that is created. The previous active receive buffer is cleared unless it has been saved with a pvm_setrbuf() call.

```
int bufid = pvm_nrecv( int tid, int msgtag )
call pvmfnrecv( tid, msgtag, bufid )
```

If the requested message has not arrived, then the nonblocking receive pvm_nrecv() returns bufid = 0. This routine can be called multiple times for the same message to check whether it has arrived, while performing useful work between calls. When no more useful work can be performed, the blocking receive pvm_recv() can be called for the same message. If a message with label msgtag has arrived from TID, pvm_nrecv() places this message in a new active receive buffer (which it creates) and returns the ID of this buffer. The previous active receive buffer is cleared unless it has been saved with a pvm_setrbuf() call. A value of -1 in msgtag or TID matches anything (wildcard).

```
int bufid = pvm_probe( int tid, int msgtag )
call pvmfprobe( tid, msgtag, bufid )
```

If the requested message has not arrived, then pvm_probe() returns bufid = 0. Otherwise, it returns a bufid for the message, but does not "receive" it. This routine can be called multiple times for the same message to check whether it has arrived, while performing useful work between calls. In addition, pvm_bufinfo() can be called with the returned bufid to determine information about the message before receiving it.

```
int bufid = pvm_trecv( int tid, int msgtag, struct timeval *tmout )
call pvmftrecv( tid, msgtag, sec, usec, bufid )
```

PVM also supplies a timeout version of receive. Consider the case where a message is never going to arrive (because of error or failure); the routine pvm_recv would block forever. To avoid such situations, the user may wish to give up after waiting for a fixed amount of time. The routine pvm_trecv() allows the user to specify a timeout period. If the timeout period is set very large, then pvm_trecv acts like pvm_recv. If the timeout period is set to zero, then pvm_trecv acts like pvm_nrecv. Thus, pvm_trecv fills the gap between the blocking and nonblocking receive functions.

```
int info = pvm_bufinfo( int bufid, int *bytes, int *msgtag, int *tid )
call pvmfbufinfo( bufid, bytes, msgtag, tid, info )
```

The routine pvm_bufinfo() returns msgtag, source TID, and length in bytes of the message identified by `bufid`. It can be used to determine the label and source of a message that was received with wildcards specified.

```
int info = pvm_precv(   int tid, int msgtag, void *vp, int cnt,
                        int type, int *rtid, int *rtag, int *rcnt )
call pvmfprecv( tid, msgtag, xp, cnt, type, rtid, rtag, rcnt, info )
```

The routine pvm_precv() combines the functions of a blocking receive and unpacking the received buffer. It does not return a `bufid`. Instead, it returns the actual values of TID, msgtag, and cnt.

```
int (*old)() = pvm_recvf(int (*new)(int buf, int tid, int tag))
```

The routine pvm_recvf() modifies the receive context used by the receive functions and can be used to extend PVM. The default receive context is to match on source and message tag. This can be modified to any user-defined comparison function. (See Appendix B for an example of creating a probe function with pvm_recf().) There is no Fortran interface routine for pvm_recvf().

5.6.4   Unpacking Data

The following C routines unpack (multiple) data types from the active receive buffer. In an application they should match their corresponding pack routines in type, number of items, and stride. `nitem` is the number of items of the given type to unpack, and `stride` is the stride.

```
int info = pvm_upkbyte(   char   *cp, int nitem, int stride )
int info = pvm_upkcplx(   float  *xp, int nitem, int stride )
int info = pvm_upkdcplx(  double *zp, int nitem, int stride )
int info = pvm_upkdouble( double *dp, int nitem, int stride )
int info = pvm_upkfloat(  float  *fp, int nitem, int stride )
int info = pvm_upkint(    int    *np, int nitem, int stride )
int info = pvm_upklong(   long   *np, int nitem, int stride )
int info = pvm_upkshort(  short  *np, int nitem, int stride )
int info = pvm_upkstr(    char   *cp )
int info = pvm_unpackf( const char *fmt, ... )
```

The routine pvm_unpackf() uses a printf-like format expression to specify what data to unpack and how to unpack it from the receive buffer.

A single Fortran subroutine handles all the unpacking functions of the above C routines.

```
call pvmfunpack( what, xp, nitem, stride, info )
```

The argument xp is the array to be unpacked into. The integer argument what specifies the type of data to be unpacked. (Same what options as for pvmfpack()).

5.7   Dynamic Process Groups

The dynamic process group functions are built on top of the core PVM routines. A separate library libgpvm3.a must be linked with user programs that make use of any of the group functions. The pvmd does not perform the group functions. This task is handled by a group server that is automatically started when the first group function is invoked. There is some debate about how groups should be handled in a message-passing interface. The issues include efficiency and reliability, and there are tradeoffs between static versus dynamic groups. Some people argue that only tasks in a group can call group functions.

In keeping with the PVM philosophy, the group functions are designed to be very general and transparent to the user, at some cost in efficiency. Any PVM task can join or leave any group at any time without having to inform any other task in the affected groups. Tasks can broadcast messages to groups of which they are not a member. In general, any PVM task may call any of the following group functions at any time. The exceptions are pvm_lvgroup(), pvm_barrier(), and pvm_reduce(), which by their nature require the calling task to be a member of the specified group.

```
int inum  = pvm_joingroup( char *group )
int info  = pvm_lvgroup( char *group )
call pvmfjoingroup( group, inum )
call pvmflvgroup( group, info )
```

These routines allow a task to join or leave a user named group. The first call to pvm_joingroup() creates a group with name group and puts the calling task in this group. pvm_joingroup() returns the instance number (inum) of the process in this group. Instance numbers run from 0 to the number of group members minus 1. In PVM 3, a task can join multiple groups.

If a process leaves a group and then rejoins it, that process may receive a different instance number. Instance numbers are recycled so a task joining a group will get the lowest available instance number. But if multiple tasks are joining a group, there is no guarantee that a task will be assigned its previous instance number.

To assist the user in maintaining a continuous set of instance numbers despite joining and leaving, the pvm_lvgroup() function does not return until the task is confirmed to have left. A pvm_joingroup() called after this return will assign the vacant instance number to the new task. It is the user's responsibility to maintain a contiguous set of instance numbers if the algorithm requires it. If several tasks leave a group and no tasks join, then there will be gaps in the instance numbers.

```
int tid = pvm_gettid( char *group, int inum )
int inum = pvm_getinst( char *group, int tid )
int size = pvm_gsize( char *group )
call pvmfgettid( group, inum, tid )
call pvmfgetinst( group, tid, inum )
call pvmfgsize( group, size )
```

The routine pvm_gettid() returns the TID of the process with a given group name and instance number. pvm_gettid() allows two tasks with no knowledge of each other to get each other's TID simply by joining a common group. The routine pvm_getinst() returns the instance number of TID in the specified group. The routine pvm_gsize() returns the number of members in the specified group.

```
int info = pvm_barrier( char *group, int count )
call pvmfbarrier( group, count, info )
```

On calling pvm_barrier() the process blocks until count members of a group have called pvm_barrier. In general count should be the total number of members of the group. A count is required because with dynamic process groups PVM cannot know how many members are in a group at a given instant. It is an error for processes to call pvm_barrier with a group it is not a member of. It is also an error if the count arguments across a given barrier call do not match. For example it is an error if one member of a group calls pvm_barrier() with a count of 4, and another member calls pvm_barrier() with a count of 5.

```
int info = pvm_bcast( char *group, int msgtag )
call pvmfbcast( group, msgtag, info )
```

pvm_bcast() labels the message with an integer identifier `msgtag` and broadcasts the message to all tasks in the specified group except itself (if it is a member of the group). For pvm_bcast() "all tasks" is defined to be those tasks the group server thinks are in the group when the routine is called. If tasks join the group during a broadcast, they may not receive the message. If tasks leave the group during a broadcast, a copy of the message will still be sent to them.

```
int info = pvm_reduce(   void (*func)(), void *data,
                         int nitem, int datatype,
                         int msgtag, char *group, int root )
call pvmfreduce(         func, data, count, datatype,
                         msgtag, group, root, info )
```

pvm_reduce() performs a global arithmetic operation across the group, for example, global sum or global max. The result of the reduction operation appears on `root`. PVM supplies four predefined functions that the user can place in `func`. These are

        PvmMax
        PvmMin
        PvmSum
        PvmProduct

The reduction operation is performed element-wise on the input data. For example, if the data array contains two floating-point numbers and func is PvmMax, then the result contains two numbers—the global maximum of each group members first number and the global maximum of each member's second number.

   In addition users can define their own global operation function to place in `func`. See Appendix B for details. An example is given in the source code for PVM. For more information see `PVM_ROOT/examples/gexamples`.

   Note: pvm_reduce() does not block. If a task calls pvm_reduce and then leaves the group before the root has called pvm_reduce, an error may occur.

6 Program Examples

In this chapter we discuss several complete PVM programs in detail. The first example, forkjoin.c, shows how to to spawn off processes and synchronize with them. The second example discusses a Fortran dot product program, PSDOT.F. The third example, failure.c, demonstrates how the user can use the `pvm_notify()` call to create fault tolerant appliations. We present an example that performs a matrix multiply. Lastly, we show how PVM can be used to compute heat diffusion through a wire.

6.1 Fork-Join

Our first example demonstrates how to spawn off PVM tasks and synchronize with them. The program spawns several tasks, three by default. The children then synchronize by sending a message to their parent task. The parent receives a message from each of the spawned tasks and prints out information about the message from the child tasks.

The fork-join program contains the code for both the parent and the child tasks. Let's examine it in more detail. The very first thing the program does is call `pvm_mytid()`. This function must be called before any other PVM call can be made. The result of the `pvm_mytid()` call should always be a positive integer. If it is not, then something is seriously wrong. In fork-join we check the value of mytid; if it indicates an error, we call `pvm_perror()` and exit the program. The `pvm_perror()` call will print a message indicating what went wrong with the last PVM call. In our example the last call was `pvm_mytid()`, so `pvm_perror()` might print a message indicating that PVM hasn't been started on this machine. The argument to `pvm_perror()` is a string that will be prepended to any error message printed by `pvm_perror()`. In this case we pass argv[0], which is the name of the program as it was typed on the command line. The `pvm_perror()` function is modeled after the Unix `perror()` function.

Assuming we obtained a valid result for mytid, we now call `pvm_parent()`. The `pvm_parent()` function will return the TID of the task that spawned the calling task. Since we run the initial fork-join program from the Unix shell, this initial task will not have a parent; it will not have been spawned by some other PVM task but will have been started manually by the user. For the initial forkjoin task the result of `pvm_parent()` will not be any particular task id but an error code, PvmNoParent. Thus we can distinguish the parent forkjoin task from the children by checking whether the result of the `pvm_parent()` call is equal to PvmNoParent. If this task is the parent, then it must spawn the children. If it is not the parent, then it must send a message to the parent.

Let's examine the code executed by the parent task. The number of tasks is taken from the command line as argv[1]. If the number of tasks is not legal, then we exit the program, calling `pvm_exit()` and then returning. The call to `pvm_exit()` is important because it tells PVM this program will no longer be using any of the PVM facilities. (In this case the task exits and PVM will deduce that the dead task no longer needs its services. Regardless, it is good style to exit cleanly.) Assuming the number of tasks is valid, forkjoin will then attempt to spawn the children.

The `pvm_spawn()` call tells PVM to start ntask tasks named argv[0]. The second parameter is the argument list given to the spawned tasks. In this case we don't care to give the children any particular command line arguments, so this value is null. The third parameter to spawn, PvmTaskDefault, is a flag telling PVM to spawn the tasks in the default location. Had we been interested in placing the children on a specific machine or a machine of a particular architecture, then we would have used PvmTaskHost or PvmTaskArch for this flag and specified the host or architecture as the fourth parameter. Since we don't care where the tasks execute, we use PvmTaskDefault for the flag and null for the fourth parameter. Finally, ntask tells spawn how many tasks to start; the integer array child will hold the task ids of the newly spawned children. The return value of `pvm_spawn()` indicates how many tasks were successfully spawned. If info is not equal to ntask, then some error occurred during the spawn. In case of an error, the error code is placed in the task id array, child, instead of the actual task id. The fork-join program loops over this array and prints the task ids or any error codes. If no tasks were successfully spawned, then the program exits.

For each child task, the parent receives a message and prints out information about that message. The `pvm_recv()` call receives a message (with that JOINTAG) from any task. The return value of `pvm_recv()` is an integer indicating a message buffer. This integer can be used to find out information about message buffers. The subsequent call to `pvm_bufinfo()` does just this; it gets the length, tag, and task id of the sending process for the message indicated by buf. In fork-join the messages sent by the children contain a single integer value, the task id of the child task. The `pvm_upkint()` call unpacks the integer from the message into the mydata variable. As a sanity check, forkjoin tests the value of mydata and the task id returned by `pvm_bufinfo()`. If the values differ, the program has a bug, and an error message is printed. Finally, the information about the message is printed, and the parent program exits.

The last segment of code in forkjoin will be executed by the child tasks. Before placing data in a message buffer, the buffer must be initialized by calling `pvm_initsend()`. The parameter PvmDataDefault indicates that PVM should do whatever data conversion is needed to ensure that the data arrives in the correct format on the destination processor. In some cases this may result in unnecessary data conversions. If the user is sure no data conversion will be needed since the destination machine uses the same data format, then he can use PvmDataRaw as a parameter to `pvm_initsend()`. The `pvm_pkint()`

call places a single integer, mytid, into the message buffer. It is important to make sure the corresponding unpack call exactly matches the pack call. Packing an integer and unpacking it as a float will not work correctly. Similarly, if the user packs two integers with a single call, he cannot unpack those integers by calling pvm_upkint() twice, once for each integer. There must be a one to one correspondence between pack and unpack calls. Finally, the message is sent to the parent task using a message tag of JOINTAG.

Fork Join Example

```
/*
    Fork Join Example
    Demonstrates how to spawn processes and exchange messages
*/

/* defines and prototypes for the PVM library */
#include <pvm3.h>

/* Maximum number of children this program will spawn */
#define MAXNCHILD    20
/* Tag to use for the joing message */
#define JOINTAG      11


int
main(int argc, char* argv[])
{

    /* number of tasks to spawn, use 3 as the default */
    int ntask = 3;
    /* return code from pvm calls */
    int info;
    /* my task id */
    int mytid;
    /* my parents task id */
    int myparent;
    /* children task id array */
    int child[MAXNCHILD];
    int i, mydata, buf, len, tag, tid;
```

```
/* find out my task id number */
mytid = pvm_mytid();

/* check for error */
if (mytid < 0) {
    /* print out the error */
    pvm_perror(argv[0]);
    /* exit the program */
    return -1;
    }
/* find my parent's task id number */
myparent = pvm_parent();

/* exit if there is some error other than PvmNoParent */
if ((myparent < 0) && (myparent != PvmNoParent)) {
    pvm_perror(argv[0]);
    pvm_exit();
    return -1;
    }


/* if i don't have a parent then i am the parent */
if (myparent == PvmNoParent) {
    /* find out how many tasks to spawn */
    if (argc == 2) ntask = atoi(argv[1]);
    /* make sure ntask is legal */
    if ((ntask < 1) || (ntask > MAXNCHILD)) { pvm_exit(); return 0; }

    /* spawn the child tasks */
    info = pvm_spawn(argv[0], (char**)0, PvmTaskDefault, (char*)0,
        ntask, child);
    /* print out the task ids */
    for (i = 0; i < ntask; i++)
        if (child[i] < 0) /* print the error code in decimal*/
            printf(" %d", child[i]);
        else  /* print the task id in hex */
            printf("t%x\t", child[i]);
```

```
    putchar('\n');

    /* make sure spawn succeeded */
    if (info == 0) { pvm_exit(); return -1; }

    /* only expect responses from those spawned correctly */
    ntask = info;

    for (i = 0; i < ntask; i++) {
        /* recv a message from any child process */
        buf = pvm_recv(-1, JOINTAG);
        if (buf < 0) pvm_perror("calling recv");
        info = pvm_bufinfo(buf, &len, &tag, &tid);
        if (info < 0) pvm_perror("calling pvm_bufinfo");
        info = pvm_upkint(&mydata, 1, 1);
        if (info < 0) pvm_perror("calling pvm_upkint");
        if (mydata != tid) printf("This should not happen!\n");
        printf("Length %d, Tag %d, Tid t%x\n", len, tag, tid);
        }
    pvm_exit();
    return 0;
    }


/* i'm a child */
info = pvm_initsend(PvmDataDefault);
if (info < 0) {
   pvm_perror("calling pvm_initsend"); pvm_exit(); return -1;
   }
info = pvm_pkint(&mytid, 1, 1);
if (info < 0) {
   pvm_perror("calling pvm_pkint"); pvm_exit(); return -1;
   }
info = pvm_send(myparent, JOINTAG);
if (info < 0) {
   pvm_perror("calling pvm_send"); pvm_exit(); return -1;
   }
pvm_exit();
```

```
% forkjoin
t10001c t40149  tc0037
Length 4, Tag 11, Tid t40149
Length 4, Tag 11, Tid tc0037
Length 4, Tag 11, Tid t10001c
% forkjoin 4
t10001e t10001d t4014b  tc0038
Length 4, Tag 11, Tid t4014b
Length 4, Tag 11, Tid tc0038
Length 4, Tag 11, Tid t10001d
Length 4, Tag 11, Tid t10001e
```

Figure 6.1
Output of fork-join program

```
    return 0;
}
```

Figure 6.1 shows the output of running forkjoin. Notice that the order the messages were received is nondeterministic. Since the main loop of the parent processes messages on a first-come first-serve basis, the order of the prints are simply determined by time it takes messages to travel from the child tasks to the parent.

6.2   Dot Product

Here we show a simple Fortran program, PSDOT, for computing a dot product. The program computes the dot product of arrays, X and Y. First PSDOT calls PVMFMYTID() and PVMFPARENT(). The PVMFPARENT call will return PVMNOPARENT if the task wasn't spawned by another PVM task. If this is the case, then PSDOT is the master and must spawn the other worker copies of PSDOT. PSDOT then asks the user for the number of processes to use and the length of vectors to compute. Each spawned process will receive $n/nproc$ elements of X and Y, where n is the length of the vectors and $nproc$ is the number of processes being used in the computation. If $nproc$ does not divide n evenly, then the master will compute the dot product on extra the elements. The subroutine SGENMAT randomly generates values for X and Y. PSDOT then spawns $nproc-1$ copies of itself and sends each new task a part of the X and Y arrays. The message contains the length of the subarrays in the message and the subarrays themselves. After the master spawns the worker processes and sends out the subvectors, the master then computes the dot product on its portion of X and Y. The master process then receives the other local dot products from the worker processes. Notice that the PVMFRECV call uses a wildcard (−1) for the task id parameter. This indicates that a message from *any* task will satisfy the receive. Using the wildcard in this manner results in a race condition. In this case the race condition does not cause a problem since addition is commutative. In other words, it doesn't matter in which order we add the partial sums from the workers. Unless one is certain that the race will not have an adverse effect on the program, race conditions should be avoided.

Once the master receives all the local dot products and sums them into a global dot product, it then calculates the entire dot product locally. These two results are then subtracted, and the difference between the two values is printed. A small difference can be expected because of the variation in floating-point roundoff errors.

If the PSDOT program is a worker then it receives a message from the master process containing subarrays of X and Y. It calculates the dot product of these subarrays and sends the result back to the master process. In the interests of brevity we do not include the SGENMAT and SDOT subroutines.

Example program: PSDOT.F

```
      PROGRAM PSDOT
*
*  PSDOT performs a parallel inner (or dot) product, where the vectors
*  X and Y start out on a master node, which then sets up the virtual
*  machine, farms out the data and work, and sums up the local pieces
*  to get a global inner product.
*
*        .. External Subroutines ..
      EXTERNAL PVMFMYTID, PVMFPARENT, PVMFSPAWN, PVMFEXIT, PVMFINITSEND
      EXTERNAL PVMFPACK, PVMFSEND, PVMFRECV, PVMFUNPACK, SGENMAT
*
*        .. External Functions ..
      INTEGER ISAMAX
      REAL SDOT
      EXTERNAL ISAMAX, SDOT
*
*        .. Intrinsic Functions ..
      INTRINSIC MOD
```

```
*
*        .. Parameters ..
         INTEGER MAXN
         PARAMETER ( MAXN = 8000 )
         INCLUDE 'fpvm3.h'
*
*        .. Scalars ..
         INTEGER N, LN, MYTID, NPROCS, IBUF, IERR
         INTEGER I, J, K
         REAL LDOT, GDOT
*
*        .. Arrays ..
         INTEGER TIDS(0:63)
         REAL X(MAXN), Y(MAXN)
*
*     Enroll in PVM and get my and the master process' task ID number
*
         CALL PVMFMYTID( MYTID )
         CALL PVMFPARENT( TIDS(0) )
*
*     If I need to spawn other processes (I am master process)
*
         IF ( TIDS(0) .EQ. PVMNOPARENT ) THEN
*
*        Get starting information
*
            WRITE(*,*) 'How many processes should participate (1-64)?'
            READ(*,*) NPROCS
            WRITE(*,2000) MAXN
            READ(*,*) N
            TIDS(0) = MYTID
            IF ( N .GT. MAXN ) THEN
               WRITE(*,*) 'N too large.  Increase parameter MAXN to run'//
     $                 'this case.'
               STOP
            END IF
*
*        LN is the number of elements of the dot product to do
```

```
*            locally.  Everyone has the same number, with the master
*            getting any left over elements.  J stores the number of
*            elements rest of procs do.
*
             J = N / NPROCS
             LN = J + MOD(N, NPROCS)
             I = LN + 1
*
*            Randomly generate X and Y
*
             CALL SGENMAT( N, 1, X, N, MYTID, NPROCS, MAXN, J )
             CALL SGENMAT( N, 1, Y, N, I, N, LN, NPROCS )
*
*            Loop over all worker processes
*
             DO 10 K = 1, NPROCS-1
*
*               Spawn process and check for error
*
                CALL PVMFSPAWN( 'psdot', 0, 'anywhere', 1, TIDS(K), IERR )
                IF (IERR .NE. 1) THEN
                   WRITE(*,*) 'ERROR, could not spawn process #',K,
     $                        '. Dying . . .'
                   CALL PVMFEXIT( IERR )
                   STOP
                END IF
*
*               Send out startup info
*
                CALL PVMFINITSEND( PVMDEFAULT, IBUF )
                CALL PVMFPACK( INTEGER4, J, 1, 1, IERR )
                CALL PVMFPACK( REAL4, X(I), J, 1, IERR )
                CALL PVMFPACK( REAL4, Y(I), J, 1, IERR )
                CALL PVMFSEND( TIDS(K), 0, IERR )
                I = I + J
   10        CONTINUE
*
*            Figure master's part of dot product
```

```
*
        GDOT = SDOT( LN, X, 1, Y, 1 )
*
*       Receive the local dot products, and
*       add to get the global dot product
*
        DO 20 K = 1, NPROCS-1
           CALL PVMFRECV( -1, 1, IBUF )
           CALL PVMFUNPACK( REAL4, LDOT, 1, 1, IERR )
           GDOT = GDOT + LDOT
  20    CONTINUE
*
*       Print out result
*
        WRITE(*,*) ' '
        WRITE(*,*) '<x,y> = ',GDOT
*
*       Do sequential dot product and subtract from
*       distributed dot product to get desired error estimate
*
        LDOT = SDOT( N, X, 1, Y, 1 )
        WRITE(*,*) '<x,y> : sequential dot product.  <x,y>^ : '//
     $            'distributed dot product.'
        WRITE(*,*) '| <x,y> - <x,y>^ | = ',ABS(GDOT - LDOT)
        WRITE(*,*) 'Run completed.'
*
*    If I am a worker process (i.e. spawned by master process)
*
     ELSE
*
*       Receive startup info
*
        CALL PVMFRECV( TIDS(0), 0, IBUF )
        CALL PVMFUNPACK( INTEGER4, LN, 1, 1, IERR )
        CALL PVMFUNPACK( REAL4, X, LN, 1, IERR )
        CALL PVMFUNPACK( REAL4, Y, LN, 1, IERR )
*
*       Figure local dot product and send it in to master
```

```
*
        LDOT = SDOT( LN, X, 1, Y, 1 )
        CALL PVMFINITSEND( PVMDEFAULT, IBUF )
        CALL PVMFPACK( REAL4, LDOT, 1, 1, IERR )
        CALL PVMFSEND( TIDS(0), 1, IERR )
     END IF
*
     CALL PVMFEXIT( 0 )
*
1000 FORMAT(I10,' Successfully spawned process #',I2,', TID =',I10)
2000 FORMAT('Enter the length of vectors to multiply (1 -',I7,'):')
     STOP
*
*    End program PSDOT
*
     END
```

6.3 Failure

The failure example demonstrates how one can kill tasks and how one can find out when tasks exit or fail. For this example we spawn several tasks, just as we did in the previous examples. One of these unlucky tasks gets killed by the parent. Since we are interested in finding out when a task fails, we call pvm_notify() after spawning the tasks. The pvm_notify() call tells PVM to send the calling task a message when certain tasks exit. Here we are interested in all the children. Note that the task calling pvm_notify() will receive the notification, *not* the tasks given in the task id array. It wouldn't make much sense to send a notification message to a task that has exited. The notify call can also be used to notify a task when a new host has been added or deleted from the virtual machine. This might be useful if a program wants to dynamically adapt to the currently available machines.

After requesting notification, the parent task then kills one of the children; in this case, one of the middle children is killed. The call to pvm_kill() simply kills the task indicated by the task id parameter. After killing one of the spawned tasks, the parent waits on a pvm_recv(-1, TASKDIED) for the message notifying it the task has died. The task id of the task that has exited is stored as a single integer in the notify message. The process unpacks the dead task's id and prints it out. For good measure it also prints out

the task id of the task it killed. These ids should be the same. The child tasks simply
wait for about a minute and then quietly exit.

Example program: failure.c

```
/*
    Failure notification example
    Demonstrates how to tell when a task exits
*/

/* defines and prototypes for the PVM library */
#include <pvm3.h>

/* Maximum number of children this program will spawn */
#define MAXNCHILD   20
/* Tag to use for the task done message */
#define TASKDIED        11


int
main(int argc, char* argv[])
{

    /* number of tasks to spawn, use 3 as the default */
    int ntask = 3;
    /* return code from pvm calls */
    int info;
    /* my task id */
    int mytid;
    /* my parents task id */
    int myparent;
    /* children task id array */
    int child[MAXNCHILD];
    int i, deadtid;
    int tid;
    char *argv[5];
```

```
/* find out my task id number */
mytid = pvm_mytid();

/* check for error */
if (mytid < 0) {
    /* print out the error */
    pvm_perror(argv[0]);
    /* exit the program */
    return -1;
    }
/* find my parent's task id number */
myparent = pvm_parent();


/* exit if there is some error other than PvmNoParent */
if ((myparent < 0) && (myparent != PvmNoParent)) {
    pvm_perror(argv[0]);
    pvm_exit();
    return -1;
    }

/* if i don't have a parent then i am the parent */
if (myparent == PvmNoParent) {
    /* find out how many tasks to spawn */
    if (argc == 2) ntask = atoi(argv[1]);
    /* make sure ntask is legal */
    if ((ntask < 1) || (ntask > MAXNCHILD)) { pvm_exit(); return 0; }

    /* spawn the child tasks */
    info = pvm_spawn(argv[0], (char**)0, PvmTaskDebug, (char*)0,
        ntask, child);

    /* make sure spawn succeeded */
    if (info != ntask) { pvm_exit(); return -1; }

    /* print the tids */
    for (i = 0; i < ntask; i++) printf("t%x\t",child[i]); putchar('\n');
```

```
            /* ask for notification when child exits */
            info = pvm_notify(PvmTaskExit, TASKDIED, ntask, child);
            if (info < 0) { pvm_perror("notify"); pvm_exit(); return -1; }


            /* reap the middle child */
            info = pvm_kill(child[ntask/2]);
            if (info < 0) { pvm_perror("kill"); pvm_exit(); return -1; }

            /* wait for the notification */
            info = pvm_recv(-1, TASKDIED);
            if (info < 0) { pvm_perror("recv"); pvm_exit(); return -1; }
            info = pvm_upkint(&deadtid, 1, 1);
            if (info < 0) pvm_perror("calling pvm_upkint");

            /* should be the middle child */
            printf("Task t%x has exited.\n", deadtid);
            printf("Task t%x is middle child.\n", child[ntask/2]);
            pvm_exit();
            return 0;
            }

    /* i'm a child */
    sleep(63);
    pvm_exit();
    return 0;
}
```

6.4 Matrix Multiply

In our next example we program a matrix-multiply algorithm described by Fox et al. in
[8]. The mmult program can be found at the end of this section. The mmult program
will calculate $C = AB$, where C, A, and B are all square matrices. For simplicity we
assume that $m \times m$ tasks will be used to calculate the solution. Each task will calculate
a subblock of the resulting matrix C. The block size and the value of m is given as a
command line argument to the program. The matrices A and B are also stored as blocks
distributed over the m^2 tasks. Before delving into the details of the program, let us first
describe the algorithm at a high level.

Assume we have a grid of $m \times m$ tasks. Each task (t_{ij} where $0 \leq i, j < m$) initially contains blocks C_{ij}, A_{ij}, and B_{ij}. In the first step of the algorithm the tasks on the diagonal (t_{ij} where $i = j$) send their block A_{ii} to all the other tasks in row i. After the transmission of A_{ii}, all tasks calculate $A_{ii} \times B_{ij}$ and add the result into C_{ij}. In the next step, the column blocks of B are rotated. That is, t_{ij} sends its block of B to $t_{(i-1)j}$. (Task t_{0j} sends its B block to $t_{(m-1)j}$.) The tasks now return to the first step; $A_{i(i+1)}$ is multicast to all other tasks in row i, and the algorithm continues. After m iterations the C matrix contains $A \times B$, and the B matrix has been rotated back into place.

Let's now go over the matrix multiply as it is programmed in PVM. In PVM there is no restriction on which tasks may communicate with which other tasks. However, for this program we would like to think of the tasks as a two-dimensional conceptual torus. In order to enumerate the tasks, each task joins the group mmult. Group ids are used to map tasks to our torus. The first task to join a group is given the group id of zero. In the mmult program, the task with group id zero spawns the other tasks and sends the parameters for the matrix multiply to those tasks. The parameters are m and *bklsize*: the square root of the number of blocks and the size of a block, respectively. After all the tasks have been spawned and the parameters transmitted, pvm_barrier() is called to make sure all the tasks have joined the group. If the barrier is not performed, later calls to pvm_gettid() might fail since a task may not have yet joined the group.

After the barrier, we store the task ids for the other tasks in our "row" in the array myrow. This is done by calculating the group ids for all the tasks in the row and asking PVM for the task id for the corresponding group id. Next we allocate the blocks for the matrices using malloc(). In an actual application program we would expect that the matrices would already be allocated. Next the program calculates the row and column of the block of C it will be computing. This is based on the value of the group id. The group ids range from 0 to $m - 1$ inclusive. Thus the integer division of ($mygid/m$) will give the task's row and ($mygid$ mod m) will give the column, if we assume a row major mapping of group ids to tasks. Using a similar mapping, we calculate the group id of the task directly *above* and *below* in the torus and store their task ids in up and down, respectively.

Next the blocks are initialized by calling InitBlock(). This function simply initializes A to random values, B to the identity matrix, and C to zeros. This will allow us to verify the computation at the end of the program by checking that $A = C$.

Finally we enter the main loop to calculate the matrix multiply. First the tasks on the diagonal multicast their block of A to the other tasks in their row. Note that the array myrow actually contains the task id of the task doing the multicast. Recall that pvm_mcast() will send to all the tasks in the tasks array except the calling task. This procedure works well in the case of mmult since we don't want to have to needlessly

handle the extra message coming into the multicasting task with an extra pvm_recv().
Both the multicasting task and the tasks receiving the block calculate the AB for the
diagonal block and the block of B residing in the task.

After the subblocks have been multiplied and added into the C block, we now shift
the B blocks vertically. Specifically, we pack the block of B into a message, send it to
the up task id, and then receive a new B block from the down task id.

Note that we use different message tags for sending the A blocks and the B blocks as
well as for different iterations of the loop. We also fully specify the task ids when doing a
pvm_recv(). It's tempting to use wildcards for the fields of pvm_recv(); however, such
a practice can be dangerous. For instance, had we incorrectly calculated the value for up
and used a wildcard for the pvm_recv() instead of down, we might have sent messages to
the wrong tasks without knowing it. In this example we fully specify messages, thereby
reducing the possibility of mistakes by receiving a message from the wrong task or the
wrong phase of the algorithm.

Once the computation is complete, we check to see that $A = C$, just to verify that the
matrix multiply correctly calculated the values of C. This check would not be done in a
matrix multiply library routine, for example.

It is not necessary to call pvm_lvgroup(), since PVM will realize the task has exited
and will remove it from the group. It is good form, however, to leave the group before
calling pvm_exit(). The reset command from the PVM console will reset all the PVM
groups. The pvm_gstat command will print the status of any groups that currently exist.

Example program: mmult.c

```
/*
    Matrix Multiply
*/

/* defines and prototypes for the PVM library */
#include <pvm3.h>
#include <stdio.h>

/* Maximum number of children this program will spawn */
#define MAXNTIDS    100
#define MAXROW      10

/* Message tags */
```

```
#define ATAG        2
#define BTAG        3
#define DIMTAG      5


void
InitBlock(float *a, float *b, float *c, int blk, int row, int col)
{
    int len, ind;
    int i,j;

    srand(pvm_mytid());
    len = blk*blk;
    for (ind = 0; ind < len; ind++)
        { a[ind] = (float)(rand()%1000)/100.0; c[ind] = 0.0; }
    for (i = 0; i < blk; i++) {
        for (j = 0; j < blk; j++) {
            if (row == col)
                b[j*blk+i] = (i==j)? 1.0 : 0.0;
            else
                b[j*blk+i] = 0.0;
        }
    }
}


void
BlockMult(float* c, float* a, float* b, int blk)
{
    int i,j,k;

    for (i = 0; i < blk; i++)
        for (j = 0; j < blk; j ++)
            for (k = 0; k < blk; k++)
                c[i*blk+j] += (a[i*blk+k] * b[k*blk+j]);
}


int
```

```
main(int argc, char* argv[])
{

    /* number of tasks to spawn, use 3 as the default */
    int ntask = 2;
    /* return code from pvm calls */
    int info;
    /* my task and group id */
    int mytid, mygid;
    /* children task id array */
    int child[MAXNTIDS-1];
    int i, m, blksize;
    /* array of the tids in my row */
    int myrow[MAXROW];
    float *a, *b, *c, *atmp;
    int row, col, up, down;

    /* find out my task id number */
    mytid = pvm_mytid();
    pvm_setopt(PvmRoute, PvmRouteDirect);

    /* check for error */
    if (mytid < 0) {
        /* print out the error */
        pvm_perror(argv[0]);
        /* exit the program */
        return -1;
        }




    /* join the mmult group */
    mygid = pvm_joingroup("mmult");
    if (mygid < 0) {
        pvm_perror(argv[0]); pvm_exit(); return -1;
        }

    /* if my group id is 0 then I must spawn the other tasks */
```

```
if (mygid == 0) {
    /* find out how many tasks to spawn */
    if (argc == 3) {
        m = atoi(argv[1]);
        blksize = atoi(argv[2]);
        }
    if (argc < 3) {
        fprintf(stderr, "usage: mmult m blk\n");
        pvm_lvgroup("mmult"); pvm_exit(); return -1;
        }

    /* make sure ntask is legal */
    ntask = m*m;
    if ((ntask < 1) || (ntask >= MAXNTIDS)) {
        fprintf(stderr, "ntask = %d not valid.\n", ntask);
        pvm_lvgroup("mmult"); pvm_exit(); return -1;
        }
    /* no need to spawn if there is only one task */
    if (ntask == 1) goto barrier;

    /* spawn the child tasks */
    info = pvm_spawn("mmult", (char**)0, PvmTaskDefault, (char*)0,
        ntask-1, child);

    /* make sure spawn succeeded */
    if (info != ntask-1) {
        pvm_lvgroup("mmult"); pvm_exit(); return -1;
        }


    /* send the matrix dimension */
    pvm_initsend(PvmDataDefault);
    pvm_pkint(&m, 1, 1);
    pvm_pkint(&blksize, 1, 1);
    pvm_mcast(child, ntask-1, DIMTAG);
    }
else {
    /* recv the matrix dimension */
```

```
        pvm_recv(pvm_gettid("mmult", 0), DIMTAG);
        pvm_upkint(&m, 1, 1);
        pvm_upkint(&blksize, 1, 1);
        ntask = m*m;
        }


    /* make sure all tasks have joined the group */
barrier:
    info = pvm_barrier("mmult",ntask);
    if (info < 0) pvm_perror(argv[0]);

    /* find the tids in my row */
    for (i = 0; i < m; i++)
        myrow[i] = pvm_gettid("mmult", (mygid/m)*m + i);

    /* allocate the memory for the local blocks */
    a = (float*)malloc(sizeof(float)*blksize*blksize);
    b = (float*)malloc(sizeof(float)*blksize*blksize);
    c = (float*)malloc(sizeof(float)*blksize*blksize);
    atmp = (float*)malloc(sizeof(float)*blksize*blksize);
    /* check for valid pointers */
    if (!(a && b && c && atmp)) {
        fprintf(stderr, "%s: out of memory!\n", argv[0]);
        free(a); free(b); free(c); free(atmp);
        pvm_lvgroup("mmult"); pvm_exit(); return -1;
        }

    /* find my block's row and column */
    row = mygid/m; col = mygid % m;
    /* calculate the neighbor's above and below */
    up = pvm_gettid("mmult", ((row)?(row-1):(m-1))*m+col);
    down = pvm_gettid("mmult", ((row == (m-1))?col:(row+1)*m+col));

    /* initialize the blocks */
    InitBlock(a, b, c, blksize, row, col);


    /* do the matrix multiply */
```

```
for (i = 0; i < m; i++) {
    /* mcast the block of matrix A */
    if (col == (row + i)%m) {
        pvm_initsend(PvmDataDefault);
        pvm_pkfloat(a, blksize*blksize, 1);
        pvm_mcast(myrow, m, (i+1)*ATAG);
        BlockMult(c,a,b,blksize);
        }
    else {
        pvm_recv(pvm_gettid("mmult", row*m + (row +i)%m), (i+1)*ATAG);
        pvm_upkfloat(atmp, blksize*blksize, 1);
        BlockMult(c,atmp,b,blksize);
        }
    /* rotate the columns of B */
    pvm_initsend(PvmDataDefault);
    pvm_pkfloat(b, blksize*blksize, 1);
    pvm_send(up, (i+1)*BTAG);
    pvm_recv(down, (i+1)*BTAG);
    pvm_upkfloat(b, blksize*blksize, 1);
    }


/* check it */
for (i = 0 ; i < blksize*blksize; i++)
    if (a[i] != c[i])
        printf("Error a[%d] (%g) != c[%d] (%g) \n", i, a[i],i,c[i]);

printf("Done.\n");
free(a); free(b); free(c); free(atmp);
pvm_lvgroup("mmult");
pvm_exit();
return 0;
}
```

6.5   One-Dimensional Heat Equation

Here we present a PVM program that calculates heat diffusion through a substrate, in this case a wire. Consider the one-dimensional heat equation on a thin wire:

$$\frac{\partial A}{\partial t} = \frac{\partial^2 A}{\partial x^2} \tag{6.5.1}$$

and a discretization of the form

$$\frac{A_{i+1,j} - A_{i,j}}{\Delta t} = \frac{A_{i,j+1} - 2A_{i,j} + A_{i,j-1}}{\Delta x^2} \tag{6.5.2}$$

giving the explicit formula

$$A_{i+1,j} = A_{i,j} + \frac{\Delta t}{\Delta x^2}(A_{i,j+1} - 2A_{i,j} + A_{i,j-1}). \tag{6.5.3}$$

initial and boundary conditions:

$A(t,0) = 0$, $A(t,1) = 0$ for all t
$A(0,x) = \sin(\pi x)$ for $0 \le x \le 1$.
The pseudo code for this computation is as follows:

```
for i = 1:tsteps-1;
    t = t+dt;
    a(i+1,1)=0;
    a(i+1,n+2)=0;
    for j = 2:n+1;
        a(i+1,j)=a(i,j) + mu*(a(i,j+1)-2*a(i,j)+a(i,j-1));
    end;
    t;
    a(i+1,1:n+2);
    plot(a(i,:))
end
```

For this example we will use a master-slave programming model. The master, heat.c, spawns five copies of the program heatslv. The slaves compute the heat diffusion for subsections of the wire in parallel. At each time step the slaves exchange boundary information, in this case the temperature of the wire at the boundaries between processors.

Let's take a closer look at the code. In heat.c the array `solution` will hold the solution for the heat diffusion equation at each time step. This array will be output at the end of the program in xgraph format. (xgraph is a program for plotting data.) First the heatslv tasks are spawned. Next, the initial data set is computed. Notice that the ends of the wires are given initial temperature values of zero.

The main part of the program is then executed four times, each with a different value for Δt. A timer is used to compute the elapsed time of each compute phase. The initial

data sets are sent to the heatslv tasks. The left and right neighbor task ids are sent
along with the initial data set. The heatslv tasks use these to communicate boundary
information. (Alternatively, we could have used the PVM group calls to map tasks
to segments of the wire. By using the group calls we would have avoided explicitly
communicating the task ids to the slave processes.)

After sending the initial data, the master process simply waits for results. When the
results arrive, they are integrated into the solution matrix, the elapsed time is calculated,
and the solution is written out to the xgraph file.

Once the data for all four phases has been computed and stored, the master program
prints out the elapsed times and kills the slave processes.

Example program: heat.c

```
/*
heat.c

    Use PVM to solve a simple heat diffusion differential equation,
    using 1 master program and 5 slaves.

    The master program sets up the data, communicates it to the slaves
    and waits for the results to be sent from the slaves.
    Produces xgraph ready files of the results.

*/

#include "pvm3.h"
#include <stdio.h>
#include <math.h>
#include <time.h>
#define SLAVENAME "heatslv"
#define NPROC 5
#define TIMESTEP 100
#define PLOTINC 10
#define SIZE 1000

int num_data = SIZE/NPROC;
```

```
main()
{   int mytid, task_ids[NPROC], i, j;
    int left, right, k, l;
    int step = TIMESTEP;
    int info;

    double init[SIZE], solution[TIMESTEP][SIZE];
    double result[TIMESTEP*SIZE/NPROC], deltax2;
    FILE *filenum;
    char *filename[4][7];
    double deltat[4];
    time_t t0;
    int etime[4];

    filename[0][0] = "graph1";
    filename[1][0] = "graph2";
    filename[2][0] = "graph3";
    filename[3][0] = "graph4";

    deltat[0] = 5.0e-1;
    deltat[1] = 5.0e-3;
    deltat[2] = 5.0e-6;
    deltat[3] = 5.0e-9;

/* enroll in pvm */
    mytid = pvm_mytid();

/* spawn the slave tasks */
    info = pvm_spawn(SLAVENAME,(char **)0,PvmTaskDefault,"",
        NPROC,task_ids);
/* create the initial data set */
    for (i = 0; i < SIZE; i++)
        init[i] = sin(M_PI * ( (double)i / (double)(SIZE-1) ));
    init[0] = 0.0;
    init[SIZE-1] = 0.0;

/* run the problem 4 times for different values of delta t */
    for (l = 0; l < 4; l++) {
```

```
        deltax2 = (deltat[l]/pow(1.0/(double)SIZE,2.0));
        /* start timing for this run */
        time(&t0);
        etime[l] = t0;
/* send the initial data to the slaves. */
/* include neighbor info for exchanging boundary data */
        for (i = 0; i < NPROC; i++) {
            pvm_initsend(PvmDataDefault);
            left = (i == 0) ? 0 : task_ids[i-1];
            pvm_pkint(&left, 1, 1);
            right = (i == (NPROC-1)) ? 0 : task_ids[i+1];
            pvm_pkint(&right, 1, 1);
            pvm_pkint(&step, 1, 1);
            pvm_pkdouble(&deltax2, 1, 1);
            pvm_pkint(&num_data, 1, 1);
            pvm_pkdouble(&init[num_data*i], num_data, 1);
            pvm_send(task_ids[i], 4);
            }


/* wait for the results */
        for (i = 0; i < NPROC; i++) {
            pvm_recv(task_ids[i], 7);
            pvm_upkdouble(&result[0], num_data*TIMESTEP, 1);
/* update the solution */
            for (j = 0; j < TIMESTEP; j++)
                for (k = 0; k < num_data; k++)
                    solution[j][num_data*i+k] = result[wh(j,k)];
            }


/* stop timing */
        time(&t0);
        etime[l] = t0 - etime[l];


/* produce the output */
        filenum = fopen(filename[l][0], "w");
        fprintf(filenum,"TitleText: Wire Heat over Delta Time: %e\n",
            deltat[l]);
        fprintf(filenum,"XUnitText: Distance\nYUnitText: Heat\n");
```

```
        for (i = 0; i < TIMESTEP; i = i + PLOTINC) {
            fprintf(filenum,"\"Time index: %d\n",i);
            for (j = 0; j < SIZE; j++)
                fprintf(filenum,"%d %e\n",j, solution[i][j]);
            fprintf(filenum,"\n");
            }
        fclose (filenum);
    }

/* print the timing information */
    printf("Problem size: %d\n",SIZE);
    for (i = 0; i < 4; i++)
        printf("Time for run %d: %d sec\n",i,etime[i]);

/* kill the slave processes */
    for (i = 0; i < NPROC; i++) pvm_kill(task_ids[i]);
    pvm_exit();
}

int wh(x, y)
int x, y;
{
    return(x*num_data+y);
}
```

The heatslv programs do the actual computation of the heat diffusion through the wire. The slave program consists of an infinite loop that receives an initial data set, iteratively computes a solution based on this data set (exchanging boundary information with neighbors on each iteration), and sends the resulting partial solution back to the master process.

Rather than using an infinite loop in the slave tasks, we could send a special message to the slave ordering it to exit. To avoid complicating the message passing, however, we simply use the infinite loop in the slave tasks and kill them off from the master program. A third option would be to have the slaves execute only once, exiting after processing a single data set from the master. This would require placing the master's spawn call inside the main for loop of heat.c. While this option would work, it would needlessly add overhead to the overall computation.

For each time step and before each compute phase, the boundary values of the temperature matrix are exchanged. The left-hand boundary elements are first sent to the left neighbor task and received from the right neighbor task. Symmetrically, the right-hand boundary elements are sent to the right neighbor and then received from the left neighbor. The task ids for the neighbors are checked to make sure no attempt is made to send or receive messages to nonexistent tasks.

Example program: heatslv.c

```
/*

heatslv.c

    The slaves receive the initial data from the host,
    exchange boundary information with neighbors,
    and calculate the heat change in the wire.
    This is done for a number of iterations, sent by the master.

*/

#include "pvm3.h"
#include <stdio.h>

int num_data;

main()
{
    int mytid, left, right, i, j, master;
    int timestep;

    double *init, *A;
    double leftdata, rightdata, delta, leftside, rightside;

/* enroll in pvm */
    mytid = pvm_mytid();
    master = pvm_parent();
```

```
/* receive my data from the master program */
  while(1) {
    pvm_recv(master, 4);
    pvm_upkint(&left, 1, 1);
    pvm_upkint(&right, 1, 1);
    pvm_upkint(&timestep, 1, 1);
    pvm_upkdouble(&delta, 1, 1);
    pvm_upkint(&num_data, 1, 1);
    init = (double *) malloc(num_data*sizeof(double));
    pvm_upkdouble(init, num_data, 1);

/* copy the initial data into my working array */

    A = (double *) malloc(num_data * timestep * sizeof(double));
    for (i = 0; i < num_data; i++) A[i] = init[i];

/* perform the calculation */

  for (i = 0; i < timestep-1; i++) {
    /* trade boundary info with my neighbors */
    /*  send left, receive right    */
    if (left != 0) {
        pvm_initsend(PvmDataDefault);
        pvm_pkdouble(&A[wh(i,0)],1,1);
        pvm_send(left, 5);
        }
    if (right != 0) {
        pvm_recv(right, 5);
        pvm_upkdouble(&rightdata, 1, 1);
    /* send right, receive left */
        pvm_initsend(PvmDataDefault);
        pvm_pkdouble(&A[wh(i,num_data-1)],1,1);
        pvm_send(right, 6);
        }
    if (left != 0) {
        pvm_recv(left, 6);
        pvm_upkdouble(&leftdata,1,1);
        }
```

```
/* do the calculations for this iteration */

    for (j = 0; j < num_data; j++) {
        leftside = (j == 0) ? leftdata : A[wh(i,j-1)];
        rightside = (j == (num_data-1)) ? rightdata : A[wh(i,j+1)];
        if ((j==0)&&(left==0))
            A[wh(i+1,j)] = 0.0;
        else if ((j==(num_data-1))&&(right==0))
            A[wh(i+1,j)] = 0.0;
        else
            A[wh(i+1,j)]=
                A[wh(i,j)]+delta*(rightside-2*A[wh(i,j)]+leftside);
        }
    }

/* send the results back to the master program */

    pvm_initsend(PvmDataDefault);
    pvm_pkdouble(&A[0],num_data*timestep,1);
    pvm_send(master,7);
    }

/* just for good measure */
  pvm_exit();
}

int wh(x, y)
int x, y;
{
    return(x*num_data+y);
}
```

6.5.1   Different Styles of Communication

In this chapter we have given a variety of example programs written in Fortran and C. These examples demonstrate various ways of writing PVM programs. Some break the code into two separate programs, while others use a single program with conditionals to handle spawning and computing phases. These examples show different styles of communication, both among worker tasks and between worker and master tasks. In some cases messages are used for synchronization; in others the master processes simply kill of the workers when they are no longer needed. We hope that these examples can be used as a basis for better understanding how to write PVM programs and for appreciating the design tradeoffs involved.

7 How PVM Works

In this chapter we describe the implementation of the PVM software and the reasons behind the basic design decisions. The most important goals for PVM 3 are fault tolerance, scalability, heterogeneity, and portability. PVM is able to withstand host and network failures. It doesn't automatically recover an application after a crash, but it does provide polling and notification primitives to allow fault-tolerant applications to be built. The virtual machine is dynamically reconfigurable. This property goes hand in hand with fault tolerance: an application may need to acquire more resources in order to continue running once a host has failed. Management is as decentralized and localized as possible, so virtual machines should be able to scale to hundreds of hosts and run thousands of tasks. PVM can connect computers of different types in a single session. It runs with minimal modification on any flavor of Unix or an operating system with comparable facilities (multitasking, networkable). The programming interface is simple but complete, and any user can install the package without special privileges.

To allow PVM to be highly portable, we avoid the use of operating system and language features that would be be hard to retrofit if unavailable, such as multithreaded processes and asynchronous I/O. These exist in many versions of Unix, but they vary enough from product to product that different versions of PVM might need to be maintained. The generic port is kept as simple as possible, though PVM can always be optimized for any particular machine.

We assume that *sockets* are used for interprocess communication and that each host in a virtual machine group can connect directly to every other host via TCP [13] and UDP [14] protocols. The requirement of full IP connectivity could be removed by specifying message routes and using the pvmds to forward messages. Some multiprocessor machines don't make sockets available on the processing nodes, but do have them on the front-end (where the pvmd runs).

7.1 Components

7.1.1 Task Identifiers

PVM uses a *task identifier* (TID) to address pvmds, tasks, and groups of tasks within a virtual machine. The TID contains four fields, as shown in Figure 7.1. Since the TID is used so heavily, it is made to fit into the largest integer data type (32 bits) available on a wide range of machines.

The fields S, G, and H have global meaning: each pvmd of a virtual machine interprets them in the same way. The H field contains a host number relative to the virtual machine. As it starts up, each pvmd is configured with a unique host number and therefore "owns"

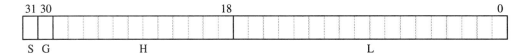

Figure 7.1
Generic task id

part of the TID address space. The maximum number of hosts in a virtual machine is limited to $2^H - 1$ (4095). The mapping between host numbers and hosts is known to each pvmd, synchronized by a global *host table*. Host number zero is used, depending on context, to refer to the local pvmd or a *shadow pvmd*, called *pvmd'* (Section 7.3.7).

The S bit is used to address pvmds, with the H field set to the host number and the L field cleared. This bit is a historical leftover and causes slightly schizoid naming; sometimes pvmds are addressed with the S bit cleared. It should someday be reclaimed to make the H or L space larger.

Each pvmd is allowed to assign private meaning to the L field (with the H field set to its own host number), except that "all bits cleared" is reserved to mean the pvmd itself. The L field is 18 bits wide, so up to $2^{18} - 1$ tasks can exist concurrently on each host. In the generic Unix port, L values are assigned by a counter, and the pvmd maintains a map between L values and Unix process id's. Use of the L field in multiprocessor ports is described in Section 7.10.

The G bit is set to form multicast addresses (GIDs), which refer to groups of tasks. Multicasting is described in Section 7.6.4.

The design of the TID enables the implementation to meet the design goals. Tasks can be assigned TIDs by their local pvmds without off-host communication. Messages can be routed from anywhere in a virtual machine to anywhere else, by hierarchical naming. Portability is enhanced because the L field can be redefined. Finally, space is reserved for error codes. When a function can return a vector of TIDs mixed with error codes, it is useful if the error codes don't correspond to legal TIDs. The TID space is divided up as follows:

Use	S	G	H	L
Task identifier	0	0	$1..H_{max}$	$1..L_{max}$
Pvmd identifier	1	0	$1..H_{max}$	0
Local pvmd (from task)	1	0	0	0
Pvmd' from master pvmd	1	0	0	0
Multicast address	0	1	$1..H_{max}$	$0..L_{max}$
Error code	1	1	(small neg. number)	

Naturally, TIDs are intended to be opaque to the application, and the programmer should not attempt to predict their values or modify them without using functions supplied in the programming library. More symbolic naming can be obtained by using a name server library layered on top of the raw PVM calls, if the convenience is deemed worth the cost of name lookup.

7.1.2 Architecture Classes

PVM assigns an *architecture name* to each kind of machine on which it runs, to distinguish between machines that run different executables, because of hardware or operating system differences. Many standard names are defined, and others can be added.

Sometimes machines with incompatible executables use the same binary data representation. PVM takes advantage of this to avoid data conversion. Architecture names are mapped to *data encoding* numbers, and the encoding numbers are used to determine when it is necessary to convert.

7.1.3 Message Model

PVM daemons and tasks can compose and send messages of arbitrary lengths containing typed data. The data can be converted using XDR [16] when passing between hosts with incompatible data formats. Messages are tagged at send time with a user-defined integer code and can be selected for receipt by source address or tag.

The sender of a message does not wait for an acknowledgment from the receiver, but continues as soon as the message has been handed to the network and the message buffer can be safely deleted or reused. Messages are buffered at the receiving end until received. PVM reliably delivers messages, provided the destination exists. Message order from each sender to each receiver in the system is preserved; if one entity sends several messages to another, they will be received in the same order.

Both blocking and nonblocking receive primitives are provided, so a task can wait for a message without (necessarily) consuming processor time by polling for it. Or, it can poll for a message without hanging. A receive with timeout is also provided, which returns after a specified time if no message has arrived.

No acknowledgments are used between sender and receiver. Messages are reliably delivered and buffered by the system. If we ignore fault recovery, then either an application will run to completion or, if some component goes down, it won't. In order to provide fault recovery, a task (T_A) must be prepared for another task $(T_B$, from which it wants a message) to crash, and must be able to take corrective action. For example, it might reschedule its request to a different server, or even start a new server. From the viewpoint of T_A, it doesn't matter specifically when T_B crashes relative to messages sent from T_A.

While waiting for T_B, T_A will receive either a message from T_B or notification that T_B has crashed. For the purposes of flow control, a fully blocking send can easily be built using the semi-synchronous send primitive.

7.1.4   Asynchronous Notification

PVM provides *notification* messages as a means to implement fault recovery in an application. A task can request that the system send a message on one of the following three events:

Type	Meaning
PvmTaskExit	Task exits or crashes
PvmHostDelete	Host is deleted or crashes
PvmHostAdd	New hosts are added to the VM

Notify requests are stored in the pvmds, attached to objects they monitor. Requests for remote events (occurring on a different host than the requester) are kept on both hosts. The remote pvmd sends the message if the event occurs, while the local one sends the message if the remote host goes down. The assumption is that a local pvmd can be trusted; if it goes down, tasks running under it won't be able to do anything, so they don't need to be notified.

7.1.5   PVM Daemon and Programming Library

PVM Daemon   One pvmd runs on each host of a virtual machine. Pvmds owned by (running as) one user do not interact with those owned by others, in order to reduce security risk, and minimize the impact of one PVM user on another.

The pvmd serves as a message router and controller. It provides a point of contact, authentication, process control, and fault detection. An idle pvmd occasionally checks that its peers are still running. Even if application programs crash, pvmds continue to run, to aid in debugging.

The first pvmd (started by hand) is designated the *master*, while the others (started by the master) are called *slaves*. During normal operation, all are considered equal. But only the master can start new slaves and add them to the configuration. Reconfiguration requests originating on a slave host are forwarded to the master. Likewise, only the master can forcibly delete hosts from the machine.

Programming Library   The libpvm library allows a task to interface with the pvmd and other tasks. It contains functions for packing (composing) and unpacking messages, and functions to perform PVM *syscalls* by using the message functions to send service requests to the pvmd. It is made as small and simple as possible. Since it shares an address space with unknown, possibly buggy, code, it can be broken or subverted. Minimal sanity-checking of parameters is performed, leaving further authentication to the pvmd.

The top level of the libpvm library, including most of the programming interface functions, is written in a machine-independent style. The bottom level is kept separate and can be modified or replaced with a new machine-specific file when porting PVM to a new environment.

7.2 Messages

7.2.1 Fragments and Databufs

The pvmd and libpvm manage message buffers, which potentially hold large amounts of dynamic data. Buffers need to be shared efficiently, for example, to attach a multicast message to several send queues (see Section 7.6.4). To avoid copying, all pointers are to a single instance of the data (a *databuf*), which is refcounted by allocating a few extra bytes for an integer at the head of the data. A pointer to the data itself is passed around, and routines subtract from it to access the refcount or free the block. When the refcount of a databuf decrements to zero, it is freed.

PVM messages are composed without declaring a maximum length ahead of time. The pack functions allocate memory in steps, using databufs to store the data, and frag descriptors to chain the databufs together.

A frag descriptor `struct frag` holds a pointer (`fr_dat`) to a block of data and its length (`fr_len`). It also keeps a pointer (`fr_buf`) to the databuf and its total length (`fr_max`); these reserve space to prepend or append data. Frags can also reference static (non-databuf) data. A frag has link pointers so it can be chained into a list. Each frag keeps a count of references to it; when the refcount decrements to zero, the frag is freed and the underlying databuf refcount is decremented. In the case where a frag descriptor is the head of a list, its refcount applies to the entire list. When it reaches zero, every frag in the list is freed. Figure 7.2 shows a list of fragments storing a message.

7.2.2 Messages in Libpvm

Libpvm provides functions to pack all of the primitive data types into a message, in one of several encoding formats. There are five sets of encoders and decoders. Each message buffer has a set associated with it. When creating a new message, the encoder set is determined by the format parameter to `pvm_mkbuf()`. When receiving a message, the decoders are determined by the encoding field of the message header. The two most commonly used ones pack data in *raw* (host native) and *default* (XDR) formats. *Inplace* encoders pack descriptors of the data (the frags point to static data), so the message is sent without copying the data to a buffer. There are no inplace decoders. *Foo* encoders use a machine-independent format that is simpler than XDR; these encoders are used when communicating with the pvmd. *Alien* decoders are installed when a received message can't be unpacked because its encoding doesn't match the data format of the host. A message in an alien data format can be held or forwarded, but any attempt to read data from it results in an error.

Figure 7.2 shows libpvm message management. To allow the PVM programmer to handle message buffers, they are labeled with integer message id's (MIDs), which are simply indices into the message heap. When a message buffer is freed, its MID is recycled. The heap starts out small and is extended if it becomes full. Generally, only a few messages exist at any time, unless an application explicitly stores them.

A vector of functions for encoding/decoding primitive types (`struct encvec`) is initialized when a message buffer is created. To pack a long integer, the generic pack function `pvm_pklong()` calls (`message_heap[mid].ub_codef->enc_long)()` of the buffer. Encoder vectors were used for speed (as opposed to having a case switch in each pack function). One drawback is that every encoder for every format is touched (by naming it in the code), so the linker must include all the functions in every executable, even when they're not used.

7.2.3   Messages in the Pvmd

By comparison with libpvm, message packing in the pvmd is very simple. Messages are handled using `struct mesg` (shown in Figure 7.3). There are encoders for signed and unsigned integers and strings, which use in the libpvm *foo* format. Integers occupy four bytes each, with bytes in network order (bits 31..24 followed by bits 23..16, ...). Byte strings are packed as an integer length (including the terminating null for ASCII strings), followed by the data and zero to three null bytes to round the total length to a multiple of four.

7.2.4   Pvmd Entry Points

Messages for the pvmd are reassembled from packets in `loclinpkt()` if from a local task, or in `netinpkt()` if from another pvmd or foreign task. Reassembled messages are passed to one of three *entry points*:

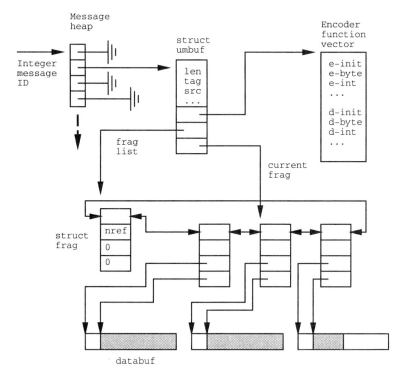

Figure 7.2
Message storage in libpvm

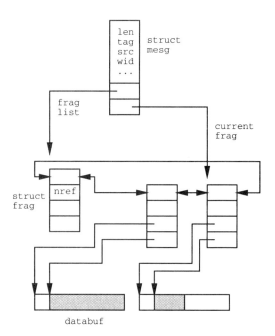

Figure 7.3
Message storage in pvmd

Function	Messages From
loclentry()	Local tasks
netentry()	Remote pvmds
schentry()	Local or remote special tasks
	(Resource manager, Hoster, Tasker)

If the message tag and contents are valid, a new thread of action is started to handle the request. Invalid messages are discarded.

7.2.5 Control Messages

Control messages are sent to a task like regular messages, but have tags in a reserved space (between TC_FIRST and TC_LAST). Normally, when a task downloads a message, it queues it for receipt by the program. Control messages are instead passed to pvmmctl() and then discarded. Like the entry points in the pvmd, pvmmctl() is an entry point in the task, causing it to take some asynchronous action. The main difference is that control messages can't be used to get the task's attention, since it must be in mxfer(), sending or receiving, in order to get them.

The following control message tags are defined. The first three are used by the direct routing mechanism (discussed in Section 7.6.3). TC_OUTPUT is used to implement pvm_catchout() (Section 7.7.2). User-definable control messages may be added in the future as a way of implementing PVM signal handlers.

Tag	Meaning
TC_CONREQ	Connection request
TC_CONACK	Connection ack
TC_TASKEXIT	Task exited/doesn't exist
TC_NOOP	Do nothing
TC_OUTPUT	Claim child stdout data
TC_SETTMASK	Change task trace mask

7.3 PVM Daemon

7.3.1 Startup

At startup, a pvmd configures itself as a master or slave, depending on its command line arguments. It creates and binds sockets to talk to tasks and other pvmds, and it opens an error log file /tmp/pvml.*uid*. A master pvmd reads the host file if supplied; otherwise it uses default parameters. A slave pvmd gets its parameters from the master pvmd via the command line and configuration messages.

After configuration, the pvmd enters a loop in function `work()`. At the core of the work loop is a call to `select()` that probes all sources of input for the pvmd (local tasks and the network). Packets are received and routed to send queues. Messages to the pvmd are reassembled and passed to the entry points.

7.3.2 Shutdown

A pvmd shuts down when it is deleted from the virtual machine, killed (signaled), loses contact with the master pvmd, or breaks (e.g., with a bus error). When a pvmd shuts down, it takes two final actions. First, it kills any tasks running under it, with signal `SIGTERM`. Second, it sends a final shutdown message (Section 7.5.2) to every other pvmd in its host table. The other pvmds would eventually discover the missing one by timing out trying to communicate with it, but the shutdown message speeds the process.

7.3.3 Host Table and Machine Configuration

A host table describes the configuration of a virtual machine. It lists the name, address and communication state for each host. Figure 7.4 shows how a host table is built from `struct htab` and `struct hostd` structures.

Host tables are issued by the master pvmd and kept synchronized across the virtual machine. The delete operation is simple: On receiving a `DM_HTDEL` message from the master, a pvmd calls `hostfailentry()` for each host listed in the message, as though the deleted pvmds crashed. Each pvmd can autonomously delete hosts from its own table on finding them unreachable (by timing out during communication). The add operation is done with a three-phase commit, in order to guarantee global availability of new hosts synchronously with completion of the add-host request. This is described in Section 7.3.8.

Each host descriptor has a refcount so it can be shared by multiple host tables. As the configuration of the machine changes, the host descriptors (except those added and deleted, of course) propagate from one host table to the next. This propagation is necessary because they hold various state information.

Host tables also serve other uses: They allow the pvmd to manipulate host sets, for example, when picking candidate hosts on which to spawn a task. Also, the advisory host file supplied to the master pvmd is parsed and stored in a host table.

Host File If the master pvmd is started with a host file, it parses the file into a host table, `filehosts`. If some hosts in the file are to be started automatically, the master sends a `DM_ADD` message to itself. The slave hosts are started just as though they had been added dynamically (Section 7.3.8).

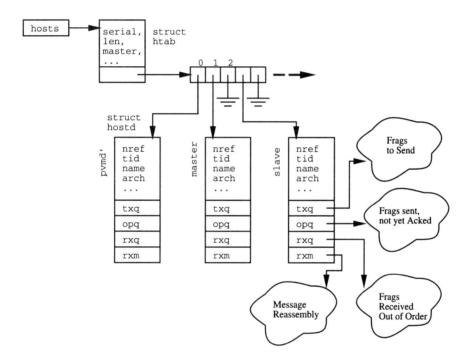

Figure 7.4
Host table

7.3.4   Tasks

Each pvmd maintains a list of all tasks under its management (Figure 7.5). Every task, regardless of state, is a member of a threaded list, sorted by task id. Most tasks are also in a second list, sorted by process id. The head of both lists is `locltasks`.

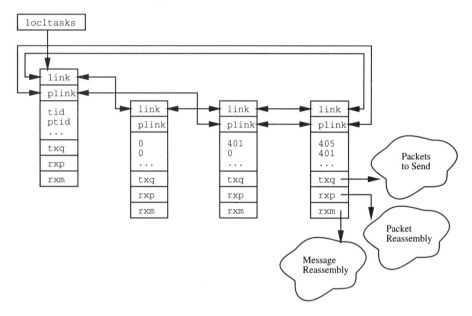

Figure 7.5
Task table

PVM provides a simple debugging system described in Section 7.7.4. More complex debuggers can be built by using a special type of task called a *tasker*, introduced in version 3.3. A tasker starts (*execs*, and is the parent of) other tasks. In general, a debugger is a process that controls the execution of other processes - can read and write their memories and start and stop instruction counters. On many species of Unix, a debugger must be the direct parent of any processes it controls. This is becoming less common with growing availability of the attachable *ptrace* interface.

The function of the tasker interface overlaps with the simple debugger starter, but is fundamentally different for two reasons: First, all tasks running under a pvmd (during the life of the tasker) may be children of a single tasker process. With `PvmTaskDebug`, a new debugger is necessarily started for each task. Second, the tasker cannot be enabled or disabled by spawn flags, so it is always in control, though this is not an important difference.

If a tasker is registered (using pvm_reg_tasker()) with a pvmd when a DM_EXEC message is received to start new tasks, the pvmd sends a SM_STTASK message to the tasker instead of calling execv(). No *SM_STTASKACK* message is required; closure comes from the task reconnecting to the pvmd as usual. The pvmd doesn't get SIGCHLD signals when a tasker is in use, because it's not the parent process of tasks, so the tasker must send notification of exited tasks to the pvmd in a SM_TASKX message.

7.3.5   Wait Contexts

The pvmd uses a wait context (waitc) to hold state when a thread of operation must be interrupted. The pvmd is not truly multithreaded but performs operations concurrently. For example, when a pvmd gets a syscall from a task and must interact with another pvmd, it doesn't block while waiting for the other pvmd to respond. It saves state in a waitc and returns immediately to the work() loop. When the reply arrives, the pvmd uses the information stashed in the waitc to complete the syscall and reply to the task. Waitcs are serial numbered, and the number is sent in the message header along with the request and returned with the reply.

For many operations, the TIDs and *kind* of wait are the only information saved. The struct waitc includes a few extra fields to handle most of the remaining cases, and a pointer, wa_spec, to a block of extra data for special cases—the spawn and host startup operations, which need to save struct waitc_spawn and struct waitc_add.

Sometimes more than one phase of waiting is necessary—in series, parallel, or nested. In the parallel case, a separate waitc is created for each foreign host. The waitcs are *peered* (linked in a list) together to indicate they pertain to the same operation. If a waitc has no peers, its peer links point to itself. Usually, peered waitcs share data, for example, wa_spec. All existing parallel operations are conjunctions; a peer group is finished when every waitc in the group is finished. As replies arrive, finished waitcs are collapsed out of the list and deleted. When the finished waitc is the only one left, the operation is complete. Figure 7.6 shows single and peered waitcs stored in waitlist (the list of all active waitcs).

When a host fails or a task exits, the pvmd searches waitlist for any blocked on this TID and terminates those operations. Waitcs from the dead host or task blocked on something else are not deleted; instead, their wa_tid fields are zeroed. This approach prevents the wait id's from being recycled while replies are still pending. Once the defunct waitcs arc satisfied, they are silently discarded.

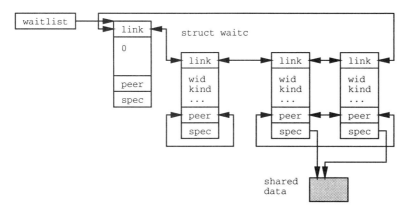

Figure 7.6
Wait context list

7.3.6   Fault Detection and Recovery

Fault detection originates in the pvmd-pvmd protocol (Section 7.5.2). When the pvmd times out while communicating with another, it calls `hostfailentry()`, which scans `waitlist` and terminates any operations waiting on the down host.

A pvmd can recover from the loss of any foreign pvmd except the master. If a slave loses the master, the slave shuts itself down. This algorithm ensures that the virtual machine doesn't become partitioned and run as two partial machines. It does, however, decrease fault tolerance of the virtual machine because the master must never crash. There is currently no way for the master to hand off its status to another pvmd, so it always remains part of the configuration. (This is an improvement over PVM 2, in which the failure of any pvmd would shut down the entire system.)

7.3.7   Pvmd'

The shadow pvmd (pvmd') runs on the master host and is used by the master to start new slave pvmds. Any of several steps in the startup process (for example, starting a shell on the remote machine) can block for seconds or minutes (or hang), and the master pvmd must be able to respond to other messages during this time. It's messy to save all the state involved, so a completely separate process is used.

The pvmd' has host number 0 and communicates with the master through the normal pvmd-pvmd interface, though it never talks to tasks or other pvmds. The normal host failure detection mechanism is used to recover in the event the pvmd' fails. The startup operation has a wait context in the master pvmd. If the pvmd' breaks, the master catches a SIGCHLD from it and calls `hostfailentry()`, which cleans up.

7.3.8   Starting Slave Pvmds

Getting a slave pvmd started is a messy task with no good solution. The goal is to get a process running on the new host, with enough identity to let it be fully configured and added as a peer.

Ideally, the mechanism used should be widely available, secure, and fast, while leaving the system easy to install. We'd like to avoid having to type passwords all the time, but don't want to put them in a file from where they can be stolen. No one system meets all of these criteria. Using `inetd` or connecting to an already-running pvmd or pvmd server at a reserved port would allow fast, reliable startup, but would require that a system administrator install PVM on each host. Starting the pvmd via `rlogin` or `telnet` with a *chat* script would allow access even to IP-connected hosts behind firewall machines and would require no special privilege to install; the main drawbacks are speed and the effort needed to get the chat program working reliably.

Two widely available systems are `rsh` and `rexec()`; we use both to cover the cases where a password does and does not need to be typed. A manual startup option allows the user to take the place of a chat program, starting the pvmd by hand and typing in the configuration. `rsh` is a privileged program that can be used to run commands on another host without a password, provided the destination host can be made to trust the source host. This can be done either by making it equivalent (requires a system administrator) or by creating a `.rhosts` file on the destination host (this isn't a great idea). The alternative, `rexec()`, is a function compiled into the pvmd. Unlike `rsh`, which doesn't take a password, `rexec()` requires the user to supply one at run time, either by typing it in or by placing it in a `.netrc` file (this is a really bad idea).

Figure 7.7 shows a host being added to the machine. A task calls `pvm_addhosts()` to send a request to its pvmd, which in turn sends a `DM_ADD` message to the master (possibly itself). The master pvmd creates a new host table entry for each host requested, looks up the IP addresses, and sets the options from host file entries or defaults. The host descriptors are kept in a `waitc_add` structure (attached to a wait context) and not yet added to the host table. The master forks the pvmd' to do the dirty work, passing it a list of hosts and commands to execute (an `SM_STHOST` message). The pvmd' uses `rsh`, `rexec()` or manual startup to start each pvmd, pass it parameters, and get a line of configuration data back. The configuration dialog between pvmd' and a new slave is as follows:

pvmd' → slave:	(exec) $PVM_ROOT/lib/pvmd -s -d8 -nhonk 1 80a9ca95:0f5a
	4096 3 80a95c43:0000
slave → pvmd':	ddpro<2312> arch<ALPHA> ip<80a95c43:0b3f> mtu<4096>
pvmd' → slave:	EOF

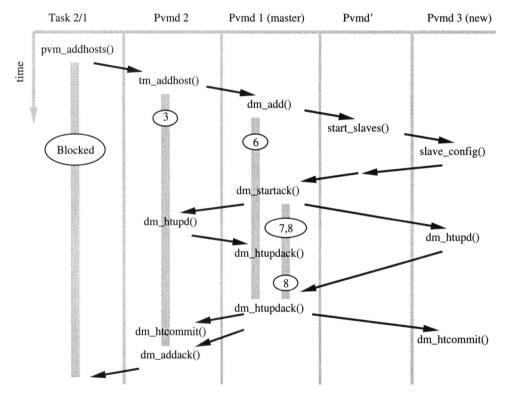

Figure 7.7
Timeline of addhost operation

The addresses of the master and slave pvmds are passed on the command line. The slave writes its configuration on standard output, then waits for an EOF from the pvmd' and disconnects. It runs in probationary status (runstate = PVMDSTARTUP) until it receives the rest of its configuration from the master pvmd. If it isn't configured within five minutes (parameter DDBAILTIME), it assumes there is some problem with the master and quits. The protocol revision (DDPROTOCOL) of the slave pvmd must match that of the master. This number is incremented whenever a change in the protocol makes it incompatible with the previous version. When several hosts are added at once, startup is done in parallel. The pvmd' sends the data (or errors) in a DM_STARTACK message to the master pvmd, which completes the host descriptors held in the wait context.

If a special task called a *hoster* is registered with the master pvmd when it receives the DM_ADD message, the pvmd' is not used. Instead, the SM_STHOST message is sent to the hoster, which starts the remote processes as described above using any mechanism it wants, then sends a SM_STHOSTACK message (same format as DM_STARTACK) back to the master pvmd. Thus, the method of starting slave pvmds is dynamically replaceable, but the hoster does not have to understand the configuration protocol. If the hoster task fails during an add operation, the pvmd uses the wait context to recover. It assumes none of the slaves were started and sends a DM_ADDACK message indicating a system error.

After the slaves are started, the master sends each a DM_SLCONF message to set parameters not included in the startup protocol. It then broadcasts a DM_HTUPD message to all new and existing slaves. Upon receiving this message, each slave knows the configuration of the new virtual machine. The master waits for an acknowledging DM_HTUPDACK message from every slave, then broadcasts an HT_COMMIT message, shifting all to the new host table. Two phases are needed so that new hosts are not advertised (e.g., by pvm_config()) until all pvmds know the new configuration. Finally, the master sends a DM_ADDACK reply to the original request, giving the new host id's.

Note: Recent experience suggests it would be cleaner to manage the pvmd' through the task interface instead of the host interface. This approach would allow multiple starters to run at once (parallel startup is implemented explicitly in a single pvmd' process).

7.3.9 Resource Manager

A *resource manager* (RM) is a PVM task responsible for making task and host scheduling (placement) decisions. The resource manager interface was introduced in version 3.3. The simple schedulers embedded in the pvmd handle many common conditions, but require the user to explicitly place program components in order to get the maximum efficiency. Using knowledge not available to the pvmds, such as host load averages, a RM can make more informed decisions automatically. For example, when spawning a task, it could pick the host in order to balance the computing load. Or, when reconfiguring the virtual machine, the RM could interact with an external queuing system to allocate a new host.

The number of RMs registered can vary from one for an entire virtual machine to one per pvmd. The RM running on the master host (where the master pvmd runs) manages any slave pvmds that don't have their own RMs. A task connecting anonymously to a virtual machine is assigned the default RM of the pvmd to which it connects. A task spawned from within the system inherits the RM of its parent task.

If a task has a RM assigned to it, service requests from the task to its pvmd are routed to the RM instead. Messages from the following libpvm functions are intercepted:

Libpvm function	Default Message	RM Message
pvm_addhost()	TM_ADDHOST	SM_ADDHOST
pvm_delhost()	TM_DELHOST	SM_DELHOST
pvm_spawn()	TM_SPAWN	SM_SPAWN

Queries also go to the RM, since it presumably knows more about the state of the virtual machine:

Libpvm function	Default Message	RM Message
pvm_config()	TM_CONFIG	SM_CONFIG
pvm_notify()	TM_NOTIFY	SM_NOTIFY
pvm_task()	TM_TASK	SM_TASK

The call to register a task as a RM (pvm_reg_rm()) is also redirected if RM is already running. In this way the existing RM learns of the new one, and can grant or refuse the request to register.

Using messages SM_EXEC and SM_ADD, the RM can directly command the pvmds to start tasks or reconfigure the virtual machine. On receiving acknowledgement for the commands, it replies to the client task. The RM is free to interpret service request parameters in any way it wishes. For example, the architecture class given to pvm_spawn() could be used to distinguish hosts by memory size or CPU speed.

7.4   Libpvm Library

7.4.1   Language Support

Libpvm is written in C and directly supports C and C++ applications. The Fortran library, libfpvm3.a (also written in C), is a set of *wrapper* functions that conform to the Fortran calling conventions. The Fortran/C linking requirements are portably met by preprocessing the C source code for the Fortran library with m4 before compilation.

7.4.2   Connecting to the Pvmd

On the first call to a libpvm function, pvm_beatask() is called to initialize the library state and connect the task to its pvmd. Connecting (for *anonymous* tasks) is slightly different from reconnecting (for spawned tasks).

The pvmd publishes the address of the socket on which it listens in /tmp/pvmd.*uid*, where *uid* is the numeric user id under which the pvmd runs. This file contains a line of the form

7f000001:06f7 or /tmp/aaa014138

This is the IP address and port number (in hexadecimal) of the socket, or the path if a Unix-domain socket. To avoid the need to read the address file, the same information is passed to spawned tasks in environment variable PVMSOCK.

To reconnect, a spawned task also needs its expected process id. When a task is spawned by the pvmd, a task descriptor is created for it during the *exec* phase. The descriptor must exist so it can stash any messages that arrive for the task before it reconnects and can receive them. During reconnection, the task identifies itself to the pvmd by its PID. If the task is always the child of the pvmd (i.e., the exact process *exec*'d by it), then it could use the value returned by getpid(). To allow for intervening processes, such as debuggers, the pvmd passes the expected PID in environment variable PVMEPID, and the task uses that value in preference to its real PID. The task also passes its real PID so it can be controlled normally by the pvmd.

pvm_beatask() creates a TCP socket and does a proper connection dance with the pvmd. Each must prove its identity to the other, to prevent a different user from spoofing the system. It does this by creating a file in /tmp writable only by the owner, and challenging the other to write in the file. If successful, the identity of the other is proven. Note that this authentication is only as strong as the filesystem and the authority of root on each machine.

A protocol serial number (TDPROTOCOL) is compared whenever a task connects to a pvmd or another task. This number is incremented whenever a change in the protocol makes it incompatible with the previous version.

Disconnecting is much simpler. It can be done forcibly by a *close* from either end, for example, by exiting the task process. The function pvm_exit() performs a clean shutdown, such that the process can be connected again later (it would get a different TID).

7.5   Protocols

PVM communication is based on TCP , UDP, and Unix-domain sockets. While more appropriate protocols exist, they aren't as generally available.

VMTP [4] is one example of a protocol built for this purpose. Although intended for RPC-style interaction (request-response), it could support PVM messages. It is packet oriented and efficiently sends short blocks of data (such as most pvmd-pvmd management messages) but also handles streaming (necessary for task-task communication). It supports multicasting and priority data (something PVM doesn't need yet). Connections don't need to be established before use; the first communication initializes the protocol drivers at each end. VMTP was rejected, however. because it is not widely available (using it requires modifying the kernel).

This section explains the PVM protocols. There are three connections to consider: Between pvmds, between pvmd and task, and between tasks.

7.5.1   Messages

The pvmd and libpvm use the same message header, shown in Figure 7.8. *Code* contains an integer tag (message type). Libpvm uses *Encoding* to pass the encoding style of the message, as it can pack in different formats. The pvmd always sets Encoding (and requires that it be set) to 1 (*foo*), Pvmds use the *Wait Context* field to pass the wait id's (if any, zero if none) of the *waitc* associated with the message. Certain tasks (resource manager, tasker, hoster) also use wait id's. The *Checksum* field is reserved for future use. Messages are sent in one or more fragments, each with its own fragment header (described below). The message header is at the beginning of the first fragment.

7.5.2   Pvmd-Pvmd

PVM daemons communicate with one another through UDP sockets. UDP is an unreliable delivery service which can lose, duplicate or reorder packets, so an acknowledgment and retry mechanism is used. UDP also limits packet length, so PVM fragments long messages.

We considered TCP, but three factors make it inappropriate. First is scalability. In

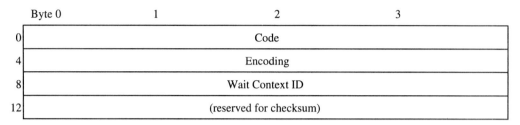

Figure 7.8
Message header

a virtual machine of N hosts, each pvmd must have connections to the other $N - 1$. Each open TCP connection consumes a file descriptor in the pvmd, and some operating systems limit the number of open files to as few as 32, whereas a single UDP socket can communicate with any number of remote UDP sockets. Second is overhead. N pvmds need $N(N - 1)/2$ TCP connections, which would be expensive to set up. The PVM/UDP protocol is initialized with no communication. Third is fault tolerance. The communication system detects when foreign pvmds have crashed or the network has gone down, so we need to set timeouts in the protocol layer. The TCP keepalive option might work, but it's not always possible to get adequate control over the parameters.

The packet header is shown in Figure 7.9. Multibyte values are sent in (Internet) *network byte order* (most significant byte first).

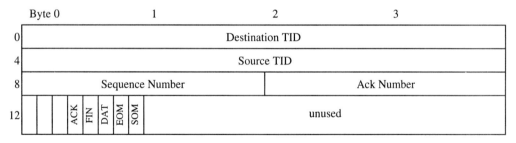

Figure 7.9
Pvmd-pvmd packet header

The source and destination fields hold the TIDs of the true source and final destination of the packet, regardless of the route it takes. Sequence and acknowledgment numbers start at 1 and increment to 65535, then wrap to zero.

SOM (EOM) – Set for the first (last) fragment of a message. Intervening fragments have both bits cleared. They are used by tasks and pvmds to delimit message boundaries.

DAT – If set, data is contained in the packet, and the sequence number is valid. The packet, even if zero length, must be delivered.

ACK – If set, the acknowledgment number field is valid. This bit may be combined with the DAT bit to piggyback an acknowledgment on a data packet.[1]

FIN – The pvmd is closing down the connection. A packet with FIN bit set (and DAT cleared) begins an orderly shutdown. When an acknowledgement arrives (ACK bit set and ack number matching the sequence number from the FIN packet), a final packet is sent with both FIN and ACK set. If the pvmd panics, (for example on a trapped segment violation) it tries to send a packet with FIN and ACK set to every peer before it exits.

The state of a connection to another pvmd is kept in its host table entry. The protocol driver uses the following fields of `struct hostd`:

Field	Meaning
hd_hostpart	TID of pvmd
hd_mtu	Max UDP packet length to host
hd_sad	IP address and UDP port number
hd_rxseq	Expected next packet number from host
hd_txseq	Next packet number to send to host
hd_txq	Queue of packets to send
hd_opq	Queue of packets sent, awaiting ack
hd_nop	Number of packets in hd_opq
hd_rxq	List of out-of-order received packets
hd_rxm	Buffer for message reassembly
hd_rtt	Estimated smoothed round-trip time

Figure 7.10 shows the host send and outstanding-packet queues. Packets waiting to be sent to a host are queued in FIFO hd_txq. Packets are appended to this queue by the routing code, described in Section 7.6.1. No receive queues are used; incoming packets are passed immediately through to other send queues or reassembled into messages (or discarded). Incoming messages are delivered to a pvmd entry point as described in Section 7.2.4.

The protocol allows multiple outstanding packets to improve performance over high-latency networks, so two more queues are required. hd_opq holds a per-host list of unacknowledged packets, and global opq lists all unacknowledged packets, ordered by time to retransmit. hd_rxq holds packets received out of sequence until they can be accepted.

The difference in time between sending a packet and getting the acknowledgement is used to estimate the round-trip time to the foreign host. Each update is filtered into the

---

[1]Currently, the pvmd generates an acknowledgement packet for each data packet.

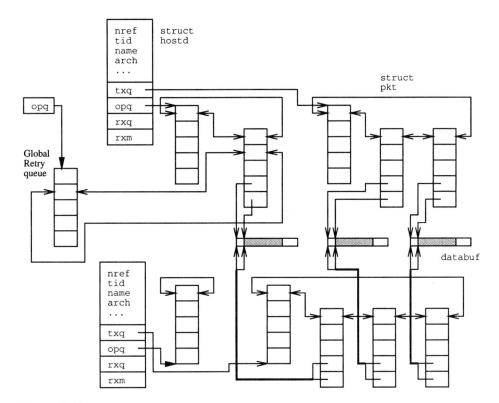

Figure 7.10
Host descriptors with send queues

estimate according to the formula

$$hd\_rtt_n = 0.75 * hd\_rtt_{n-1} + 0.25 * \Delta t.$$

When the acknowledgment for a packet arrives, the packet is removed from hd_opq and opq and discarded. Each packet has a retry timer and count, and each is resent until acknowledged by the foreign pvmd. The timer starts at $3 * hd\_rtt$, and doubles for each retry up to 18 seconds. hd_rtt is limited to nine seconds, and backoff is bounded in order to allow at least 10 packets to be sent to a host before giving up. After three minutes of resending with no acknowledgment, a packet expires.

If a packet expires as a result of timeout, the foreign pvmd is assumed to be down or unreachable, and the local pvmd gives up on it, calling hostfailentry()

7.5.3 Pvmd-Task and Task-Task

A task talks to its pvmd and other tasks through TCP sockets. TCP is used because it delivers data reliably. UDP can lose packets even within a host. Unreliable delivery requires retry (with timers) at both ends: since tasks can't be interrupted while computing to perform I/O, we can't use UDP.

Implementing a packet service over TCP is simple because of its reliable delivery. The packet header is shown in Figure 7.11. No sequence numbers are needed, and only flags *SOM* and *EOM* (these have the same meaning as in Section 7.5.2). Since TCP provides no record marks to distinguish back-to-back packets from one another, the length is sent in the header. Each side maintains a FIFO of packets to send, and switches between reading the socket when data is available and writing when there is space.

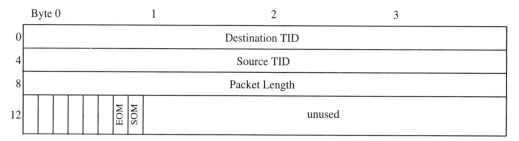

Figure 7.11
Pvmd-task packet header

The main drawback to TCP (as opposed to UDP) is that more system calls are needed to transfer each packet. With UDP, a single sendto() and single recvfrom() are required. With TCP, a packet can be sent by a single write() call, but must be received by two read() calls, the first to get the header and the second to get the data.

When traffic on the connection is heavy, a simple optimization reduces the average number of reads back to about one per packet. If, when reading the packet body, the requested length is increased by the size of a packet header, the read may succeed in getting both the packet body and header of the next packet at once. We have the header for the next packet for free and can repeat this process.[2]

Version 3.3 introduced the use of Unix-domain stream sockets as an alternative to TCP for local communication, to improve latency and transfer rate (typically by a factor of two). If enabled (the system is built without the `NOUNIXDOM` option), stream sockets are used between the pvmd and tasks as well as between tasks on the same host.

7.6   Message Routing

7.6.1   Pvmd

Packet Buffers   Packet descriptors (`struct pkt`) track message fragments through the pvmd. Fields `pk_buf`, `pk_max`, `pk_dat` and `pk_len` are used in the same ways as similarly named fields of a frag, described in Section 7.2.1. Besides data, pkts contain state to operate the pvmd-pvmd protocol.

Message Routing   Messages are sent by calling `sendmessage()`, which routes by destination address. Messages for other pvmds or tasks are linked to packet descriptors and attached to a send queue. If the pvmd addresses a message to itself, `sendmessage()` passes the whole message descriptor to `netentry()`, avoiding the packet layer entirely. This loopback interface is used often by the pvmd. During a complex operation, `netentry()` may be reentered several times as the pvmd sends itself messages.

Messages to the pvmd are reassembled from packets in message reassembly buffers, one for each local task and remote pvmd. Completed messages are passed to entry points (Section 7.2.4).

Packet Routing   A graph of packet and message routing inside the pvmd is shown in Figure 7.12. Packets are received from the network by `netinput()` directly into buffers long enough to hold the largest packet the pvmd will receive (its MTU in the host table). Packets from local tasks are read by `loclinput()`, which creates a buffer large enough for each packet after it reads the header. To route a packet, the pvmd chains it onto the queue for its destination. If a packet is multicast (see Section 7.6.4), the descriptor is replicated, counting extra references on the underlying databuf. One copy is placed in each send queue. After the last copy of the packet is sent, the databuf is freed.

---

[2]This was once implemented, but was removed while the code was updated and hasn't been reintroduced.

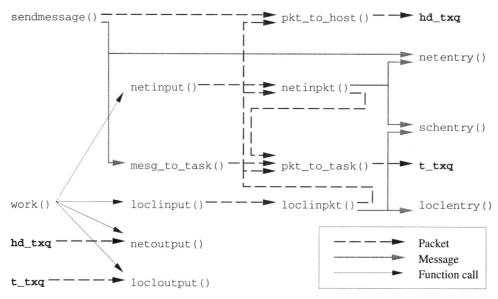

Figure 7.12
Packet and message routing in pvmd

Refragmentation   Messages are generally built with fragment length equal to the
MTU of the host's pvmd, allowing them to be forwarded without refragmentation. In
some cases, the pvmd can receive a packet (from a task) too long to be sent to another
pvmd. The pvmd refragments the packet by replicating its descriptor as many times as
necessary. A single databuf is shared between the descriptors. The pk_dat and pk_len
fields of the descriptors cover successive chunks of the original packet, each chunk small
enough to send. The SOM and EOM flags are adjusted (if the original packet is the start
or end of a message). At send time, netoutput() saves the data under where it writes
the packet header, sends the packet, and then restores the data.

7.6.2   Pvmd and Foreign Tasks

Pvmds usually don't communicate with foreign tasks (those on other hosts). The pvmd
has message reassembly buffers for each foreign pvmd and each task it manages. What
it doesn't want is to have reassembly buffers for foreign tasks. To free up the reassembly
buffer for a foreign task (if the task dies), the pvmd would have to request notification
from the task's pvmd, causing extra communication.

For the sake of simplicity the pvmd local to the sending task serves as a message
repeater. The message is reassembled by the task's local pvmd as if it were the receiver,

then forwarded all at once to the destination pvmd, which reassembles the message again. The source address is preserved, so the sender can be identified.

Libpvm maintains dynamic reassembly buffers, so messages from pvmd to task do not cause a problem.

7.6.3 Libpvm

Four functions handle all packet traffic into and out of libpvm. `mroute()` is called by higher-level functions such as `pvm_send()` and `pvm_recv()` to copy messages into and out of the task. It establishes any necessary routes before calling `mxfer()`. `mxfer()` polls for messages, optionally blocking until one is received or until a specified timeout. It calls `mxinput()` to copy fragments into the task and reassemble messages. In the generic version of PVM, `mxfer()` uses `select()` to poll all routes (sockets) in order to find those ready for input or output. `pvmmctl()` is called by `mxinput()` when a control message (Section 7.2.5) is received.

Direct Message Routing   Direct routing allows one task to send messages to another through a TCP link, avoiding the overhead of forwarding through the pvmds. It is implemented entirely in libpvm, using the notify and control message facilities. By default, a task routes messages to its pvmd, which forwards them on. If direct routing is enabled (`PvmRouteDirect`) when a message (addressed to a task) is passed to `mroute()`, it attempts to create a direct route if one doesn't already exist. The route may be granted or refused by the destination task, or fail (if the task doesn't exist). The message is then passed to `mxfer()`.

Libpvm maintains a protocol control block (`struct ttpcb`) for each active or denied connection, in list `ttlist`. The state diagram for a ttpcb is shown in Figure 7.13. To request a connection, `mroute()` makes a ttpcb and socket, then sends a `TC_CONREQ` control message to the destination via the default route. At the same time, it sends a `TM_NOTIFY` message to the pvmd, to be notified if the destination task exits, with closure (message tag) `TC_TASKEXIT`. Then it puts the ttpcb in state `TTCONWAIT`, and calls `mxfer()` in blocking mode repeatedly until the state changes.

When the destination task enters `mxfer()` (for example, to receive a message), it receives the `TC_CONREQ` message. The request is granted if its routing policy (`pvmrouteopt != PvmDontRoute`) and implementation allow a direct connection, it has resources available, and the protocol version (`TDPROTOCOL`) in the request matches its own. It makes a ttpcb with state `TTGRNWAIT`, creates and listens on a socket, and then replies with a `TC_CONACK` message. If the destination denies the connection, it nacks, also with a `TC_CONACK` message. The originator receives the `TC_CONACK` message, and either opens the connection (`state = TTOPEN`) or marks the route denied (`state = TTDENY`). Then, mroute() passes the original message to mxfer(), which sends it. Denied connections are cached in order to prevent repeated negotiation.

If the destination doesn't exist, the TC_CONACK message never arrives because the TC_CONREQ message is silently dropped. However, the TC_TASKEXIT message generated by the notify system arrives in its place, and the ttpcb state is set to TTDENY.

This connect scheme also works if both ends try to establish a connection at the same time. They both enter TTCONWAIT, and when they receive each other's TC_CONREQ messages, they go directly to the TTOPEN state.

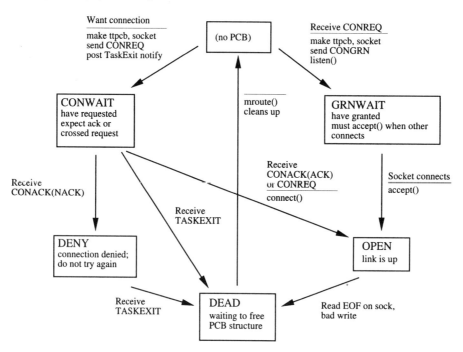

Figure 7.13
Task-task connection state diagram

7.6.4 Multicasting

The libpvm function pvm_mcast() sends a message to multiple destinations simultaneously. The current implementation only routes multicast messages through the pvmds. It uses a 1:N fanout to ensure that failure of a host doesn't cause the loss of any messages (other than ones to that host). The packet routing layer of the pvmd cooperates with the libpvm to multicast a message.

To form a multicast address TID (GID), the G bit is set (refer to Figure 7.1). The L field is assigned by a counter that is incremented for each multicast, so a new multicast address is used for each message, then recycled.

To initiate a multicast, the task sends a TM_MCA message to its pvmd, containing a list of recipient TIDs. The pvmd creates a multicast descriptor (struct mca) and GID. It sorts the addresses, removes bogus ones, and duplicates and caches them in the mca. To each destination pvmd (ones with destination tasks), it sends a DM_MCA message with the GID and destinations on that host. The GID is sent back to the task in the TM_MCA reply message.

The task sends the multicast message to the pvmd, addressed to the GID. As each packet arrives, the routing layer copies it to each local task and foreign pvmd. When a multicast packet arrives at a destination pvmd, it is copied to each destination task. Packet order is preserved, so the multicast address and data packets arrive in order at each destination. As it forwards multicast packets, each pvmd eavesdrops on the header flags. When it sees a packet with EOM flag set, it flushes the mca.

7.7 Task Environment

7.7.1 Environment Variables

Experience seems to indicate that inherited environment (Unix environ) is useful to an application. For example, environment variables can be used to distinguish a group of related tasks or to set debugging variables.

PVM makes increasing use of environment, and may eventually support it even on machines where the concept is not native. For now, it allows a task to export any part of environ to tasks spawned by it. Setting variable PVM_EXPORT to the names of other variables causes them to be exported through spawn. For example, setting

```
PVM_EXPORT=DISPLAY:SHELL
```

exports the variables DISPLAY and SHELL to children tasks (and PVM_EXPORT too).

The following environment variables are used by PVM. The user may set these:

PVM_ROOT	Root installation directory
PVM_EXPORT	Names of environment variables to inherit through spawn
PVM_DPATH	Default slave pvmd install path
PVM_DEBUGGER	Path of debugger script used by spawn

The following variables are set by PVM and should not be modified:

PVM_ARCH	PVM architecture name
PVMSOCK	Address of the pvmd local socket; see Section 7.4.2
PVMEPID	Expected PID of a spawned task
PVMTMASK	Libpvm Trace mask

7.7.2 Standard Input and Output

Each task spawned through PVM has /dev/null opened for *stdin*. From its parent, it inherits a *stdout sink*, which is a *(TID, code)* pair. Output on *stdout* or *stderr* is read by the pvmd through a pipe, packed into PVM messages and sent to the TID, with message tag equal to the code. If the output TID is set to zero (the default for a task with no parent), the messages go to the master pvmd, where they are written on its error log.

Children spawned by a task inherit its stdout sink. Before the spawn, the parent can use pvm_setopt() to alter the output TID or code. This doesn't affect where the output of the parent task itself goes. A task may set output TID to one of three settings: the value inherited from its parent, its own TID, or zero. It can set output code only if output TID is set to its own TID. This means that output can't be assigned to an arbitrary task.

Four types of messages are sent to an stdout sink. The message body formats for each type are as follows:

Spawn:	(code) {		Task has been spawned
		int tid,	Task id
		int -1,	Signals spawn
		int ptid	TID of parent
	}		
Begin:	(code) {		First output from task
		int tid,	Task id
		int -2,	Signals task creation
		int ptid	TID of parent
	}		
Output:	(code) {		Output from a task
		int tid,	Task id
		int count,	Length of output fragment
		char data[count]	Output fragment
	}		
End:	(code) {		Last output from a task
		int tid,	Task id
		int 0	Signals EOF
	}		

The first two items in the message body are always the task id and output count, which allow the receiver to distinguish between different tasks and the four message types. For each task, one message each of types *Spawn*, *Begin*, and *End* is sent, along with zero or more messages of class *Output*, (`count > 0`). Classes *Begin*, *Output* and *End* will be received in order, as they originate from the same source (the pvmd of the target task). Class *Spawn* originates at the (possibly different) pvmd of the parent task, so it can be received in any order relative to the others. The output sink is expected to understand the different types of messages and use them to know when to stop listening for output from a task (EOF) or group of tasks (global EOF).

The messages are designed so as to prevent race conditions when a task spawns another task, then immediately exits. The output sink might get the *End* message from the parent task and decide the group is finished, only to receive more output later from the child task. According to these rules, the *Spawn* message for the second task must arrive before the *End* message from the first task. The *Begin* message itself is necessary because the *Spawn* message for a task may arrive after the *End* message for the same task. The state transitions of a task as observed by the receiver of the output messages are shown in Figure 7.14.

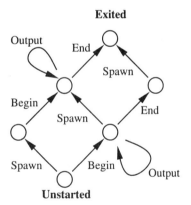

Figure 7.14
Output states of a task

The libpvm function `pvm_catchout()` uses this output collection feature to put the output from children of a task into a file (for example, its own stdout). It sets output TID to its own task id, and the output code to control message TC_OUTPUT. Output from children and grandchildren tasks is collected by the pvmds and sent to the task, where it is received by `pvmmctl()` and printed by `pvmclaimo()`.

7.7.3   Tracing

The libpvm library has a tracing system that can record the parameters and results of all calls to interface functions. Trace data is sent as messages to a trace sink task just as output is sent to an stdout sink (Section 7.7.2). If the trace output TID is set to zero (the default), tracing is disabled.

Besides the trace sink, tasks also inherit a trace mask, used to enable tracing function-by-function. The mask is passed as a (printable) string in environment variable PVMTMASK. A task can manipulate its own trace mask or the one to be inherited from it. A task's trace mask can also be set asynchronously with a TC_SETTMASK control message.

Constants related to trace messages are defined in public header file pvmtev.h. Trace data from a task is collected in a manner similar to the output redirection discussed above. Like the type *Spawn*, *Begin*, and *End* messages which bracket output from a task, TEV_SPNTASK, TEV_NEWTASK and TEV_ENDTASK trace messages are generated by the pvmds to bracket trace messages.

The tracing system was introduced in version 3.3 and is still expected to change somewhat.

7.7.4   Debugging

PVM provides a simple but extensible debugging facility. Tasks started by hand could just as easily be run under a debugger, but this procedure is cumbersome for those spawned by an application, since it requires the user to comment out the calls to pvm_spawn() and start tasks manually. If PvmTaskDebug is added to the flags passed to pvm_spawn(), the task is started through a debugger script (a normal shell script), $PVM_ROOT/lib/debugger.

The pvmd passes the name and parameters of the task to the debugger script, which is free to start any sort of debugger. The script provided is very simple. In an *xterm* window, it runs the correct debugger according to the architecture type of the host. The script can be customized or replaced by the user. The pvmd can be made to execute a different debugger via the bx= host file option or the PVM_DEBUGGER environment variable.

7.8   Console Program

The PVM console is used to manage the virtual machine—to reconfigure it or start and stop processes. In addition, it's an example program that makes use of most of the libpvm functions.

pvm_getfds() and select() are used to check for input from the keyboard and messages from the pvmd simultaneously. Keyboard input is passed to the command interpreter, while messages contain notification (for example, HostAdd) or output from a task.

The console can collect output or trace messages from spawned tasks, using the redirection mechanisms described in Section 7.7.2 and Section 7.7.3, and write them to the screen or a file. It uses the *begin* and *end* messages from child tasks to maintain groups of tasks (or *jobs*), related by common ancestors. Using the `PvmHostAdd` notify event, it informs the user when the virtual machine is reconfigured.

7.9   Resource Limitations

Resource limits imposed by the operating system and available hardware are in turn passed to PVM applications. Whenever possible, PVM avoids setting explicit limits; instead, it returns an error when resources are exhausted. Competition between users on the same host or network affects some limits dynamically.

7.9.1   In the PVM Daemon

How many tasks each pvmd can manage is limited by two factors: the number of processes allowed a user by the operating system, and the number of file descriptors available to the pvmd. The limit on processes is generally not an issue, since it doesn't make sense to have a huge number of tasks running on a uniprocessor machine.

Each task consumes one file descriptor in the pvmd, for the pvmd-task TCP stream. Each spawned task (not ones connected anonymously) consumes an extra descriptor, since its output is read through a pipe by the pvmd (closing stdout and stderr in the task would reclaim this slot). A few more file descriptors are always in use by the pvmd for the local and network sockets and error log file. For example, with a limit of 64 open files, a user should be able to have up to 30 tasks running per host.

The pvmd may become a bottleneck if all these tasks try to talk to one another through it.

The pvmd uses dynamically allocated memory to store message packets en route between tasks. Until the receiving task accepts the packets, they accumulate in the pvmd in an FIFO procedure. No flow control is imposed by the pvmd: it will happily store all the packets given to it, until it can't get any more memory. If an application is designed so that tasks can keep sending even when the receiving end is off doing something else and not receiving, the system will eventually run out of memory.

7.9.2   In the Task

As with the pvmd, a task may have a limit on the number of others it can connect to directly. Each direct route to a task has a separate TCP connection (which is bidirectional), and so consumes a file descriptor. Thus, with a limit of 64 open files, a task can establish direct routes to about 60 other tasks. Note that this limit is in effect only when using task-task direct routing. Messages routed via the pvmds use only the default pvmd-task connection.

The maximum size of a PVM message is limited by the amount of memory available to the task. Because messages are generally packed using data existing elsewhere in memory, and they must be reside in memory between being packed and sent, the largest possible message a task can send should be somewhat less than half the available memory. Note that as a message is sent, memory for packet buffers is allocated by the pvmd, aggravating the situation. In-place message encoding alleviates this problem somewhat, because the data is not copied into message buffers in the sender. However, on the receiving end, the entire message is downloaded into the task before the receive call accepts it, possibly leaving no room to unpack it.

In a similar vein, if many tasks send to a single destination all at once, the destination task or pvmd may be overloaded as it tries to store the messages. Keeping messages from being freed when new ones are received by using **pvm_setrbuf()** also uses up memory.

These problems can sometimes be avoided by rearranging the application code, for example, to use smaller messages, eliminate bottlenecks, and process messages in the order in which they are generated.

7.10   Multiprocessor Systems

Developed initially as a parallel programming environment for Unix workstations, PVM has gained wide acceptance and become a de facto standard for message-passing programming. Users want the same programming environment on multiprocessor computers so they can move their applications onto these systems. A common interface would also allow users to write vendor-independent programs for parallel computers and to do part or most of the development work on workstations, freeing up the multiprocessor supercomputers for production runs.

With PVM, multiprocessor systems can be included in the same configuration with workstations. For example, a PVM task running on a graphics workstation can display the results of computations carried out on a massively parallel processing supercomputer. Shared-memory computers with a small number of processors can be linked to deliver supercomputer performance.

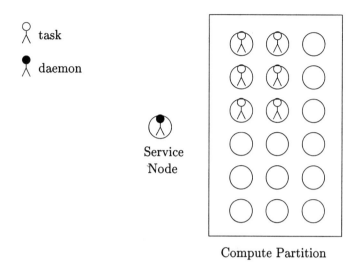

Figure 7.15
PVM daemon and tasks on MPP host

The virtual machine hides the configuration details from the programmer. The physical processors can be a network of workstations, or they can be the nodes of a multicomputer. The programmer doesn't have to know how the tasks are created or where they are running; it is the responsibility of PVM to schedule user's tasks onto individual processors. The user can, however, tune the program for a specific configuration to achieve maximum performance, at the expense of its portability.

Multiprocessor systems can be divided into two main categories: message passing and shared memory. In the first category, PVM is now supported on Intel's iPSC/860 and Paragon, as well as Thinking Machine's CM-5. Porting PVM to these platforms is straightforward, because the message-passing functions in PVM map quite naturally onto the native system calls. The difficult part is the loading and management of tasks. In the second category, message passing can be done by placing the message buffers in shared memory. Access to these buffers must be synchronized with mutual exclusion locks. PVM 3.3 shared memory ports include SGI multiprocessor machines running IRIX 5.x and Sun Microsystems, Inc., multiprocessor machines running Solaris 2.3 (This port also runs on the Cray Research, Inc., CS6400). In addition, CRAY and DEC have created PVM ports for their T3D and DEC 2100 shared memory multiprocessors, respectively.

7.10.1 Message-Passing Architectures

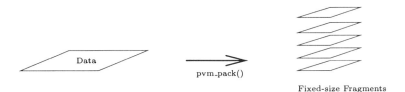

Figure 7.16
Packing: breaking data into fixed-size fragments

A typical MPP system has one or more service nodes for user logins and a large number of compute nodes for number crunching. The PVM daemon runs on one of the service nodes and serves as the gateway to the outside world. A task can be started on any one of the service nodes as a Unix process and enrolls in PVM by establishing a TCP socket connection to the daemon. The only way to start PVM tasks on the compute nodes is via pvm_spawn(). When the daemon receives a request to spawn new tasks, it will allocate a set of nodes if necessary, and load the executable onto the specified number of nodes.

The way PVM allocates nodes is system dependent. On the CM-5, the entire partition is allocated to the user. On the iPSC/860, PVM will get a subcube big enough to accommodate all the tasks to be spawned. Tasks created with two separate calls to pvm_spawn() will reside in different subcubes, although they can exchange messages directly by using the physical node address. The NX operating system limits the number of active subcubes system-wide to 10. Pvm_spawn will fail when this limit is reached or when there are not enough nodes available. In the case of the Paragon, PVM uses the default partition unless a different one is specified when pvmd is invoked. Pvmd and the spawned tasks form one giant parallel application. The user can set the appropriate NX environment variables such as NX_DFLT_SIZE before starting PVM, or he can specify the equivalent command-line arguments to pvmd (i.e., pvmd -sz 32).

PVM message-passing functions are implemented in terms of the native send and receive system calls. The "address" of a task is encoded in the task id, as illustrated in Figure 7.17. This enables the messages to be sent directly to the target task, without any

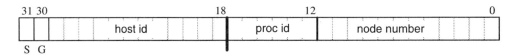

Figure 7.17
How TID is used to distinguish tasks on MPP

help from the daemon. The node number is normally the logical node number, but the

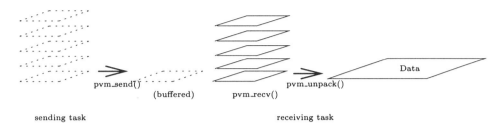

Figure 7.18
Buffering: buffering one fragment by receiving task until pvm_recv() is called

physical address is used on the iPSC/860 to allow for direct intercube communication. The instance number is used to distinguish tasks running on the same node.

PVM normally uses asynchronous send primitives to send messages. The operating system can run out of message handles very quickly if a lot of small messages or several large messages are sent at once. PVM will be forced to switch to synchronous send when there are no more message handles left or when the system buffer gets filled up. To improve performance, a task should call pvm_send() as soon as the data becomes available, so (one hopes) when the other task calls pvm_recv(), the message will already be in its buffer. PVM buffers one incoming packet between calls to pvm_send()/pvm_recv(). A large message, however, is broken up into many fixed-size fragments during packing, and each piece is sent separately. Buffering one of these fragments is not sufficient unless pvm_send() and pvm_recv() are synchronized. Figures 7.16 and 7.18 illustrate this process.

The front end of an MPP system is treated as a regular workstation. Programs to be run there should be linked with the regular PVM library, which relies on Unix sockets to transmit messages. Normally one should avoid running processes on the front end, because communication between those processes and the node processes must go through the PVM daemon and a TCP socket link. Most of the computation and communication should take place on the compute nodes in order to take advantage of the processing power of these nodes and the fast interconnects between them.

Since the PVM library for the front end is different from the one for the nodes, the executable for the front end must be different from the one compiled for the nodes. An SPMD program, for example, has only one source file, but the object code must be linked with the front end and node PVM libraries separately to produce two executables if it is to be started from the front end. An alternative would be a "hostless" SPMD program, which could be spawned from the PVM console.

Table 7.1 shows the native system calls used by the corresponding PVM functions on

Table 7.1
Implementation of PVM system calls

PVM	iPSC860	Paragon	CM-5
pvm_spawn	getcube/load	nx_loadve	fork
pvm_send	isend/csend	isend/csend	CMMD_send_async/_noblock
pvm_recv	irecv	irecv	CMMD_receive_async
pvm_mcast	gsendx	gsendx	CMMD_send_async/_noblock

various platforms.

The CM-5 is somewhat different from the Intel systems because it requires a special host process for each group of tasks spawned. This process enrolls in PVM and relays messages between pvmd and the node programs. This, needless to say, adds even more overhead to daemon-task communications.

Another restrictive feature of the CM-5 is that all nodes in the same partition are scheduled as a single unit. The partitions are normally configured by the system manager and each partition must contain at least 16 processors. User programs are run on the entire partition by default. Although it is possible to idle some of the processors in a partition, as PVM does when fewer nodes are called for, there is no easy way to harness the power of the idle processors. Thus, if PVM spawns two groups of tasks, they will time-share the partition, and any intergroup traffic must go through pvmd.

Additionally, CMMD has no support for multicasting. Thus, pvm_mcast() is implemented with a loop of CMMD_async_send().

7.10.2 Shared-Memory Architectures

The shared-memory architecture provides a very efficient medium for processes to exchange data. In our implementation, each task owns a shared buffer created with the shmget() system call. The task id is used as the "key" to the shared segment. If the key is being used by another user, PVM will assign a different id to the task. A task communicates with other tasks by mapping their message buffers into its own memory space.

To enroll in PVM, the task first writes its Unix process id into pvmd's incoming box. It then looks for the assigned task id in pvmd's pid→TID table.

The message buffer is divided into pages, each of which holds one fragment (Figure 7.19). PVM's page size can be a multiple of the system page size. Each page has a header, which contains the lock and the reference count. The first few pages are used as the incoming box, while the rest of the pages hold outgoing fragments (Figure 7.20).

Page Layout

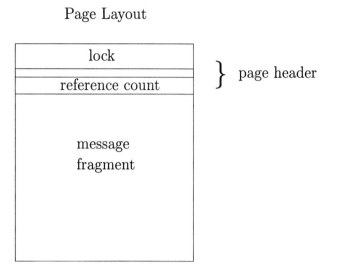

Figure 7.19
Structure of a PVM page

To send a message, the task first packs the message body into its buffer, then delivers the message header (which contains the sender's TID and the location of the data) to the incoming box of the intended recipient. When pvm_recv() is called, PVM checks the incoming box, locates and unpacks the messages (if any), and decreases the reference count so the space can be reused. If a task is not able to deliver the header directly because the receiving box is full, it will block until the other task is ready.

Inevitably some overhead will be incurred when a message is packed into and unpacked from the buffer, as is the case with all other PVM implementations. If the buffer is full, then the data must first be copied into a temporary buffer in the process's private space and later transferred to the shared buffer.

Memory contention is usually not a problem. Each process has its own buffer, and each page of the buffer has its own lock. Only the page being written to is locked, and no process should be trying to read from this page because the header has not been sent out. Different processes can read from the same page without interfering with each other, so multicasting will be efficient (they do have to decrease the counter afterwards, resulting in some contention). The only time contention occurs is when two or more processes trying to deliver the message header to the same process at the same time. But since the header is very short (16 bytes), such contention should not cause any significant delay.

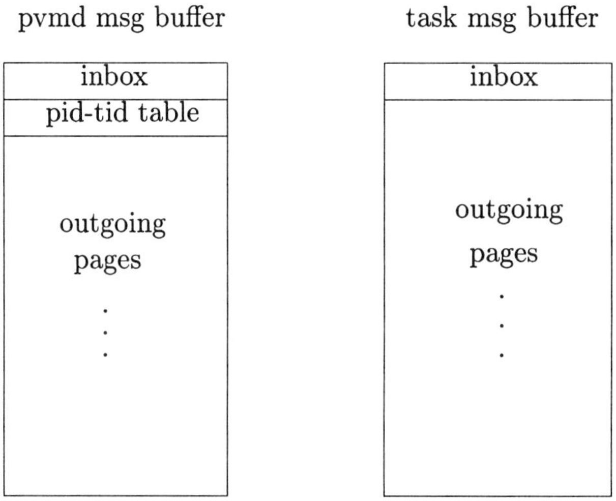

pvmd msg buffer   task msg buffer

inbox
pid-tid table
outgoing
pages
.
.
.

inbox
outgoing
pages
.
.
.

Figure 7.20
Structures of shared message buffers

To minimize the possibility of page faults, PVM attempts to use only a small number of pages in the message buffer and recycle them as soon as they have been read by all intended recipients.

Once a task's buffer has been mapped, it will not be unmapped unless the system limits the number of mapped segments. This strategy saves time for any subsequent message exchanges with the same process.

7.10.3 Optimized Send and Receive on MPP

In the original implementation, all user messages are buffered by PVM. The user must pack the data into a PVM buffer before sending it, and unpack the data after it has been received into an internal buffer. This approach works well on systems with relatively high communication latency, such as the Ethernet. On MPP systems the packing and unpacking introduce substantial overhead. To solve this problem we added two new PVM functions, namely pvm_psend() and pvm_precv(). These functions combine packing/unpacking and sending/receiving into one single step. They could be mapped directly into the native message passing primitives available on the system, doing away with internal buffers altogether. On the Paragon these new functions give almost the same performance as the native ones.

Although the user can use both pvm_psend() and pvm_send() in the same program, on MPP the pvm_psend() must be matched with pvm_precv(), and pvm_send() with pvm_recv().

8 Advanced Topics

8.1 XPVM

It is often useful and always reassuring to be able to see the present configuration of the virtual machine and the status of the hosts. It would be even more useful if the user could also see what his program is doing—what tasks are running, where messages are being sent, etc. The PVM GUI called XPVM was developed to display this information, and more.

XPVM combines the capabilities of the PVM console, a performance monitor, and a call-level debugger into a single, easy-to-use X-Windows interface. XPVM is available from netlib in the directory pvm3/xpvm. It is distributed as precompiled, ready-to-run executables for SUN4, RS6K, ALPHA, SUN4SOL2, HPPA, and SGI5. The XPVM source is also available for compiling on other machines.

XPVM is written entirely in C using the TCL/TK [12] toolkit and runs just like another PVM task. If a user wishes to build XPVM from the source, he must first obtain and install the TCL/TK software on his system. TCL and TK were developed by John Ousterhout at Berkeley and can be obtained by anonymous ftp to sprite.berkeley.edu The TCL and XPVM source distributions each contain a README file that describes the most up-to-date installation procedure for each package respectively.

Figure 8.1 shows a snapshot of XPVM in use.

Like the PVM console, XPVM will start PVM if PVM is not already running, or will attach to the local pvmd if it is. The console can take an optional hostfile argument whereas XPVM always reads $HOME/.xpvm_hosts as its hostfile. If this file does not exist, then XPVM just starts PVM on the local host (or attaches to the existing PVM). In typical use, the hostfile .xpvm_hosts contains a list of hosts prepended with an &. These hostnames then get added to the *Hosts* menu for addition and deletion from the virtual machine by clicking on them.

The top row of buttons perform console-like functions. The *Hosts* button displays a menu of hosts. Clicking on a host toggles whether it is added or deleted from the virtual machine. At the bottom of the menu is an option for adding a host not listed. The *Tasks* button brings up a menu whose most-used selection is *spawn*. Selecting spawn brings up a window where one can set the executable name, spawn flags, start position, number of copies to start, etc. By default, XPVM turns on tracing in all tasks (and their children) started inside XPVM. Clicking on *Start* in the spawn window starts the task, which will then appear in the space-time view. The *Reset* button has a menu for resetting PVM (i.e., kill all PVM tasks) or resetting different parts of XPVM. The *Quit* button exits

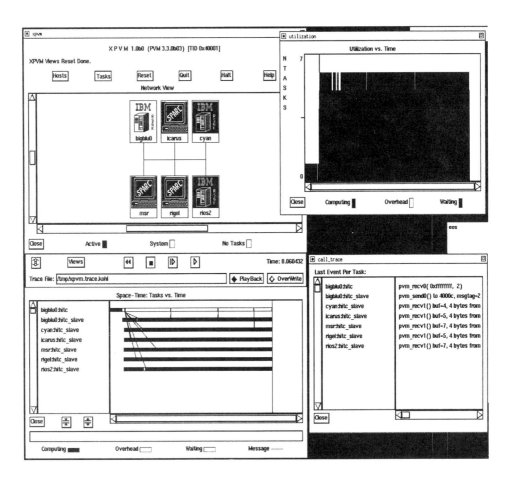

Figure 8.1
XPVM interface - snapshot during use

XPVM while leaving PVM running. If XPVM is being used to collect trace information, the information will not be collected if XPVM is stopped. The *Halt* button is used when one is through with PVM. Clicking on this button kills all running PVM tasks, shuts down PVM cleanly, and exits the XPVM interface. The *Help* button brings up a menu of topics the user can get help about.

During startup, XPVM joins a group called xpvm. The intention is that tasks started outside the XPVM interface can get the TID of XPVM by doing `tid = pvm_gettid( xpvm, 0 )`. This TID would be needed if the user wanted to manually turn on tracing inside such a task and pass the events back to XPVM for display. The expected TraceCode for these events is 666.

While an application is running, XPVM collects and displays the information in real time. Although XPVM updates the views as fast as it can, there are cases when XPVM cannot keep up with the events and it falls behind the actual run time.

In the middle of the XPVM interface are tracefile controls. It is here that the user can specify a tracefile—a default tracefile in /tmp is initially displayed. There are buttons to specify whether the specified tracefile is to be played back or overwritten by a new run. XPVM saves trace events in a file using the "self defining data format" (SDDF) described in Dan Reed's Pablo [15] trace playing package. The analysis of PVM traces can be carried out on any of a number of systems such as Pablo.

XPVM can play back its own SDDF files. The tape-player-like buttons allow the user to rewind the tracefile, stop the display at any point, and step through the execution. A time display specifies the number of seconds from when the trace display began.

The *Views* button allows the user to open or close any of several views presently supplied with XPVM. These views are described below.

8.1.1   Network View

The *Network* view displays the present virtual machine configuration and the activity of the hosts. Each host is represented by an icon that includes the PVM_ARCH and host name inside the icon. In the initial release of XPVM, the icons are arranged arbitrarily on both sides of a bus network. In future releases the view will be extended to visualize network activity as well. At that time the user will be able to specify the network topology to display.

These icons are illuminated in different colors to indicate their status in executing PVM tasks. Green implies that at least one task on that host is busy executing useful work. Yellow indicates that no tasks are executing user computation, but at least one task is busy executing PVM system routines. When there are no tasks on a given host, its icon is left uncolored or white. The specific colors used in each case are user customizable.

The user can tell at a glance how well the virtual machine is being utilized by his

PVM application. If all the hosts are green most of the time, then machine utilization is good. The Network view does not display activity from other users' PVM jobs or other processes that may be running on the hosts.

In future releases the view will allow the user to click on a multiprocessor icon and get information about the number of processors, number of PVM tasks, etc., that are running on the host.

8.1.2   Space-Time View

The *Space-Time* view displays the activities of individual PVM tasks that are running on the virtual machine. Listed on the left-hand side of the view are the executable names of the tasks, preceded by the host they are running on. The task list is sorted by host so that it is easy to see whether tasks are being clumped on one host. This list also shows the task-to-host mappings (which are not available in the Network view).

The Space-Time view combines three different displays. The first is like a Gantt chart. Beside each listed task is a horizontal bar stretching out in the "time" direction. The color of this bar at any time indicates the state of the task. Green indicates that user computations are being executed. Yellow marks the times when the task is executing PVM routines. White indicates when a task is waiting for messages. The bar begins at the time when the task starts executing and ends when the task exits normally. The specific colors used in each case are user customizable.

The second display overlays the first display with the communication activity among tasks. When a message is sent between two tasks, a red line is drawn starting at the sending task's bar at the time the message is sent and ending at the receiving task's bar when the message is received. Note that this is not necessarily the time the message arrived, but rather the time the task returns from pvm_recv(). Visually, the patterns and slopes of the red lines combined with white "waiting" regions reveal a lot about the communication efficiency of an application.

The third display appears only when a user clicks on interesting features of the Space-Time view with the left mouse button. A small "pop-up" window appears giving detailed information regarding specific task states or messages. If a task bar is clicked on, the state begin and end times are displayed, along with the last PVM system call information. If a message line is clicked on, the window displays the send and receive time as well as the number of bytes in the message and the message tag.

When the mouse is moved inside the Space-Time view, a blue vertical line tracks the cursor and the time corresponding to this vertical line is displayed as Query time at the bottom of the display. This vertical line also appears in the other "something vs. time" views so the user can correlate a feature in one view with information given in another view.

The user can zoom into any area of the Space-Time view by dragging the vertical line with the middle mouse button. The view will unzoom back one level when the right mouse button is clicked. It is often the case that very fine communication or waiting states are only visible when the view is magnified with the zoom feature. As with the Query time, the other views also zoom along with the Space-Time view.

8.1.3 Other Views

XPVM is designed to be extensible. New views can be created and added to the *Views* menu. At present, there are three other views: task utilization vs. time view, call trace view, and task output view. Unlike the Network and Space-Time views, these views are closed by default. XPVM attempts to draw the views in real time; hence, the fewer open views, the faster XPVM can draw.

The Utilization view shows the number of tasks computing, in overhead, or waiting for each instant. It is a summary of the Space-Time view for each instant. Since the number of tasks in a PVM application can change dynamically, the scale on the Utilization view will change dynamically when tasks are added, but not when they exit. When the number of tasks changes, the displayed portion of the Utilization view is completely redrawn to the new scale.

The Call Trace view provides a textual record of the last PVM call made in each task. The list of tasks is the same as in the Space-Time view. As an application runs, the text changes to reflect the most recent activity in each task. This view is useful as a call level debugger to identify where a PVM program's execution hangs.

Unlike the PVM console, XPVM has no natural place for task output to be printed. Nor is there a flag in XPVM to tell tasks to redirect their standard output back to XPVM. This flag is turned on automatically in all tasks spawned by XPVM after the Task Output view is opened. This view gives the user the option to also redirect the output into a file. If the user types a file name in the "Task Output" box, then the output is printed in the window and into the file.

As with the trace events, a task started outside XPVM can be programmed to send standard output to XPVM for display by using the options in pvm_setopt(). XPVM expects the OutputCode to be set to 667.

8.2 Porting PVM to New Architectures

PVM has been ported to three distinct classes of architecture:

- Workstations and PCs running some version of Unix
- Distributed-memory multiprocessors like the Intel hypercubes

- Shared-memory multiprocessors like the SGI Challenge

Each of these classes requires a different approach to make PVM exploit the capabilities of the respective architecture. The workstations use TCP/IP to move data between hosts, the distributed-memory multiprocessors use the native message-passing routines to move data between nodes, and the shared-memory multiprocessors use shared memory to move data between the processors. The following sections describe the steps for porting the PVM source to each of these classes.

Porting PVM to non-Unix operating systems can be very difficult. Nonetheless, groups outside the PVM team have developed PVM ports for DEC's VMS and IBM's OS/2 operating systems. Such ports can require extensive rewriting of the source and are not described here.

8.2.1   Unix Workstations

PVM is supported on most Unix platforms. If an architecture is not listed in the file $PVM_ROOT/docs/arches, the following description should help you to create a new PVM port. Anything from a small amount of tweaking to major surgery may be required, depending on how accomodating your version of Unix is.

The PVM source directories are organized in the following manner: Files in **src** form the core for PVM (pvmd and libpvm); files in **console** are for the PVM console, which is just a special task; source for the FORTRAN interface and group functions are in the libfpvm and pvmgs directories, respectively.

In each of the source directories, the file **Makefile.aimk** is the generic makefile for all uniprocessor platforms. System-specific definitions are kept in the **conf** directory under $(PVM_ARCH).def. The script lib/aimk, invoked by the top-level makefile, determines the value of PVM_ARCH, then chooses the appropriate makefile for a particular architecture. It first looks in the PVM_ARCH subdirectory for a makefile; if none is found, the generic one is used. The custom information stored in the **conf** directory is prepended to the head of the chosen makefile, and the build begins. The generic makefiles for MPP and shared-memory systems are Makefile.mimd and Makefile.shmem, respectively. System-specific rules are kept in the makefile under the PVM_ARCH subdirectory.

The steps to create a new architecture (for example *ARCH*) are:

- Add a rule to the script lib/pvmgetarch so it returns *ARCH*. PVM uses this program to determine machine architecture at run time. pvmgetarch tries to use the **uname** or **arch** command (supplied by many vendors). If there is no such command, we check for the existence of a file or device unique to a machine – try to find one that doesn't depend on configuration options. Don't break the existing architectures when adding a new one, unless you won't be sharing the code or just want to hack it together. At worst, you can override pvmgetarch by setting PVM_ARCH in your .cshrc file.

- Create files *ARCH*.def and *ARCH*.m4 in pvm3/conf. As a first try, copy them from another architecture similar to yours (you'll have to figure that out). *ARCH*.def is a machine-dependent header used with the generic makefiles (for example see the file src/Makefile.aimk). It defines the following variables (and possibly others):

  - PVM_ARCH – This is set to the architecture name, *ARCH*.

  - ARCHCFLAGS – This lists any special C compiler flags needed, for example, optimizer limits or floating-point switches (Not, for example, -O). It also defines macros needed to switch in optional PVM source code, for example, -DSYSVSIGNAL. Common compiler macros are explained below.

  - ARCHDLIB – This lists any special libraries needed to link with the pvmd, for example -lsocket. You'll need to set this if there are symbols undefined while linking the pvmd. You can use nm and grep to find the missing functions in /usr/lib/lib*.a. They may occur in multiple libraries, but are probably defined in only one.

  - ARCHLIB – This lists any special libraries needed to link with tasks (anything linked with *libpvm*). It is probably a supeset of ARCHDLIB, because libpvm uses mostly the same functions as the pvmd, and also uses XDR.

  - HASRANLIB – This should be set to t if your machine has the ranlib command, and f otherwise.

  Compiler macros imported from conf/*ARCH*.def are listed at the top of the file named src/Makefile.aimk. They enable options that are common to several machines and so generally useful. New ones are added occasionally. The macro IMA_*ARCH* can be used to enable code that only applies to a single architecture. The ones most commonly used are:

  - FDSETPATCH – If fd_set definitions are missing from the system (rare these days).

  - HASSTDLIB – If system has <stdlib.h>.

  - NOGETDTBLSIZ – If system doesn't have getdtablesize() (uses sysconf(_SC_OPEN_MAX) instead).

  - NOREXEC – If system doesn't have rexec() function.

  - NOSOCKOPT – If system doesn't have setsockopt() function, or it doesn't work.

  - NOSTRCASE – If system doesn't have strcasecmp() or strncasecmp() (includes replacements).

  - NOTMPNAM – If system doesn't have tmpnam() function, or it's broken.

  - NOUNIXDOM – To disable use of Unix-domain sockets for local communication.

  - NOWAIT3 – If system doesn't have wait3() function (uses waitpid()).

  - NOWAITPID – If system doesn't have waitpid() function either (uses wait()).

  - RSHCOMMAND – If rsh command isn't named "/usr/ucb/rsh".

  - SHAREDTMP – If /tmp directory is shared between machines in a cluster.

- SOCKADHASLEN – If `struct sockaddr` has an `sa_len` field.

- SYSVBFUNC – If system doesn't have `bcopy()` but does have `memcpy()`.

- SYSVSIGNAL – If system has System-5 signal handling (signal handlers are uninstalled after each signal).

- SYSVSTR – If system doesn't have `index()` but does have `strchr()`.

- UDPMAXLEN – To set a different maximum UDP packet length (the default is 4096).

ARCH.m4 is a file of commands for the `m4` macro processor, that edits the libfpvm C source code to conform to FORTRAN calling conventions, which vary from machine to machine. The two main things you must determine about your FORTRAN are: 1. How FORTRAN subroutine names are converted to linker symbols. Some systems append an underscore to the name; others convert to all capital letters. 2. How strings are passed in FORTRAN – One common method is to pass the address in a `char*`, and pass corresponding lengths after all remaining parameters. The easiest way to discover the correct choices may be to try every common case (approximately three) for each. First, get the function names right, then make sure you can pass string data to FORTRAN tasks.

- Add *ARCH* to the `arches[]` array in `src/pvmarchc.c`. You must determine the *data format* of your machine to know which class to assign it to. Machines with the same `arches[i].archnum` have the same binary representations for integers and floating point numbers. At worst, put the new machine in a class by itself.

- Modify the source if it still doesn't work. Use `cpp` symbol IMA_*ARCH* to include modifications that only apply to *ARCH*, so they don't affect other ports.

8.2.2 Multiprocessors

Porting to MPP systems is more difficult because most of them do not offer a standard Unix environment on the nodes. We discuss some of these limitations below.

Processes running on the nodes of an Intel iPSC/860 have no Unix process id's and they cannot receive Unix signals. There is a similar problem for the Thinking Machine's CM-5.

If a node process forks, the behavior of the new process is machine dependent. In any event it would not be allowed to become a new PVM task. In general, processes on the nodes are not allowed to enroll unless they were spawned by PVM.

By default, pvm_spawn() starts tasks on the (compute) nodes. To spawn multiple copies of the same executable, the programmer should call pvm_spawn() once and specify the number of copies.

On some machines (e.g., iPSC/860), only one process is allowed on each node, so the total number of PVM tasks on these machines cannot exceed the number of nodes available.

Several functions serve as the multiprocessor "interface" for PVM. They are called by pvmd to spawn new tasks and to communicate with them. The implementation of these functions is system dependent; the source code is kept in the src/PVM_ARCH/pvmdmimd.c (message passing) or src/PVM_ARCH/pvmdshmem.c (shared memory). We give a brief description of each of these functions below. Note that pvmdmimd.c can be found in the subdirectory PVM_ARCH because MPP platforms are very different from one another, even those from the same vendor.

```
void mpp_init(int argc, char **argv);
     Initialization. Called once when PVM is started. Arguments argc and argv
     are passed from pvmd main().

int mpp_load(int flags, char *name, char *argv, int count, int *tids, int ptid);
     Create partition if necessary. Load executable onto nodes; create new
     entries in task table, encode node number and process type into task IDs.
     flags:   exec options;
     name:    executable to be loaded;
     argv:    command line argument for executable;
     count:   number of tasks to be created;
     tids:    array to store new task IDs;
     ptid:    parent task ID.

void mpp_output(struct task *tp, struct pkt *pp);
     Send all pending packets to nodes via native send. Node number and process
     type are extracted from task ID.
     tp: destination task;
     pp: packet.

int mpp_mcast(struct pkt pp, int *tids, int ntask);
     Global send.
     pp:      packet;
     tids:    list of destination task IDs;
     ntask:   how many.

int mpp_probe();
     Probe for pending packets from nodes (non-blocking). Returns 1 if packets
     are found, otherwise 0.

void mpp_input();
     Receive pending packets (from nodes) via native receive.
```

```
void mpp_free(int tid)
    Remove node/process-type from active list.
    tid: task ID.
```

In addition to these functions, the message exchange routine in libpvm, mroute(),
must also be implemented in the most efficient native message-passing primitives. The
following macros are defined in src/pvmmimd.h:

```
ASYNCRECV(buf,len)
    Non-blocking receive. Returns immediately with a message handle.
    buf: (char *), buffer to place the data;
    len: (int), size of buffer in bytes.

ASYNCSEND(tag,buf,len,dest,ptype)
    Non-blocking send. Returns immediately with a message handle.
    tag: (int), message tag;
    buf: (char *), location of data;
    len: (int), size of data in bytes;
    dest: (long), address of destination node;
    ptype: instance number of destination task.

ASYNCWAIT(mid)
    Blocks until operation associated with mid has completed.
    mid: message handle (its type is system-dependent).

ASYNCDONE(mid)
    Returns 1 if operation associated with mid has completed, and 0 otherwise.
    mid: message handle (its type is system-dependent).

MSGSIZE(mid)
    Returns size of message most recently arrived.
    mid: message handle (its type is system-dependent).

MSGSENDER(mid)
    Returns node number of the sender of most recently received message.
    mid: message handle (its type is system-dependent).

PVMCRECV(tag,buf,len)
    Blocks until message has been received into buffer.
    tag: (int), expected message tag;
    buf: (char *), buffer to place the data;
    len: (int), size of buffer in bytes;
```

```
PVMCSEND(tag,buf,len,dest,ptype)
     Blocks until send operation is complete and buffer can be reused.
     Non-blocking send. Returns immediately with a message handle.
     tag: (int), message tag;
     buf: (char *), location of data;
     len: (int), size of data in bytes;
     dest: (long), address of destination node;
     ptype: instance number of destination task.
```

These functions are used by mroute() on MPP systems. The source code for mroute
for multiprocessors is in `src/lpvmmimd.c` or `src/lpvmshmem.c` depending on the class.

For shared-memory implementations, the following macros are defined in the file
`src/pvmshmem.h`:

```
PAGEINITLOCK(lp)
     Initialize the lock pointed to by lp.
```

```
PAGELOCK(lp)
     Locks the lock pointed to by lp.
```

```
PAGEUNLOCK(lp)
     Unlocks the lock pointed to by lp.
```

In addition, the file `pvmshmem.c` contains routines used by both pvmd and libpvm.

9 Troubleshooting

This chapter attempts to answer some of the most common questions encountered by users when installing PVM and running PVM programs. It also covers debugging the system itself, which is sometimes necessary when doing new ports or trying to determine whether an application or PVM is at fault. The material here is mainly taken from other sections of the book, and rearranged to make answers easier to find. As always, RTFM pages first. Printed material always lags behind reality, while the online documentation is kept up-to-date with each release. The newsgroup *comp.parallel.pvm* is available to post questions and discussions.

If you find a problem with PVM, please tell us about it. A bug report form is included with the distribution in $PVM_ROOT/doc/bugreport. Please use this form or include equivalent information.

Some of the information in this chapter applies only to the generic Unix implementation of PVM, or describes features more volatile than the standard documented ones. It is presented here to aid with debugging, and tagged with a ♣ to warn you of its nature.

Examples of shell scripts are for either C-shell (csh, tcsh) or Bourne shell (sh, ksh). If you use some other shell, you may need to modify them somewhat, or use csh while troubleshooting.

9.1 Getting PVM Installed

You can get a copy of PVM for your own use or share an already-installed copy with other users. The installation process for either case more or less the same.

9.1.1 Set PVM_ROOT

Make certain you have environment variable PVM_ROOT set (and exported, if applicable) to directory where PVM is installed before you do anything else. This directory is where the system executables and libraries reside. Your application executables go in a private directory, by default $HOME/pvm3/bin/$PVM_ARCH. If PVM is already installed at your site you can share it by setting PVM_ROOT to that path, for example /usr/local/pvm3. If you have your own copy, you could install it in $HOME/pvm3.

If you normally use csh, add a line like this to your .cshrc file:

```
setenv PVM_ROOT $HOME/pvm3
```

If you normally use sh, add these lines to your .profile:

```
PVM_ROOT=$HOME/pvm3 PVM_DPATH=$HOME/pvm3/lib/pvmd export PVM_ROOT PVM_DPATH
```

Make sure these are set in your current session too.

Older versions of PVM assumed an installation path of $HOME/pvm3. Versions 3.3 and later require that the PVM_ROOT variable always be set. Note: For compatibility with older versions of PVM and some command shells that don't execute a startup file, newer versions guess $HOME/pvm3 if it's not set, but you shouldn't depend on that.

9.1.2   On-Line Manual Pages

On-line manual pages compatible with most Unix machines are shipped with the source distribution. These reside in $PVM_ROOT/man and can be copied to some other place (for example /usr/local/man or used in-place. If the man program on your machine uses the MANPATH environment variable, try adding something like the following near the end of your .cshrc or .login file:

```
if (! $?MANPATH) setenv MANPATH /usr/man:/usr/local/man
setenv MANPATH ${MANPATH}:$PVM_ROOT/man
```

Then you should be able to read both normal system man pages and PVM man pages by simply typing man *subject*.

9.1.3   Building the Release

The following commands download, unpack, build and install a release:

```
(start in directory just above PVM root, for example $HOME or /usr/local)
% ftp netlib2.cs.utk.edu
Name:  anonymous
Password:  your id, user@host.domain
ftp> cd pvm3
ftp> bin
ftp> get pvm3.3.tar.z.uu   (or the most recent version)
ftp> quit
% uudecode pvm3.3.tar.z.uu
% zcat pvm3.3.tar.Z | tar xf -
% cd pvm3
% setenv PVM_ROOT $cwd
% make
```

9.1.4   Errors During Build

The compiler may print a few warning messages; we suggest you ignore these unless the build doesn't complete or until you have some other reason to think there is a problem. If you can't build the unmodified distribution "out of the box" on a supported architecture, let us know.

9.1.5   Compatible Versions

The protocols used in building PVM are evolving, with the result that newer releases are not compatible with older ones. Compatibility is determined by the pvmd-task and task-task protocol revision numbers. These are compared when two PVM entities connect; they will refuse to interoperate if the numbers don't match. The protocol numbers are defined in src/ddpro.h and src/tdpro.h (DDPROTOCOL, TDPROTOCOL).

As a general rule, PVM releases with the same second digit in their version numbers (for example 3.2.0 and 3.2.6) will interoperate. Changes that result in incompatibility are held until a major version change (for example, from 3.2 to 3.3).

9.2   Getting PVM Running

To get PVM running, you must start either a pvmd or the PVM console by hand. The executables are named **pvmd3** and **pvm**, respectively, and reside in directory $PVM_ROOT/lib/ $PVM_ARCH. We suggest using the **pvmd** or **pvm** script in $PVM_ROOT/lib instead, as this simplifies setting your shell path. These scripts determine the host architecture and run the correct executable, passing on their command line arguments.

Problems when starting PVM can be caused by system or network trouble, running out of resources (such as disk space), incorrect installation or a bug in the PVM code.

9.2.1   Pvmd Log File

The pvmd writes errors on both its standard error stream (only until it is fully started) and a log file, named /tmp/pvml.*uid*. *uid* is your numeric user id (generally the number in the third colon-separated field of your *passwd* entry). If PVM was built with the SHAREDTMP option (used when a cluster of machines shares a /tmp directory), the log file will instead be named /tmp/pvml.*uid*.*hostname*.

If you have trouble getting PVM started, always check the log file for hints about what went wrong. If more than one host is involved, check the log file on each host. For example, when adding a new host to a virtual machine, check the log files on the *master* host and the new host.

Try the following command to get your uid:

```
(grep `whoami` /etc/passwd || ypmatch `whoami` passwd) \
  | awk -F: '{print $3;exit}'
```

9.2.2 Pvmd Socket Address File

The pvmd publishes the address of the socket to which local tasks connect in a file named /tmp/pvmd.*uid*. *uid* is your numeric user id (generally in the third field of your *passwd* entry). If PVM was built with the SHAREDTMP option (used when a cluster of machines shares a /tmp directory), the file will be named /tmp/pvmd.*uid*.*hostname*. See §7.4.2 for more information on how this file is used.

The pvmd creates the socket address file while starting up, and removes it while shutting down. If while starting up, it finds the file already exists, it prints an error message and exits. If the pvmd can't create the file because the permissions of /tmp are set incorrectly or the filesystem is full, it won't be able to start up.

If the pvmd is killed with un uncatchable signal or other catastrophic event such as a (Unix) machine crash, you must remove the socket address file before another pvmd will start on that host.

Note that if the pvmd is compiled with option OVERLOADHOST, it will start up even if the address file already exists (creating it if it doesn't). It doesn't consider the existence of the address file an error. This allows disjoint virtual machines owned by the same user to use overlapping sets of hosts. Tasks not spawned by PVM can only connect to the first pvmd running on an overloaded host, however, unless they can somehow guess the correct socket address of one of the other pvmds.

9.2.3 Starting PVM from the Console

PVM is normally started by invoking the console program, which starts a pvmd if one is not already running and connects to it. The syntax for starting a PVM console is:

pvm [-d*debugmask*] [-n*hostname*] [*hostfile*]

If the console can't start the pvmd for some reason, you may see one of the following error messages. Check the pvmd log file for error messages. The most common ones are described below.

Can't start pvmd – This message means that the console either can't find the pvmd executable or the pvmd is having trouble starting up. If the pvmd complains that it can't bind a socket, perhaps the host name set for the machine does not resolve to an IP address of one of its interfaces, or that interface is down. The console/pvmd option -n*name* can be used to change the default.

Can't contact local daemon – If a previously running pvmd crashed, leaving behind its *socket address* file, the console may print this message. The pvmd will log error message pvmd already running?. Find and delete the address file.

`Version mismatch` – The console (libpvm) and pvmd protocol revision numbers don't match. The protocol has a revision number so that incompatible versions won't attempt to interoperate. Note that having different protocol revisions doesn't necessarily cause this message to be printed; instead the connecting side may simply hang.

9.2.4 Starting the Pvmd by Hand

It is necessary to start the master pvmd by hand if you will use the *so=pw* or *so=ms* options in the host file or when adding hosts. These options require direct interaction with the pvmd when adding a host. If the pvmd is started by the console, or otherwise backgrounded, it will not be able to read passwords from a TTY.

The syntax to start the master pvmd by hand is:

$$\texttt{\$PVM\_ROOT/lib/pvmd} \ \texttt{[-d}debugmask\texttt{]} \ \texttt{[-n}hostname\texttt{]} \ \texttt{[}hostfile\texttt{]}$$

If you start a PVM console or application, use another window. When the pvmd finishes starting up, it prints out a line like either: `80a95ee4:0a9a` or `/tmp/aaa026175`. If it can't start up, you may not see an error message, depending on whether the problem occurs before or after the pvmd stops logging to its standard error output. Check the pvmd log file for a complete record.

9.2.5 Adding Hosts to the Virtual Machine

This section also applies to hosts started via a host file, because the same mechanism is used in both cases. The master pvmd starts up, reads the host file, then sends itself a request to add more hosts. The PVM console (or an application) can return an error when adding hosts to the virtual machine. Check the pvmd log file on the master host and the failing host for additional clues to what went wrong.

`No such host` – The master pvmd couldn't resolve the the host name (or name given in `ip=` option) to an IP address. Make sure you have the correct host name.

`Can't start pvmd` – This message means that the master pvmd failed to start the slave pvmd process. This can be caused by incorrect installation, network or permission problems. The master pvmd must be able to resolve the host name (get its IP address) and route packets to it. The pvmd executable and shell script to start it must be installed in the correct location. You must avoid printing anything in your `.cshrc` (or equivalent) script, because it will confuse the pvmd communication. If you must print something, either move it to your `.login` file or enclose it in a conditional:

```
if ( { tty -s } && $?prompt ) then
    echo terminal type is $TERM
    stty erase '^?' kill '^u' intr '^c' echo
endif
```

To test all the above, try running the following command by hand on the master host:

rsh *host* $PVM_ROOT/lib/pvmd -s

where *host* is the name of the slave host you want to test. You should see a message similar to the following from the slave pvmd and nothing else:

```
[pvmd pid12360] slave_config: bad args
[pvmd pid12360] pvmbailout(0)
```

Version mismatch – This message indicates that the protocol revisions of the master and slave pvmd are incompatible. You must install the same (or compatible) versions everywhere.

Duplicate host – This message means that PVM thinks there is another pvmd (owned by the same user) already running on the host. If you're not already using the host in the current virtual machine or a different one, the socket address file (§9.2.2) must be left over from a previous run. Find and delete it.

9.2.6 PVM Host File

A *host file* may be supplied to the pvmd (or console, which passes it to the pvmd) as a command-line parameter. Each line of the file contains a host name followed by option parameters. Hosts not preceded by '&' are started automatically as soon as the master pvmd is ready. The syntax:

```
    * option option ...
```

changes the default parameters for subsequent hosts (both those in the host file and those added later). Default statements are not cumulative; each applies to the *system* defaults. For example, after the following two host file entries:

```
    * dx=pvm3/lib/pvmd
    * ep=/bin:/usr/bin:pvm3/bin/$PVM_ARCH
```

only ep is changed from its system default (dx is reset by the second line). To set multiple defaults, combine them into a single line.

9.2.7 Shutting Down

The preferred way to shut down a virtual machine is to type halt at the PVM console, or to call libpvm function pvm_halt(). When shutting PVM down from the console, you may see an error message such as *EOF on pvmd sock*. This is normal and can be ignored.

You can instead kill the pvmd process; it will shut down, killing any local tasks with SIGTERM. If you kill a slave pvmd, it will be deleted from the virtual machine. If you kill the master pvmd, the slaves will all exit too. Always kill the pvmd with a *catchable* signal, for example SIGTERM. If you kill it with SIGKILL, it won't be able to clean up after itself, and you'll have to do that by hand.

9.3   Compiling Applications

9.3.1   Header Files

PVM applications written in C should include header file pvm3.h, as follows:

#include <pvm3.h>

Programs using the trace functions should additionally include pvmtev.h, and resource manager programs should include pvmsdpro.h. You may need to specify the PVM include directory in the compiler flags as follows:

cc ...   -I$PVM_ROOT/include ...

A header file for Fortran (fpvm3.h) is also supplied. Syntax for including files in Fortran is variable; the header file may need to be pasted into your source. A statement commonly used is:

INCLUDE '/usr/local/pvm/include/fpvm3.h'

9.3.2   Linking

PVM applications written in C must be linked with at least the base PVM library, *libpvm3*. Fortran applications must be linked with both *libfpvm3* and *libpvm3*. Programs that use group functions must also be linked with *libgpvm3*. On some operating systems, PVM programs must be linked with still other libraries (for the socket or XDR functions).

Note that the order of libraries in the link command is important; Unix machines generally process the list from left to right, searching each library once. You may also need to specify the PVM library directory in the link command. A correct order is shown below (your compiler may be called something other than cc or f77).

```
cc/f77 [ compiler flags ] [ source files ] [ loader flags ]
       -L$PVM_ROOT/lib/$PVM_ARCH -lfpvm3 -lgpvm3 -lpvm3
       [ libraries needed by PVM ] [ other libraries ]
```

The aimk program supplied with PVM automatically sets environment variable PVM_ARCH to the PVM architecture name and ARCHLIB to the necessary system libraries. Before running aimk, you must have PVM_ROOT set to the path where PVM is installed. You can use these variables to write a portable, shared makefile (Makefile.aimk).

9.4   Running Applications

9.4.1   Spawn Can't Find Executables

No such file – This error code is returned instead of a task id when the pvmd fails to find a program executable during spawn.

Remember that task placement decisions are made before checking the existence of executables. If an executable is not installed on the selected host, PVM returns an error instead of trying another one. For example, if you have installed *myprog* on 4 hosts of a 7 host virtual machine, and spawn 7 instances of *myprog* with default placement, only 4 will succeed. Make sure executables are built for each architecture you're using, and installed in the correct directory. By default, PVM searches first in pvm3/bin/$PVM_ARCH (the pvmd default working directory is $HOME) and then in $PVM_ROOT/bin/$PVM_ARCH. This path list can be changed with host file option ep=. If your programs aren't on a filesystem shared between the hosts, you must copy them to each host manually.

9.4.2   Group Functions

failed to start group server – This message means that a function in the group library (libgpvm3.a) could not spawn a *group server task* to manage group membership lists. Tasks using group library functions must be able to communicate with this server. It is started automatically if one is not already running. The group server executable (pvmgs) normally resides in $PVM_ROOT/bin/$PVM_ARCH, which must be in the pvmd search path. If you change the path using the host file ep= option, make sure this directory is still included. The group server may be spawned on any host, so be sure one is installed and your path is set correctly everywhere.

9.4.3   Memory Use

Tasks and pvmds allocate some memory (using malloc()) as they run. Malloc never gives memory back to the system, so the data size of each process only increases over its lifetime. Message and packet buffers (the main users of dynamic memory in PVM) are recycled, however.

The things that most commonly cause PVM to use a large amount of memory are passing huge messages, certain communication patterns and memory leaks.

A task sending a PVM message doesn't necessarily block until the corresponding receive is executed. Messages are stored at the destination until claimed, allowing some leeway when programming in PVM. The programmer should be careful to limit the number of outstanding messages. Having too many causes the receiving task (and its pvmd if the task is busy) to accumulate a lot of dynamic memory to hold all the messages.

There is nothing to stop a task from sending a message which is never claimed (because receive is never called with a wildcard pattern). This message will be held in memory until the task exits.

Make sure you're not accumulating old message buffers by moving them aside. The `pvm_initsend()` and receive functions automatically free the current buffer, but if you use the `pvm_set[sr]buf()` routines, then the associated buffers may not be freed. For example, the following code fragment allocates message buffers until the system runs out of memory:

```
while (1) {
    pvm_initsend(PvmDataDefault);    /* make new buffer */
    pvm_setsbuf(0);
    /* now buffer won't be freed by next initsend */
}
```

♣ As a quick check, look at the message handles returned by initsend or receive functions. Message ids are taken from a pool, which is extended as the number of message buffers in use increases. If there is a buffer leak, message ids will start out small and increase steadily.

♣ Two undocumented functions in libpvm dump information about message buffers:

umbuf_dump(int mid, int level),
umbuf_list(int level).

Function `umbuf_dump()` dumps a message buffer by id (`mid`). Parameter `level` is one of:

Level	Information dumped
0	One-line summary
1	List of data fragments
2	All data packed in message

Function `umbuf_list()` calls `umbuf_dump()` for each message in the message heap.

9.4.4 Input and Output

Each task spawned through PVM has its *stdout* and *stderr* files connected to a pipe that is read by the pvmd managing the task. Anything printed by the task is packed into a PVM message by the pvmd and sent to the task's *stdout sink*. The implementation of this mechanism is described in §7.7.2. Each spawned task has /dev/null opened as *stdin*.

Output from a task running on any host in a virtual machine (unless redirected by the console, or a parent task) is written in the log file of the *master* pvmd by default.

You can use the console spawn command with flag `->` to collect output from an application (the spawned tasks and any others they in turn spawn). Use function `pvm_catchout()` to collect output within an application.

The C *stdio* library (`fgets()`, `printf()`, etc.) buffers input and output whenever possible, to reduce the frequency of actual `read()` or `write()` system calls. It decides whether to buffer by looking at the underlying file descriptor of a stream. If the file is a tty, it buffers only a line at a time, that is, the buffer is flushed whenever the newline character is encountered. If the descriptor is a file, pipe, or socket, however, stdio buffers up much more, typically 4k bytes.

A task spawned by PVM writes output through a pipe back to its pvmd, so the stdout buffer isn't flushed after every line (stderr probably is). The `pvm_exit()` function closes the stdio streams, causing them to be flushed so you should eventually see all your output. You can flush stdout by calling `fflush(stdout)` anywhere in your program. You can change the buffering mode of stdout to line-oriented for the entire program by calling `setlinebuf(stdout)` near the top of the program.

Fortran systems handle output buffering in many different ways. Sometimes there is a FLUSH subroutine, sometimes not.

In a PVM task, you can open a file to read or write, but remember that spawned components inherit the working directory (by default `$HOME`) from the pvmd so the file path you open must be relative to your home directory (or an absolute path). You can change the pvmd (and therefore task) working directory (per-host) by using the host file option `wd=`.

9.4.5 Scheduling Priority

♣ PVM doesn't have a built-in facility for running programs at different priorities (as with `nice`), but you can do it yourself. You can call `setpriority()` (or perhaps `nice()`) in your code or replace your program with a shell script wrapper as follows:

```
cd ~/pvm3/bin/SUN4
mv prog prog-
echo 'P=$0"-"; shift; exec nice -10 $P $@' > prog
chmod 755 prog
```

When `prog` is spawned, the shell script execs `prog-` at a new priority level.

You could be even more creative and pass an environment variable through PVM to the shell script, to allow varying the priority without editing the script. If you want to have real fun, hack the *tasker* example to do the work, then you won't have to replace all the programs with wrappers.

One reason for changing the scheduling priority of a task is to allow it to run on a workstation without impacting the performance of the machine for someone sitting at the console. Longer response time seems to *feel* worse than lower throughput. Response time is affected most by tasks that use a lot of memory, stealing all the physical pages from other programs. When interactive input arrives, it takes the system time to reclaim all the pages. Decreasing the priority of such a task may not help much, because if it's allowed to run for a few seconds, it accumulates pages again. In contrast, cpu bound jobs with small working set sizes may hardly affect the response time at all, unless you have many of them running.

9.4.6   Resource Limitations

Available memory limits the maximum size and number of outstanding messages the system can handle. The number of file descriptors (I/O channels) available to a process limits the number of *direct route* connections a task can establish to other tasks, and the number of tasks a single pvmd can manage. The number of processes allowed to a user limits the number of tasks that can run on a single host, and so on.

An important thing to know is that you may not see a message when you reach a resource limit. PVM tries to return an error code to the offending task and continue operation, but can't recover from certain events (running out of memory is the worst).

See §7.9 for more information on how resource limits affect PVM.

9.5   Debugging and Tracing

First, the bad news. Adding `printf()` calls to your code is still a state-of-the-art methodology.

PVM tasks can be started in a debugger on systems that support X-Windows. If `PvmTaskDebug` is specified in `pvm_spawn()`, PVM runs `$PVM_ROOT/lib/debugger`, which opens an *xterm* in which it runs the task in a debugger defined in `pvm3/lib/debugger2`. The `PvmTaskDebug` flag is not inherited, so you must modify each call to spawn. The `DISPLAY` environment variable can be exported to a remote host so the xterm will always be displayed on the local screen. Use the following command before running the application:

```
setenv PVM_EXPORT DISPLAY
```

Make sure `DISPLAY` is set to the name of your host (not `unix:0`) and the host name is fully qualified if your virtual machine includes hosts at more than one administrative site. To spawn a task in a debugger from the console, use the command:

```
spawn -? [ rest of spawn command ]
```

You may be able to use the libpvm trace facility to isolate problems, such as hung processes. A task has a *trace mask*, which allows each function in libpvm to be selectively traced, and a *trace sink*, which is another task to which trace data is sent (as messages). A task's trace mask and sink are inherited by any tasks spawned by it.

The console can spawn a task with tracing enabled (using the `spawn -@`), collect the trace data and print it out. In this way, a whole *job* (group of tasks related by parentage) can be traced. The console has a `trace` command to edit the mask passed to tasks it spawns. Or, XPVM can be used to collect and display trace data graphically.

It is difficult to start an application by hand and trace it, though. Tasks with no parent (anonymous tasks) have a default trace mask and sink of NULL. Not only must the first task call `pvm_setopt()` and `pvm_settmask()` to initialize the tracing parameters, but it must collect and interpret the trace data. If you must start a traced application from a TTY, we suggest spawning an xterm from the console:

```
spawn -@ /usr/local/X11R5/bin/xterm -n PVMTASK
```

The task context held open by the xterm has tracing enabled. If you now run a PVM program in the xterm, it will reconnect to the task context and trace data will be sent back to the PVM console. Once the PVM program exits, you must spawn a new xterm to run again, since the task context will be closed.

Because the libpvm library is linked with your program, it can't be trusted when debugging. If you overwrite part of its memory (for example by overstepping the bounds of an array) it may start to behave erratically, making the fault hard to isolate. The pvmds are somewhat more robust and attempt to sanity-check messages from tasks, but can still be killed by errant programs.

The `pvm_setopt()` function can be used to set the debug mask for PVM message-passing functions, as described in §9.6.1. Setting this mask to 3, for example, will force PVM to log for every message sent or received by that task, information such as the source, destination, and length of the message. You can use this information to trace lost or stray messages.

9.6   Debugging the System

You may need to debug the PVM system when porting it to a new architecture, or because an application is not running correctly. If you've thoroughly checked your application and can't find a problem, then it may lie in the system itself. This section describes a few tricks and undocumented features of PVM to help you find out what's going on.

9.6.1   Runtime Debug Masks

♣ The pvmd and libpvm each have a debugging mask that can be set to enable logging of various information. Logging information is divided into classes, each enabled separately by a bit in the debug mask. The pvmd and console have a command line option (-d) to set the debug mask of the pvmd to the (hexadecimal) value specified; the default is zero. Slave pvmds inherit the debug mask of the master as they are started. The debug mask of a pvmd can be set at any time using the console `tickle` command on that host. The debug mask in libpvm can be set in the task with `pvm_setopt()`.

The pvmd debug mask bits are defined in ddpro.h, and the libpvm bits in lpvm.c. The meanings of the bits are not well defined, since they're only intended to be used when fixing or modifying the pvmd or libpvm. At present, the bits in the debug mask are as follows:

Name	Bit	Debug Messages about
pkt	0x1	Packet routing
msg	2	Message routing
tsk	4	Task management
slv	8	Slave pvmd startup
hst	10	Host table updates
sel	20	Select loop (below packet routing layer)
net	40	Network twiddling
mpp	80	MPP port specific
sch	100	Resource manager interface

9.6.2   Tickle the Pvmd

♣ The tickle function is a simple, extensible interface that allows a task to poke at its local pvmd as it runs. It is not formally specified, but has proven to be very useful in debugging the system. Tickle is accessible from the console (`tickle` command) or libpvm. Function `pvm_tickle()` sends a TM_TICKLE message to the pvmd containing a short (maximum of ten) array of integers and receives an array in reply. The first element of the array is a subcommand, and the remaining elements are parameters. The commands currently defined are:

Args	Return	Action
0	-	Dump instrumented heap (§9.6.4) to pvmd log file
1	-	Dump host table
2	-	Dump task table
3	-	Dump waitc list
4	-	Dump class-name list
5	*mask*	Get pvmd debug mask
6 *mask*	-	Set pvmd debug mask to *mask*
7 *max*	-	Set max outstanding packets to *max*
8 *tid*	-	Trigger host fail for host *tid*
9 *flag*	-	Dump pvmd statistics (§9.6.5); clear if *flag* nonzero

New tickle commands are generally added to the end of the list.

9.6.3   Starting Pvmd under a Debugger

If the pvmd breaks, you may need to start it under a debugger. The master pvmd can be started by hand under a debugger, and the PVM console started on another terminal. To start a slave pvmd under a debugger, use the manual startup (so=ms) host file option so the master pvmd will allow you to start the slave by hand. Or, use the dx= host file option to execute a script similar to lib/debugger, and run the pvmd in a debugger in an *xterm* window.

9.6.4   Sane Heap

♣ To help catch memory allocation errors in the system code, the pvmd and libpvm use a sanity-checking library called *imalloc*. Imalloc functions are wrappers for the regular *libc* functions malloc(), realloc(), and free(). Upon detecting an error, the imalloc functions abort the program so the fault can be traced.

The following checks and functions are performed by imalloc:

1. The length argument to malloc is checked for insane values. A length of zero is changed to one so it succeeds.

2. Each allocated block is tracked in a hash table to detect when free() is called more than once on a block or on something not from malloc().

3. i_malloc() and i_realloc() write pads filled with a pseudo-random pattern outside the bounds of each block, which are checked by i_free() to detect when something writes past the end of a block.

4. i_free() zeros each block before it frees it so further references may fail and make themselves known.

5. Each block is tagged with a serial number and string to indicate its use. The heap space can be dumped or sanity-checked at any time by calling i_dump(). This helps find

memory leaks.

Since the overhead of this checking is quite severe, it is disabled at compile time by default. Defining USE_PVM_ALLOC in the source makefile(s) switches it on.

9.6.5 Statistics

♣ The pvmd includes several registers and counters to sample certain events, such as the number of calls made to select() or the number of packets refragmented by the network code. These values can be computed from a debug log, but the counters have less adverse impact on the performance of the pvmd than would generating a huge log file. The counters can be dumped or reset using the pvm_tickle() function or the console tickle command. The code to gather statistics is normally switched out at compile time. To enable it, one edits the makefile and adds -DSTATISTICS to the compile options.

Glossary

asynchronous Not guaranteed to enforce coincidence in clock time. In an asynchronous communication operation, the sender and receiver may or may not both be engaged in the operation at the same instant in clock time.

atomic Not interruptible. An atomic operation is one that always appears to have been executed as a unit.

bandwidth A measure of the speed of information transfer typically used to quantify the communication capability of multicomputer and multiprocessor systems. Bandwidth can express point-to-point or collective (bus) communications rates. Bandwidths are usually expressed in megabytes per second.

barrier synchronization An event in which two or more processes belonging to some implicit or explicit group block until all members of the group have blocked. They may then all proceed. No member of the group may pass a barrier until all processes in the group have reached it.

big-endian A binary data format in which the most significant byte or bit comes first. See also *little-endian.*

bisection bandwidth The rate at which communication can take place between one half of a computer and the other. A low bisection bandwidth or a large disparity between the maximum and minimum bisection bandwidths achieved by cutting the computers elements in different ways is a warning that communications bottlenecks may arise in some calculations.

broadcast To send a message to all possible recipients. Broadcast can be implemented as a repeated send or in a more efficient method, for example, over a spanning tree where each node propagates the message to its descendents.

buffer A temporary storage area in memory. Many methods for routing messages between processors use buffers at the source and destination or at intermediate processors.

bus A single physical communications medium shared by two or more devices. The network shared by processors in many distributed computers is a bus, as is the shared data path in many multiprocessors.

cache consistency The problem of ensuring that the values associated with a particular variable in the caches of several processors are never visibly different.

channel A point-to-point connection through which messages can be sent. Programming systems that rely on channels are sometimes called connection oriented, to distinguish them from connectionless systems in which messages are sent to named destinations rather than through named channels.

circuit A network where connections are established between senders and receivers, reserving network resources. Compare with *packet switching.*

combining Joining messages together as they traverse a network. Combining may be done to reduce the total traffic in the network, to reduce the number of times the start-up penalty of messaging is incurred, or to reduce the number of messages reaching a particular destination.

communication overhead A measure of the additional workload incurred in a parallel algorithm as a result of communication between the nodes of the parallel system.

computation-to-communication ratio The ratio of the number of calculations a process does to the total size of the messages it sends; alternatively, the ratio of time spent calculating to time spent communicating, which depends on the relative speeds of the processor and communications medium, and on the startup cost and latency of communication.

contention Conflict that arises when two or more requests are made concurrently for a resource that cannot be shared. Processes running on a single processor may contend for CPU time, or a network may suffer from contention if several messages attempt to traverse the same link at the same time.

context switching Saving the state of one process and replacing it with that of another. If little time is required to switch contexts, processor overloading can be an effective way to hide latency in a message-passing system.

daemon A special-purpose process that runs on behalf of the system, for example, the pvmd process or group server task.

data encoding A binary representation for data objects (e.g., integers, floating-point numbers) such as XDR or the native format of a microprocessor. PVM messages can contain data in XDR, native, or *foo* format.

data parallelism A model of parallel computing in which a single operation can be applied to all elements of a data structure simultaneously. Typically, these data structures are arrays, and the operations act independently on every array element or reduction operations.

deadlock A situation in which each possible activity is blocked, waiting on some other activity that is also blocked.

distributed computer A computer made up of smaller and potentially independent computers, such as a network of workstations. This architecture is increasingly studied because of its cost effectiveness and flexibility. Distributed computers are often heterogeneous.

distributed memory Memory that is physically distributed among several modules. A distributed-memory architecture may appear to users to have a single address space and a single shared memory or may appear as disjoint memory made up of many separate address spaces.

DMA *Direct memory access,* allowing devices on a bus to access memory without interfering with the CPU.

efficiency A measure of hardware utilization, equal to the ratio of speedup achieved on P processors to P itself.

Ethernet A popular LAN technology invented by Xerox. Ethernet is a 10-Mbit/S CSMA/CD (Carrier Sense Multiple Access with Collision Detection) bus. Computers on an Ethernet send data packets directly to one another. They listen for the network to become idle before transmitting, and retransmit in the event that multiple stations simultaneously attempt to send.

FDDI *Fiber Distributed Data Interface,* a standard for local area networks using optical fiber and a 100-Mbit/s data rate. A *token* is passed among the stations to control access to send on the network. Networks can be arranged in topologies such as stars, trees, and rings. Independent *counter-rotating* rings allow the network to continue to function in the event that a station or link fails.

FLOPS *Floating-Point Operations per Second,* a measure of memory access performance, equal to the rate at which a machine can perform single-precision floating-point calculations.

fork To create another copy of a running process; fork returns twice. Compare with *spawn.*

fragment A contiguous part of a message. Messages are fragmented so they can be sent over a network having finite maximum packet length.

group A set of tasks assigned a common symbolic name, for addressing purposes.

granularity The size of operations done by a process between communications events. A fine-grained process may perform only a few arithmetic operations between processing one message and the next, whereas a coarse-grained process may perform millions.

heterogeneous Containing components of more than one kind. A heterogeneous architecture may be one in which some components are processors, and others memories, or it may be one that uses different types of processor together.

hierarchical routing Messages are routed in PVM based on a hierarchical address (a TID). TIDs are divided into host and local parts to allow efficient local and global routing.

HiPPI *High Performance Parallel Interface*, a point-to-point 100-MByte/sec interface standard used for networking components of high-performance multicomputers together.

host A computer, especially a self-complete one on a network with others. Also, the front-end support machine for, for example, a multiprocessor.

hoster A special PVM task that performs slave pvmd startup for the master pvmd.

interval routing A routing algorithm that assigns an integer identifier to each possible destination and then labels the outgoing links of each node with a single contiguous interval or window so that a message can be routed simply by sending it out the link in whose interval its destination identifier falls.

interrupt-driven system A type of message-passing system. When a message is delivered to its destination process, it interrupts execution of that process and initiates execution of an interrupt handler, which may either process the message or store it for subsequent retrieval. On completion of the interrupt handler (which may set some flag or sends some signal to denote an available message), the original process resumes execution.

IP *Internet Protocol*, the Internet standard protocol that enables sending datagrams (blocks of data) between hosts on interconnected networks. It provides a connectionless, best-effort delivery service. IP and the ICMP control protocol are the building blocks for other protocols such as TCP and UDP.

kernel A program providing basic services on a computer, such as managing memory, devices, and file systems. A kernel may provide minimal service (as on a multiprocessor *node*) or many features (as on a Unix machine). Alternatively, a kernel may be a basic computational building-block (such as a fast Fourier transform) used iteratively or in parallel to perform a larger computation.

latency The time taken to service a request or deliver a message that is independent of the size or nature of the operation. The latency of a message-passing system is the minimum time to deliver any message.

Libpvm The core PVM programming library, allowing a task to interface with the pvmd and other tasks.

linear speedup The case when a program runs faster in direct proportion to the number of processors used.

little-endian A binary data format is which the least significant byte or bit comes first. See also *big-endian*.

load balance The degree to which work is evenly distributed among available processors. A program executes most quickly when it is perfectly load balanced, that is, when every processor has a share of the total amount of work to perform so that all processors complete their assigned tasks at the same time. One measure of load imbalance is the ratio of the difference between the finishing times of the first and last processors to complete their portion of the calculation to the time taken by the last processor.

locality The degree to which computations done by a processor depend only on data held in memory that is *close* to that processor. Also, the degree to which computations done on part of a data structure depend only on neighboring values. Locality can be measured by the ratio of local to nonlocal data accesses, or by the distribution of distances of, or times taken by, nonlocal accesses.

lock A device or algorithm the use of which guarantees some type of exclusive access to a shared resource.

loose synchronization The situation when the nodes on a computer are constrained to intermittently synchronize with each other via some communication. Frequently, some global computational parameter such as a time or iteration count provides a natural synchronization reference. This parameter divides the running program into compute and communication cycles.

mapping An allocation of processes to processors; allocating work to processes is usually called scheduling.

memory protection Any system that prevents one process from accessing a region of memory being used by another. Memory protection is supported in most serial computers by the hardware and the operating system and in most parallel computers by the hardware kernel and service kernel of the processors.

mesh A topology in which nodes form a regular acyclic d-dimensional grid, and each edge is parallel to a grid axis and joins two nodes that are adjacent along that axis. The architecture of many multicomputers is a two- or three-dimensional mesh; meshes are also the basis of many scientific calculations, in which each node represents a point in space, and the edges define the neighbors of a node.

message ID An integer handle used to reference a message buffer in libpvm.

message passing A style of interprocess communication in which processes send discrete messages to one another. Some computer architectures are called message-passing architectures because they support this model in hardware, although message passing has often been used to construct operating systems and network software for uniprocessors and distributed computers.

message tag An integer code (chosen by the programmer) bound to a message as it is sent. Messages can be accepted by tag value and/or source address at the destination.

message typing The association of information with a message that identifies the nature of its contents. Most message-passing systems automatically transfer information about a message's sender to its receiver. Many also require the sender to specify a type for the message, and let the receiver select which types of messages it is willing to receive. See *message tag*.

MIMD *Multiple-Instruction Multiple-Data*, a category of Flynn's taxonomy in which many instruction streams are concurrently applied to multiple data sets. A MIMD architecture is one in which heterogeneous processes may execute at different rates.

multicast To send a message to many, but not necessarily all possible recipient processes.

multicomputer A computer in which processors can execute separate instruction streams, can have their own private memories, and cannot directly access one another's memories. Most multicomputers are disjoint memory machines, constructed by joining nodes (each containing a microprocessor and some memory) via links.

multiprocessor A computer in which processors can execute separate instruction streams, but have access to a single address space. Most multiprocessors are shared-memory machines, constructed by connecting several processors to one or more memory banks through a bus or switch.

multiprocessor host The front-end support machine of, for example, a multicomputer. It may serve to boot the multicomputer, provide network access, file service, etc. Utilities such as compilers may run only on the front-end machine.

multitasking Executing many processes on a single processor. This is usually done by time-slicing the execution of individual processes and performing a context switch each time a process is swapped in or out, but is supported by special-purpose hardware in some computers. Most operating systems support multitasking, but it can be costly if the need to switch large caches or execution pipelines makes context switching expensive in time.

mutual exclusion A situation in which at most one process can be engaged in a specified activity at any time. Semaphores are often used to implement this.

network A physical communication medium. A network may consist of one or more buses, a switch, or the links joining processors in a multicomputer.

network byte order The Internet standard byte order (big-endian).

node Basic compute building block of a multicomputer. Typically a node refers to a processor with a memory system and a mechanism for communicating with other processors in the system.

non-blocking An operation that does not block the execution of the process using it. The term is usually applied to communications operations, where it implies that the communicating process may perform other operations before the communication has completed.

notify A message generated by PVM on a specified event. A task may request to be notified when another task exits or the virtual machine configuration changes.

NUMA *Non-Uniform Memory Access*, an architecture that does not support constant-time read and write operations. In most NUMA systems, memory is organized hierarchically, so that some portions can be read and written more quickly than others by a given processor.

packet A quantity of data sent over the network.

packet switching A network in which limited-length packets are routed independently from source to destination. Network resources are not reserved. Compare with *circuit*.

parallel computer A computer system made up of many identifiable processing units working together in parallel. The term is often used synonymously with concurrent computer to include both multiprocessor and multicomputer. The term *concurrent* is more commonly used in the United States, whereas the term *parallel* is more common in Europe.

parallel slackness Hiding the latency of communication by giving each processor many different tasks, and having the processors work on the tasks that are ready while other tasks are blocked (waiting on communication or other operations).

PID *Process Identifier* (in UNIX) that is native to a machine or operating system.

polling An alternative to interrupting in a communication system. A node inspects its communication hardware (typically a flag bit) to see whether information has arrived or departed.

private memory Memory that appears to the user to be divided between many address spaces, each of which can be accessed by only one process. Most operating systems rely on some memory protection mechanism to prevent one process from accessing the private memory of another; in disjoint-memory machines, the problem is usually finding a way to emulate shared memory using a set of private memories.

process An address space, I/O state, and one or more threads of program control.

process creation The act of forking or spawning a new process. If a system permits only static process creation, then all processes are created at the same logical time, and no process may interact with any other until all have been created. If a system permits dynamic process creation, then one process can create another at any time. Most first and second generation multicomputers only supported static process creation, while most multiprocessors, and most operating systems on uniprocessors, support dynamic process creation.

process group A set of processes that can be treated as a single entity for some purposes, such as synchronization and broadcast or multicast operations. In some parallel programming systems there is only one process group, which implicitly contains all processes; in others, programmers can assign processes to groups statically when configuring their program, or dynamically by having processes create, join and leave groups during execution.

process migration Changing the processor responsible for executing a process during the lifetime of that process. Process migration is sometimes used to dynamically load balance a program or system.

pvmd *PVM daemon*, a process that serves as a message router and virtual machine coordinator. One PVD daemon runs on each host of a virtual machine.

race condition A situation in which the result of operations being executed by two or more processes depends on the order in which those processes execute, for example, if two processes A and B are to write different values V_A and V_B to the same variable.

randomized routing A routing technique in which each message is sent to a randomly chosen node, which then forwards it to its final destination. Theory and practice show that this can greatly reduce the amount of contention for access to links in a multicomputer.

resource manager A special task that manages other tasks and the virtual machine configuration. It intercepts requests to create/destroy tasks and add/delete hosts.

route The act of moving a message from its source to its destination. A routing algorithm is a rule for deciding, at any intermediate node, where to send a message next; a routing technique is a way of handling the message as it passes through individual nodes.

RTFM *Read The Fine Manual*

scalable Capable of being increased in size; More important, capable of delivering an increase in performance proportional to an increase in size.

scheduling Deciding the order in which the calculations in a program are to be executed and by which processes. Allocating processes to processors is usually called mapping.

self-scheduling Automatically allocating work to processes. If T tasks are to be done by P processors, and $P < T$, then they may be self-scheduled by keeping them in a central pool from which each processor claims a new job when it finishes executing its old one.

semaphore A data type for controlling concurrency. A semaphore is initialized to an integer value. Two operations may be applied to it: *signal* increments the semaphore's value by one, and *wait* blocks its caller until the semaphore's value is greater than zero, then decrements the semaphore. A binary semaphore is one that can only take on the values 0 and 1. Any other synchronization primitive can be built in terms of semaphores.

sequential bottleneck A part of a computation for which there is little or no parallelism.

sequential computer Synonymous with a Von Neumann computer, that is, a "conventional" computer in which only one processing element works on a problem at a given time.

shared memory Real or virtual memory that appears to users to constitute a single address space, but which is actually physically disjoint. Virtual shared memory is often implemented using some combination of hashing and local caching. Memory that appears to the user to be contained in a single address space and that can be accessed by any process. In a uniprocessor or multiprocessor there is typically a single memory unit, or several memory units interleaved to give the appearance of a single memory unit.

shared variables Variables to which two or more processes have access, or a model of parallel computing in which interprocess communication and synchronization are managed through such variables.

signal

SIMD *Single-Instruction Multiple-Data*, a category of Flynn's taxonomy in which a single instruction stream is concurrently applied to multiple data sets. A SIMD architecture is one in which homogeneous processes synchronously execute the same instructions on their own data, or one in which an operation can be executed on vectors of fixed or varying size.

socket An endpoint for network communication. For example, on a Unix machine, a TCP/IP connection may terminate in a socket, which can be read or written through a file descriptor.

space sharing Dividing the resources of a parallel computer among many programs so they can run simultaneously without affecting one another's performance.

spanning tree A tree containing a subset of the edges in a graph and including every node in that graph. A spanning tree can always be constructed so that its depth (the greatest distance between its root and any leaf) is no greater than the diameter of the graph. Spanning trees are frequently used to implement broadcast operations.

spawn To create a new process or PVM task, possibly different from the parent. Compare with fork.

speedup The ratio of two program execution times, particularly when times are from execution on 1 and P nodes of the same computer. Speedup is usually discussed as a function of the number of processors, but is also a function (implicitly) of the problem size.

SPMD *Single-Program Multiple-Data*, a category sometimes added to Flynn's taxonomy to describe programs made up of many instances of a single type of process, each executing the same code independently. SPMD can be viewed either as an extension of SIMD or as a restriction of MIMD.

startup cost The time taken to initiate any transaction with some entity. The startup cost of a message-passing system, for example, is the time needed to send a message of zero length to nowhere.

supercomputer A time-dependent term that refers to the class of most powerful computer systems worldwide at the time of reference.

switch A physical communication medium containing nodes that perform only communications functions. Examples include crossbar switches, in which $N + M$ buses cross orthogonally at NM switching points to connect N objects of one type to M objects of another, and multistage switches in which several layers of switching nodes connect N objects of one type to N objects of another type.

synchronization The act of bringing two or more processes to known points in their execution at the same clock time. Explicit synchronization is not needed in SIMD programs (in which every processor either executes the same operation as every other or does nothing) but is often necessary in SPMD and MIMD programs. The time wasted by processes waiting for other processes to synchronize with them can be a major source of inefficiency in parallel programs.

synchronous Occurring at the same clock time. For example, if a communication event is synchronous, then there is some moment at which both the sender and the receiver are engaged in the operation.

task The smallest component of a program addressable in PVM. A task is generally a native "process" to the machine on which it runs.

tasker A special task that manages other tasks on the same host. It is the parent of the target tasks, allowing it to manipulate them (e.g., for debugging or other instrumentation).

TCP *Transmission Control Protocol*, a reliable host-host stream protocol for packet-switched interconnected networks such as IP.

thread A thread of program control sharing resources (memory, I/O state) with other threads. A lightweight process.

TID *Task Identifier*, an address used in PVM for tasks, pvmds, and multicast groups.

time sharing Sharing a processor among multiple programs. Time sharing attempts to better utilize a CPU by overlapping I/O in one program with computation in another.

trace scheduling A compiler optimization technique that vectorizes the most likely path through a program as if it were a single basic block, includes extra instructions at each branch to undo any ill effects of having made a wrong guess, vectorizes the next most likely branches, and so on.

topology the configuration of the processors in a multicomputer and the circuits in a switch. Among the most common topologies are the mesh, the hypercube, the butterfly, the torus, and the shuffle exchange network.

tuple An ordered sequence of fixed length of values of arbitrary types. Tuples are used for both data storage and interprocess communication in the generative communication paradigm.

tuple space A repository for tuples in a generative communication system. Tuple space is an associative memory.

UDP User Datagram Protocol, a simple protocol allowing datagrams (blocks of data) to be sent between hosts interconnected by networks such as IP. UDP can duplicate or lose messages, and imposes a length limit of 64 kbytes.

uniprocessor A computer containing a single processor. The term is generally synonymous with scalar processor.

virtual channel A logical point-to-point connection between two processes. Many virtual channels may time share a single link to hide latency and to avoid deadlock.

virtual concurrent computer A computer system that is programmed as a concurrent computer of some number of nodes P but that is implemented either on a real concurrent computer of some number of nodes less than P or on a uniprocessor running software to emulate the environment of a concurrent machine. Such an emulation system is said to provide virtual nodes to the user.

virtual cut-through A technique for routing messages in which the head and tail of the message both proceed as rapidly as they can. If the head is blocked because a link it wants to cross is being used by some other message, the tail continues to advance, and the message's contents are put into buffers on intermediate nodes.

virtual machine A multicomputer composed of separate (possibly self-complete) machines and a *software backplane* to coordinate operation.

virtual memory Configuration in which portions of the address space are kept on a secondary medium, such as a disk or auxiliary memory. When a reference is made to a location not resident in main memory, the virtual memory manager loads the location from secondary storage before the access completes. If no space is available in main memory, data is written to secondary storage to make some available. Virtual memory is used by almost all uniprocessors and multiprocessors to increase apparent memory size, but is not available on some array processors and multicomputers.

virtual shared memory   Memory that appears to users to constitute a single address space, but that is actually physically disjoint. Virtual shared memory is often implemented using some combination of hashing and local caching.

Von Neumann architecture   Any computer that does not employ concurrency or parallelism. Named after John Von Neumann (1903–1957), who is credited with the invention of the basic architecture of current sequential computers.

wait context   A data structure used in the pvmd to hold state when a thread of operation must be suspended, for example, when calling a pvmd on another host.

working set   Those values from shared memory that a process has copied into its private memory, or those pages of virtual memory being used by a process. Changes a process makes to the values in its working set are not automatically seen by other processes.

XDR   *eXternal Data Representation*   An Internet standard data encoding (essentially just big-endian integers and IEEE format floating point numbers). PVM converts data to XDR format to allow communication between hosts with different native data formats.

A History of PVM Versions

This appendix contains a list of all the versions of PVM that have been released from the first one in February 1991 through August 1994. Along with each version we include a brief synopsis of the improvements made in this version. Although not listed here, new ports were being added to PVM with each release. PVM continues to evolve driven by new technology and user feedback. Newer versions of PVM beyond those listed here may exist at the time of reading. The latest version can always be found on *netlib*.

```
PVM 1.0  (never released)
    any of the several initial experimental PVM versions
    used to study heterogeneous distributed computing issues.

PVM 2.0  (Feb. 1991)
    + Complete rewrite of in-house experimental PVM software (v1.0),
    + cleaned up the specification and implementation
      to improve robustness and portablility.

PVM 2.1  (Mar. 1991)
    + process-process messages switched to XDR
      to improve protability of source in heterogeneous environments.
    + Simple console interpreter added to master pvmd.

PVM 2.2  (April 1991)
    + pvmd-pvmd message format switched to XDR.
    + Get and put functions vectorized to improve performance.
    + broadcast function --> deprecated

PVM 2.3.2  (June 1991)
    + improved password-less startup via rsh/rcmd
    + added per-host options to hostfile format:
        ask for password
        specify alternate loginname
        specify alternate pvmd executable location
    + pvmd-pvmd protocol version checked to prevent mixed versions
      interoperating.
    + added support for short and long integers in messages.
    + added 'reset' pvmd command to reset the vm.
```

```
    + can specify "." as host to initiateM() to create on localhost

PVM 2.3.3  (July 1991)
    + added 'barr' command to check barrier/ready status
    + pstatus() libpvm call added to return size of virtual machine

PVM 2.3.4  (Oct. 1991)
    + pvmds negotiate maximum UDP message length at startup.
    + removed static limitation on number of hosts (used to be 40).

PVM 2.4.0  (Feb. 1992)
    + added direct-connect TCP message transfer available through
      vsnd() and vrcv() to improve communication performance.
    + added option to specify user executable path on each host.
    + version check added between pvmd and libpvm to prevent running
      incompatible versions.
    + libpvm automatically prints error messages.
    + libpvm error codes standardized and exported in "pvmuser.h".
    + includes instrumented heap to aid system debugging.
    + host file default parameters can be set with '*'.
    + libpvm returns error code instead of exiting in case
      of fatal error.

PVM 2.4.1  (June 1992)
    + added new ports and bug fixes

PVM 2.4.2  (Dec. 1992)
    + pvmuser.h made compatible with C++.
    + can force messages to be packed in raw data format to avoid XDR.
    + rcv() will return BadMsg if message can't be decoded.

PVM 3.0  (Feb. 1993)
    Complete redesign of PVM software both the user interface and
    the implementation in order to:
    + allow scalability to hundreds of hosts.
    + allow portability to multiprocessors / operating systems
      other than Unix.
    + allows dynamic reconfiguration of the virtual machine,
```

+ allows fault tolerance
+ allows asynchronous task notification - task exit,
  machine reconfiguration.
+ includes dynamic process groups,
+ separate PVM console task.

PVM 3.1 (April 1993)
    + added task-task direct routing via TCP
      using normal send and receive calls.

PVM 3.1.1 (May 1993) Five bug fix patches released for PVM 3.1
PVM 3.1.2 (May 1993)
PVM 3.1.3 (June 1993)
PVM 3.1.4 (July 1993)
PVM 3.1.5 (Aug. 1993)

PVM 3.2 (Aug. 1993)
    + distributed memory ports merged with Unix port source.
      Ports include I860, PGON, CM5.

    + conf/ARCH.def files created for per-machine configuration
      to improve source portability and package size.

    + pvmd adds new slave hosts in parallel to improve performance.

    + stdout and stderr from tasks can be redirected to a task/console.

    + option OVERLOADHOST allows virtual machines running under the
      same login to overlap i.e. user can have multiple overlapping vm.

    + new printf-like pack and unpack routines pvm_packf() and
      pvm_unpackf() available to C and C++ programmers.

    + added pack, unpack routines for unsigned integers.

    + environment passed through spawn(), controlled by
      variable PVM_EXPORT.

    + many enhancements and features added to PVM console program.

    + pvmd and libpvm use PVM_ROOT and PVM_ARCH environment
      variables if set.

PVM 3.2.1 (Sept. 1993)   Six bug fix patches released for PVM 3.2
PVM 3.2.2 (Sept. 1993)
PVM 3.2.3 (Oct. 1993)
PVM 3.2.4 (Nov. 1993)
PVM 3.2.5 (Dec. 1993)
PVM 3.2.6 (Jan. 1994)

PVM 3.3.0 (June 1994)

    + PVM_ROOT environment variable now must be set.
      $HOME/pvm3 is no longer assumed.

    + shared-memory ports merged with Unix and distributed memory ports.
      Ports include SUNMP and SGIMP.

    + New functions pvm_psend() and pvm_precv() send and receive raw
      data buffers, enabling more efficient implementation on machines
      such as multiprocessors.

    + new function pvm_trecv() blocks until a message is received or a
      specified timeout (in seconds and usec) improves fault tolerance.

    + Inplace packing implemented for dense data reducing packing costs.

    + Resource Manager, Hoster and Tasker interfaces defined
      to allow third party debuggers and resource managers to use PVM.

    + libpvm parameter/result tracing implemented to drive XPVM tool.
      tasks inherit trace destination and per-call event mask.

    + XPVM, a graphical user interface for PVM, is released.

+ added collective communication routines to group library.
  global reduce and scatter/gather

+ libpvm function pvm_catchout() collects output of children tasks.
    output can be appended to any FILE* (e.g. stdout).

+ new hostfile option "wd=" sets the working directory of the pvmd.

+ environment variables expanded when setting ep= or
  bp= in the hostfile.

PVM 3.3.1   (June 1994)   bug fix patches for PVM 3.3
PVM 3.3.2   (July 1994)
PVM 3.3.3   (August 1994)

B PVM 3 Routines

This appendix contains an alphabetical listing of all the PVM 3 routines. Each routine is described in detail for both C and Fortran use. There are examples and diagnostics for each routine.

pvmfaddhost()   pvm_addhosts()

Adds one or more hosts to the virtual machine.

Synopsis

C   `int info = pvm_addhosts( char **hosts, int nhost, int *infos )`
Fortran   `call pvmfaddhost( host, info )`

Parameters

hosts   –   an array of pointers to character strings containing the names of the machines to be added.
nhost   –   integer specifying the number of hosts to be added.
infos   –   integer array of length nhost which contains the status code returned by the routine for the individual hosts. Values less than zero indicate an error.
host   –   character string containing the name of the machine to be added.
info   –   integer status code returned by the routine. Values less than nhost indicate partial failure; values less than 1 indicate total failure.

Discussion

The routine pvm_addhosts adds the list of computers pointed to in hosts to the existing configuration of computers making up the virtual machine. If pvm_addhosts is successful, info will be equal to nhost. Partial success is indicated by 1 <=info<nhost, and total failure by info< 1. The array infos can be checked to determine which host caused the error.

The Fortran routine pvmfaddhost adds a single host to the configuration with each call.

If a host fails, the PVM system will continue to function. The user can use this routine to increase the fault tolerance of his PVM application. The status of hosts can be requested by the application using pvm_mstat and pvm_config. If a host has failed, it will be automatically deleted from the configuration. With pvm_addhosts a replacement host can be added by the application. It is still the responsibility of the application developer to make the application tolerant of host failure. Another use of this feature would be to add more hosts as they become available (for example, on a weekend) or if the application dynamically determines it could use more computational power.

Examples

C:

```
static char *hosts[] = {
        "sparky",
        "thud.cs.utk.edu",
};
info = pvm_addhosts( hosts, 2, infos );
```

Fortran:

```
CALL PVMFADDHOST( 'azure', INFO )
```

Errors

The following error conditions can be returned by **pvm_addhosts**

Name	Possible Cause
PvmBadParam	giving an invalid argument value.
PvmAlready	already been added.
PvmSysErr	local pvmd is not responding.

The following error conditions can be returned in **infos**

Name	Possible Cause
PvmBadParam	bad hostname syntax.
PvmNoHost	no such host.
PvmCantStart	failed to start pvmd on host.
PvmDupHost	host already in configuration.
PvmBadVersion	remote pvmd version doesn't match.
PvmOutOfRes	PVM has run out of system resources.

pvmfbarrier()   pvm_barrier()

Blocks the calling process until all processes in a group have called it.

Synopsis
C   int info = pvm_barrier(char *group, int count)
Fortran call pvmfbarrier(group, count, info)

Parameters
group – character string group name. The group must exist and the call-
          ing process must be a member of the group.
count – integer specifying the number of group members that must call
          pvm_barrier before they are all released. Though it can be differ-
          ent, the count is expected to be the total number of members of
          the specified group.
info   – integer status code returned by the routine. Values less than zero
          indicate an error.

Discussion
The routine pvm_barrier blocks the calling process until count members of the group
have called pvm_barrier. The count argument is required because processes could be
joining the given group after other processes have called pvm_barrier. Thus PVM doesn't
know how many group members to wait for at any given instant. Although count can
be set less, it is typically the total number of members of the group. Hence, the logical
function of the pvm_barrier call is to provide a group synchronization. During any given
barrier call all participating group members must call barrier with the same count value.
Once a given barrier has been successfully passed, pvm_barrier can be called again by
the same group using the same group name.

As a special case, if count equals -1 then PVM will use the value of pvm_gsize() (i.e., all
the group members). This case is useful after a group is established and not changing
during an application.

If pvm_barrier is successful, info will be 0. If some error occurs, info will be < 0.

Examples

C:

```
inum = pvm_joingroup( "worker" );

        .

        .

info = pvm_barrier( "worker", 5 );
```

Fortran:

```
CALL PVMFJOINGROUP( "shakers", INUM )
COUNT = 10
CALL PVMFBARRIER( "shakers", COUNT, INFO )
```

Errors

The following error conditions can be returned by **pvm_barrier**.

Name	Possible Cause
PvmSysErr	pvmd was not started or has crashed.
PvmBadParam	giving a count < 1.
PvmNoGroup	giving a nonexistent group name.
PvmNotInGroup	calling process is not in specified group.

pvmfbcast()   pvm_bcast()

Broadcasts the data in the active message buffer.

Synopsis

C   int info = pvm_bcast(char *group, int msgtag)
Fortran   call pvmfbcast(group, msgtag, info)

Parameters

group   –   character string group name of an existing group.
msgtag   –   integer message tag supplied by the user. msgtag should be $>= 0$.
             It allows the user's program to distinguish between different kinds
             of messages.
info   –   integer status code returned by the routine. Values less than zero
             indicate an error.

Discussion

The routine pvm_bcast broadcasts a message stored in the active send buffer to all the
members of group. In PVM 3.2 the broadcast message is not sent back to the sender.
Any PVM task can call pvm_bcast(); it need not be a member of the group. The content
of the message can be distinguished by msgtag. If pvm_bcast is successful, info will be
0. If some error occurs, info will be < 0.

pvm_bcast is asynchronous. Computation on the sending processor resumes as soon as
the message is safely on its way to the receiving processors. This procedure is in contrast
to synchronous communication, during which computation on the sending processor halts
until a matching receive is executed by all the receiving processors.

pvm_bcast first determines the tids of the group members by checking a group database.
A multicast is performed to these tids. If the group is changed during a broadcast, the
change will not be reflected in the broadcast. Multicasting is not supported by most
multiprocessor vendors. Typically their native calls support only broadcasting to *all* the
user's processes on a multiprocessor. Because of this omission, pvm_bcast may not be
an efficient communication method on some multiprocessors.

Examples

C:

```
        info = pvm_initsend( PvmDataRaw );
        info = pvm_pkint( array, 10, 1 );
        msgtag = 5 ;
        info = pvm_bcast( "worker", msgtag );
```

Fortran:

```
        CALL PVMFINITSEND( PVMDEFAULT )
        CALL PVMFPKFLOAT( DATA, 100, 1, INFO )
        CALL PVMFBCAST( 'worker', 5, INFO )
```

Errors

The following error conditions can be returned by **pvm_bcast**.

Name	Possible Cause
PvmSysErr	pvmd was not started or has crashed.
PvmBadParam	giving a negative msgtag.
PvmNoGroup	giving a nonexistent group name.

pvmfbufinfo()   pvm_bufinfo()

Returns information about the requested message buffer.

Synopsis
C   int info = pvm_bufinfo(int bufid, int *bytes,
                                       int *msgtag, int *tid)
Fortran   call pvmfbufinfo(bufid, bytes, msgtag, tid, info)

Parameters
bufid   –   integer specifying a particular message buffer identifier.
bytes   –   integer returning the length in bytes of the entire message.
msgtag –   integer returning the message label.
tid   –   integer returning the source of the message.
info   –   integer status code returned by the routine. Values less than zero
            indicate an error.

Discussion
The routine pvm_bufinfo returns information about the requested message buffer. Typically it is used to determine facts about the last received message such as its size or source. pvm_bufinfo is especially useful when an application is able to receive any incoming message. The action taken depends on the source tid and the msgtag associated with the message that comes in first. If pvm_bufinfo is successful, info will be 0. If some error occurs, info will be < 0.

Examples
C:
                bufid = pvm_recv(-1, -1);
                info = pvm_bufinfo(bufid, &bytes, &type, &source);
Fortran:
                CALL PVMFRECV(-1, -1, BUFID)
                CALL PVMFBUFINFO(BUFID, BYTES, TYPE, SOURCE, INFO)

Errors
The following error conditions can be returned by pvm_bufinfo.

Name	Possible Cause
PvmNoSuchBuf	specified buffer does not exist.
PvmBadParam	invalid argument.

pvmfcatchout()   pvm_catchout()

Catches output from child tasks.

Synopsis

C   #include <stdio.h>
            int bufid = pvm_catchout(FILE *ff)
Fortran   call pvmfcatchout(onoff)

Parameters

ff   –   File descriptor on which to write collected output.
onoff –   Integer parameter. Turns output collection on or off.

Discussion

The routine pvm_catchout causes the calling task (the parent) to catch output from tasks spawned after the call to pvm_catchout. Characters printed on *stdout* or *stderr* in children tasks are collected by the pvmds and sent in control messages to the parent task, which tags each line and appends it to the specified file. Output from grandchildren (spawned by children) tasks is also collected, provided the children don't reset PvmOutputTid.

Each line of output has one of the following forms:

```
[txxxxx] BEGIN
[txxxxx] (text from child task)
[txxxxx] END
```

The output from each task includes one BEGIN line and one END line, with whatever the task prints in between.

In C, the output file descriptor may be specified. Giving a null pointer turns output collection off. **Note:** The file option is not implemented in PVM 3.3.0; output goes to calling task's stdout.

In Fortran, output collection can only be turned on or off, and is logged to stdout of the parent task.

If pvm_exit is called while output collection is in effect, it will block until all tasks sending it output have exited, in order to print all their output. To avoid this, one can turn off the output collection by calling pvm_catchout(0) before calling pvm_exit.

pvm_catchout() always returns PvmOk.

Examples

C:

```
#include <stdio.h>
pvm_catchout(stdout);
```

Fortran:

```
CALL PVMFCATCHOUT( 1 )
```

Errors

No error conditions are returned by **pvm_catchout**.

pvmfconfig()   pvm_config()

Returns information about the present virtual machine configuration.

Synopsis

C
```
int info = pvm_config( int *nhost, int *narch,
            struct pvmhostinfo **hostp )
struct pvmhostinfo {
    int  hi_tid;
    char *hi_name;
    char *hi_arch;
    int  hi_speed;
} hostp;
```
Fortran
```
call pvmfconfig( nhost, narch, dtid,
                 name, arch, speed, info )
```

Parameters

nhost – integer returning the number of hosts (pvmds) in the virtual machine.

narch – integer returning the number of different data formats being used.

hostp – pointer to an array of structures that contain information about each host, including its pvmd task ID, name, architecture, and relative speed.

dtid – Integer returning pvmd task ID for this host.

name – Character string returning name of this host.

arch – Character string returning name of host architecture.

speed – Integer returning relative speed of this host. Default value is 1000.

info – integer status code returned by the routine. Values less than zero indicate an error.

Discussion

The routine pvm_config returns information about the present virtual machine. The information returned is similar to that available from the console command conf. The C function returns information about the entire virtual machine in one call. The Fortran function returns information about one host per call and cycles through all the hosts.

Thus, if pvmfconfig is called nhost times, the entire virtual machine will be represented. If pvm_config is successful, `info` will be 0. If some error occurs, `info` will be < 0.

Examples

C:

```
info = pvm_config( &nhost, &narch, &hostp );
```

Fortran:

```
Do i=1, NHOST
  CALL PVMFCONFIG( NHOST,NARCH,DTID(i),HOST(i),ARCH(i),
                        SPEED(i),INFO )
Enddo
```

Errors

The following error condition can be returned by **pvm_config**

Name	Possible Cause
PvmSysErr	pvmd not responding.

pvmfdelhost()   pvm_delhosts()

Deletes one or more hosts from the virtual machine.

Synopsis
C   int info = pvm_delhosts(char **hosts, int nhost, int *infos)
Fortran   call pvmfdelhost(host, info)

Parameters
hosts   –   an array of pointers to character strings containing the names of
            the machines to be deleted.
nhost   –   integer specifying the number of hosts to be deleted.
infos   –   integer array of length nhost which contains the status code re-
            turned by the routine for the individual hosts. Values less than
            zero indicate an error.
host   –   character string containing the name of the machine to be deleted.
info   –   integer status code returned by the routine. Values less than
            nhost indicate partial failure; values less than 1 indicate total
            failure.

Discussion
The routine pvm_delhosts deletes from the virtual machine one or more computers
pointed to in hosts. All PVM processes and the pvmd running on these computers
are killed as the computer is deleted. If pvm_delhosts is successful, info will be nhost.
Partial success is indicated by $1 <= $ info $<$ nhost, and total failure by info < 1. The
array infos can be checked to determine which host caused the error.

The Fortran routine pvmfdelhost deletes a single host from the configuration with each
call.

If a host fails, the PVM system will continue to function and will automatically delete
this host from the virtual machine. An application can be notified of a host failure by
calling pvm_notify. It is still the responsibility of the application developer to make his
application tolerant of host failure.

Examples

C:

```
static char *hosts[] = {
        "sparky",
        "thud.cs.utk.edu",
};
info = pvm_delhosts( hosts, 2 );
```

Fortran:

```
CALL PVMFDELHOST( 'azure', INFO )
```

Errors

The following error conditions can be returned by pvm_delhosts.

Name	Possible cause
PvmBadParam	giving an invalid argument value.
PvmSysErr	local pvmd not responding.
PvmOutOfRes	PVM has run out of system resources.

pvmfexit()   pvm_exit()

Tells the local pvmd that this process is leaving PVM.

Synopsis

C	`int info = pvm_exit( void )`
Fortran	`call pvmfexit( info )`

Parameters

info – integer status code returned by the routine. Values less than zero
indicate an error.

Discussion

The routine **pvm_exit** tells the local pvmd that this process is leaving PVM. This routine
does not kill the process, which can continue to perform tasks just like any other serial
process.

Pvm_exit should be called by all PVM processes before they stop or exit for good. It
must be called by processes that were not started with pvm_spawn.

Examples

C:

```
/* Program done */
pvm_exit();
exit();
```

Fortran:

```
CALL PVMFEXIT(INFO)
STOP
```

Errors

The following error condition can be returned by **pvm_exit()**.

Name	Possible Cause
PvmSysErr	pvmd not responding

pvmffreebuf()   pvm_freebuf()

Disposes of a message buffer.

Synopsis

C   int info = pvm_freebuf(int bufid)
Fortran   call pvmffreebuf(bufid, info)

Parameters

bufid   –   integer message buffer identifier.

info   –   integer status code returned by the routine. Values less than zero
            indicate an error.

Discussion

The routine pvm_freebuf frees the memory associated with the message buffer identified by bufid. Message buffers are created by pvm_mkbuf, pvm_initsend, and pvm_recv. If pvm_freebuf is successful, info will be 0. If some error occurs, info will be < 0.

pvm_freebuf can be called for a send buffer created by pvm_mkbuf after the message has been sent and is no longer needed.

Receive buffers typically do not have to be freed unless they have been saved in the course of using multiple buffers. But pvm_freebuf can be used to destroy receive buffers as well. Therefore, messages that arrive but are no longer needed as a result of some other event in an application can be destroyed so they will not consume buffer space.

Typically, multiple send and receive buffers are not needed, and the user can simply use the pvm_initsend routine to reset the default send buffer.

There are several cases where multiple buffers are useful. One example involves libraries or graphical interfaces that use PVM and interact with a running PVM application but do not want to interfere with the application's own communication. When multiple buffers are used, they generally are made and freed for each message that is packed. In fact, pvm_initsend simply does a pvm_freebuf followed by a pvm_mkbuf for the default buffer.

Examples

    C:

```
          bufid = pvm_mkbuf( PvmDataDefault );
                  :
          info = pvm_freebuf( bufid );
```

    Fortran:

```
          CALL PVMFMKBUF( PVMDEFAULT, BUFID )
                  :
          CALL PVMFFREEBUF( BUFID, INFO )
```

Errors

The following error conditions can be returned by **pvm_freebuf**.

Name	Possible Cause
PvmBadParam	giving an invalid argument value.
PvmNoSuchBuf	giving an invalid bufid value.

pvmfgetinst()   pvm_getinst()

Returns the instance number in a group of a PVM process.

Synopsis

C   `int inum = pvm_getinst( char *group, int tid )`
Fortran `call pvmfgetinst( group, tid, inum )`

Parameters

group — character string group name of an existing group.

tid — integer task identifier of a PVM process.

inum — integer instance number returned by the routine. Instance numbers start at 0 and count up. Values less than zero indicate an error.

Discussion

The routine pvm_getinst takes a group name group and a PVM task identifier tid and returns the unique instance number that corresponds to the input. If pvm_getinst is successful, inum will be $>= 0$. If some error occurs, inum will be < 0.

Examples

C:

```
        inum = pvm_getinst( "worker", pvm_mytid() );
        --------
        inum = pvm_getinst( "worker", tid[i] );
```
Fortran:

```
        CALL PVMFGETINST( 'GROUP3', TID, INUM )
```

Errors

The following error conditions can be returned by pvm_getinst.

Name	Possible Cause
PvmSysErr	pvmd was not started or has crashed.
PvmBadParam	giving an invalid tid value.
PvmNoGroup	giving a nonexistent group name.
PvmNotInGroup	specifying a group in which the tid is not a member.

pvmfgetopt( )   pvm_getopt( )

Shows various libpvm options.

Synopsis

C   int val = pvm_getopt(int what)
Fortran   call pvmfgetrbuf(what, val)

Parameters

what   –   Integer defining what to get. Options include the following:

Option value		Meaning
PvmRoute	1	routing policy
PvmDebugMask	2	debugmask
PvmAutoErr	3	auto error reporting
PvmOutputTid	4	stdout device for children
PvmOutputCode	5	output msgtag
PvmTraceTid	6	trace device for children
PvmTraceCode	7	trace msgtag
PvmFragSize	8	message fragment size
PvmResvTids	9	Allow messages to reserved tags and TIDs

val   –   Integer specifying value of option. Predefined route values are as follows:

Option value		Meaning
PvmRoute	1	routing policy
PvmDontRoute	1	
PvmAllowDirect	2	
PvmRouteDirect	3	

Discussion

The routine pvm_getopt allows the user to see the value of options set in PVM. See pvm_setopt for a description of options that can be set.

Examples

C:

```
        route_method = pvm_getopt( PvmRoute );
```
Fortran:

```
        CALL PVMFGETOPT( PVMAUTOERR, VAL )
```

Errors

The following error conditions can be returned by **pvm_getopt**.

Name	Possible Cause
PvmBadParam	giving an invalid argument.

pvmfgetrbuf()   pvm_getrbuf()

Returns the message buffer identifier for the active receive buffer.

Synopsis
```
C        int bufid = pvm_getrbuf( void )
Fortran  call pvmfgetrbuf( bufid )
```

Parameters
bufid   –   integer the returned message buffer identifier for the active receive
            buffer.

Discussion

The routine pvm_getrbuf returns the message buffer identifier bufid for the active receive
buffer or 0 if there is no current buffer.

Examples
C:
```
        bufid = pvm_getrbuf();
```
Fortran:
```
        CALL PVMFGETRBUF( BUFID )
```

Errors

No error conditions are returned by pvm_getrbuf.

pvmfgetsbuf()   pvm_getsbuf()

Returns the message buffer identifier for the active send buffer.

Synopsis

C   int bufid = pvm_getsbuf(void)
Fortran call pvmfgetsbuf(bufid)

Parameters

bufid – integer the returned message buffer identifier for the active send
           buffer.

Discussion

The routine pvm_getsbuf returns the message buffer identifier bufid for the active send
buffer or 0 if there is no current buffer.

Examples

C:
        bufid = pvm_getsbuf();
Fortran:
        CALL PVMFGETSBUF(BUFID)

Errors

No error conditions are returned by pvm_getsbuf.

pvmfgettid()   pvm_gettid()

Returns the tid of the process identified by a group name and instance number.

Synopsis
```
C        int tid = pvm_gettid( char *group, int inum )
Fortran  call pvmfgettid( group, inum, tid )
```

Parameters
group – character string that contains the name of an existing group.
inum   – integer instance number of the process in the group.
tid   – integer task identifier returned.

Discussion
The routine pvm_gettid returns the tid of the PVM process identified by the group name group and the instance number inum. If pvm_gettid is successful, tid will be > 0. If some error occurs, tid will be < 0.

Examples
C:
```
            tid = pvm_gettid("worker",0);
```
Fortran:
```
            CALL PVMFGETTID('worker',5,TID)
```

Errors
The following error conditions can be returned by pvm_gettid.

Name	Possible Cause
PvmSysErr	Cannot contact the local pvmd (most likely, it is not running).
PvmBadParam	Bad parameter (most likely, a NULL character string).
PvmNoGroup	No group exists by that name.
PvmNoInst	No such instance in the group.

pvmfgsize()   pvm_gsize()

Returns the number of members currently in the named group.

Synopsis

```
C         int size = pvm_gsize( char *group )
Fortran   call pvmfgsize( group, size )
```

Parameters

group – character string group name of an existing group.

size   – integer returning the number of members presently in the group.
          Values less than zero indicate an error.

Discussion

The routine pvm_gsize returns the size of the group named group. If there is an error, size will be negative.

Since groups can change dynamically in PVM 3, this routine can guarantee only to return the instantaneous size of a given group.

Examples

C:

```
        size = pvm_gsize( "worker" );
```

Fortran:

```
        CALL PVMFGSIZE( 'group2', SIZE )
```

Errors

The following error conditions can be returned by pvm_gsize.

Name	Possible Cause
PvmSysErr	pvmd was not started or has crashed.
PvmBadParam	giving an invalid group name.

pvmfhalt   pvm_halt()

Shuts down the entire PVM system.

Synopsis

C   int info = pvm_halt(void)
Fortran   call pvmfhalt(info)

Parameters

info –   Integer returns the error status.

Discussion

The routine **pvm_halt** shuts down the entire PVM system including remote tasks, remote pvmd, the local tasks (including the calling task), and the local pvmd.

Errors

The following error condition can be returned by **pvm_halt**.

Name	Possible Cause
PvmSysErr	local pvmd is not responding.

pvmfhostsync()   pvm_hostsync()

Gets time-of-day clock from PVM host.

Synopsis
C   #include <sys/time.h>
           int info = pvm_hostsync(int host, struct timeval *clk,
                                           struct timeval *delta)
Fortran   call pvmfhostsync(host, clksec, clkusec,
                                    deltasec, deltausec, info)

Parameters
host   –   TID of host.
clk or
clksec and
clkusec)   –   Returns time-of-day clock sample from host.
delta or
deltasec and
deltausec)   –   Returns difference between local clock and remote host clock.

Discussion
pvm_hostsync() samples the time-of day clock of a host in the virtual machine and returns both the clock value and the difference between local and remote clocks.

To reduce the delta error due to message transit time, local clock samples are taken before and after reading the remote clock. Delta is the difference between the mean local clocks and remote clock.

Note that the delta time can be negative. The microseconds field is always normalized to 0..999999, while the sign of the seconds field gives the sign of the delta.

In C, if clk or delta is input as a null pointer, that parameter is not returned.

Errors
The following error conditions can be returned by .pvm_synchost

Name	Possible Cause
PvmSysErr	Local pvmd is not responding.
PvmNoHost	no such host.
PvmHostFail	host is unreachable (and thus possibly failed).

pvmfinitsend()   pvm_initsend()

Clears default send buffer and specifies message encoding.

Synopsis

C   `int bufid = pvm_initsend( int encoding )`
Fortran   `call pvmfinitsend( encoding, bufid )`

Parameters

encoding   – integer specifying the next message's encoding scheme.
             Options in C are as follows:

Encoding value		Meaning
PvmDataDefault	0	XDR
PvmDataRaw	1	no encoding
PvmDataInPlace	2	data left in place

bufid   – integer message buffer identifier. Values less than zero indicate
             an error.

Discussion

The routine pvm_initsend clears the send buffer and prepares it for packing a new message. The encoding scheme used for this packing is set by encoding. XDR encoding is used by default because PVM cannot know whether the user is going to add a heterogeneous machine before this message is sent. If the user knows that the next message will be sent only to a machine that understands the native format, he can use *PvmDataRaw* encoding and save on encoding costs.

PvmDataInPlace encoding specifies that data be left in place during packing. The message buffer contains only the sizes and pointers to the items to be sent. When pvm_send is called, the items are copied directly out of the user's memory. This option decreases the number of times a message is copied, at the expense of requiring that the user not modify the items between the time they are packed and the time they are sent. The PvmDataInPlace is not implemented in PVM 3.2.

If pvm_initsend is successful, bufid will contain the message buffer identifier. If some error occurs, bufid will be < 0.

See also pvm_mkbuf.

Examples

C:

```
bufid = pvm_initsend( PvmDataDefault );
info = pvm_pkint( array, 10, 1 );
msgtag = 3 ;
info = pvm_send( tid, msgtag );
```

Fortran:

```
CALL PVMFINITSEND(PVMRAW, BUFID)
CALL PVMFPACK( REAL4, DATA, 100, 1, INFO )
CALL PVMFSEND( TID, 3, INFO )
```

Errors

The following error conditions can be returned by **pvm_initsend**.

Name	Possible Cause
PvmBadParam	giving an invalid encoding value.
PvmNoMem	Malloc has failed. There is not enough memory to create the buffer.

pvmfjoingroup()   pvm_joingroup()

Enrolls the calling process in a named group.

Synopsis
```
C         int inum = pvm_joingroup( char *group )
Fortran   call pvmfjoingroup( group, inum )
```

Parameters
group – character string group name of an existing group.

inum   – integer instance number returned by the routine. Instance num-
          bers start at 0 and count up. Values less than zero indicate an
          error.

Discussion
The routine pvm_joingroup enrolls the calling task in the group named **group** and returns
the instance number **inum** of this task in this group. If there is an error, **inum** will be
negative.

Instance numbers start at 0 and count up. When using groups, a (group, inum) pair
uniquely identifies a PVM process. This is consistent with the previous PVM naming
schemes. If a task leaves a group by calling pvm_lvgroup and later rejoins the same group,
the task is not guaranteed to get the same instance number. PVM attempts to reuse
old instance numbers; thus, when a task joins a group, it will get the lowest available
instance number. A PVM 3 task can be a member of multiple groups simultaneously.

Examples
C:
```
        inum = pvm_joingroup( "worker" );
```
Fortran:
```
        CALL PVMFJOINGROUP( 'group2', INUM )
```

Errors
The following error conditions can be returned by pvm_joingroup.

Name	Possible Cause
PvmSysErr	pvmd was not started or has crashed.
PvmBadParam	giving a NULL group name.
PvmDupGroup	trying to join a group one is already in.

pvmfkill()   pvm_kill()

Terminates a specified PVM process.

Synopsis

C   int info = pvm_kill(int tid)
Fortran call pvmfkill(tid, info)

Parameters

tid   –   integer task identifier of the PVM process to be killed (not
          yourself).
info –   integer status code returned by the routine. Values less than zero
          indicate an error.

Discussion

The routine pvm_kill sends a terminate (SIGTERM) signal to the PVM process identified by tid. In the case of multiprocessors the terminate signal is replaced with a
host-dependent method for killing a process. If pvm_kill is successful, info will be 0. If
some error occurs, info will be < 0.

pvm_kill is not designed to kill the calling process. To kill yourself in C call pvm_exit()
followed by exit(). To kill yourself in Fortran, call pvmfexit followed by stop.

Examples

C:
        info = pvm_kill(tid);
Fortran:
        CALL PVMFKILL(TID, INFO)

Errors

The following error conditions can be returned by pvm_kill.

Name	Possible Cause
PvmBadParam	giving an invalid tid value.
PvmSysErr	pvmd not responding.

pvmflvgroup()   pvm_lvgroup()

Unenrolls the calling process from a named group.

Synopsis

C   int info = pvm_lvgroup(char *group)
Fortran   call pvmflvgroup(group, info)

Parameters

group   –   character string group name of an existing group.
info   –   integer status code returned by the routine. Values less than zero
            indicate an error.

Discussion

The routine **pvm_lvgroup** unenrolls the calling process from the group named **group**. If
there is an error, **info** will be negative.

If a process leaves a group by calling either pvm_lvgroup or pvm_exit, and later rejoins
the same group, the process may be assigned a new instance number. Old instance
numbers are reassigned to processes calling pvm_joingroup.

Examples

C:
        info = pvm_lvgroup("worker");
Fortran:
        CALL PVMFLVGROUP('group2', INFO)

Errors

The following error conditions can be returned by **pvm_lvgroup**.

Name	Possible Cause
PvmSysErr	pvmd not responding.
PvmBadParam	giving a NULL group name.
PvmNoGroup	giving a nonexistent group name.
PvmNotInGroup	asking to leave a group one is not a member of.

pvmfmcast()   pvm_mcast()

Multicasts the data in the active message buffer to a set of tasks.

Synopsis

C   `int info = pvm_mcast( int *tids, int ntask, int msgtag )`

Fortran   `call pvmfmcast( ntask, tids, msgtag, info )`

Parameters

ntask   –   integer specifying the number of tasks to be sent to.

tids   –   integer array of length at least `ntask` containing the task IDs of the tasks to be sent to.

msgtag   –   integer message tag supplied by the user. msgtag should be $>= 0$.

info   –   integer status code returned by the routine. Values less than zero indicate an error.

Discussion

The routine pvm_mcast multicasts a message stored in the active send buffer to `ntask` tasks specified in the `tids` array. The message is not sent to the caller even if its tid is in `tids`. The content of the message can be distinguished by `msgtag`. If pvm_mcast is successful, `info` will be 0. If some error occurs, `info` will be < 0.

The receiving processes can call either pvm_recv or pvm_nrecv to receive their copy of the multicast. pvm_mcast is asynchronous. Computation on the sending processor resumes as soon as the message is safely on its way to the receiving processors. This is in contrast to synchronous communication, during which computation on the sending processor halts until the matching receive is executed by the receiving processor.

pvm_mcast first determines which other pvmds contain the specified tasks. Then passes the message to these pvmds, which in turn distribute the message to their local tasks without further network traffic.

Multicasting is not supported by most multiprocessor vendors. Typically their native calls support only broadcasting to *all* the user's processes on a multiprocessor. Because of this omission, pvm_mcast may not be an efficient communication method on some multiprocessors except in the special case of broadcasting to all PVM processes.

Examples

C:

```
        info = pvm_initsend( PvmDataRaw );
        info = pvm_pkint( array, 10, 1 );
        msgtag = 5 ;
        info = pvm_mcast( tids, ntask, msgtag );
```

Fortran:

```
        CALL PVMFINITSEND(PVMDEFAULT)
        CALL PVMFPACK( REAL4, DATA, 100, 1, INFO )
        CALL PVMFMCAST( NPROC, TIDS, 5, INFO )
```

Errors

The following error conditions can be returned by **pvm_mcast**..

Name	Possible Cause
PvmBadParam	giving a msgtag < 0.
PvmSysErr	pvmd not responding.
PvmNoBuf	no send buffer.

pvmfmkbuf() pvm_mkbuf()

Creates a new message buffer.

Synopsis

```
C        int bufid = pvm_mkbuf( int encoding )
Fortran  call pvmfmkbuf( encoding, bufid )
```

Parameters

encoding – integer specifying the buffer's encoding scheme. Options in C are as follows:

Encoding value		Meaning
PvmDataDefault	0	XDR
PvmDataRaw	1	no encoding
PvmDataInPlace	2	data left in place

bufid – integer message buffer identifier returned. Values less than zero indicate an error.

Discussion

The routine pvm_mkbuf creates a new message buffer and sets its encoding status to encoding. If pvm_mkbuf is successful, bufid will be the identifier for the new buffer, which can be used as a send buffer. If some error occurs, bufid will be < 0.

With the default setting XDR encoding is used when packing the message because PVM cannot know whether the user is going to add a heterogeneous machine before this message is sent. The other options to encoding allow the user to take advantage of knowledge about his virtual machine even when it is heterogeneous. For example, if the user knows that the next message will be sent only to a machine that understands the native format, he can use PvmDataRaw encoding and save on encoding costs.

PvmDataInPlace encoding specifies that data be left in place during packing. The message buffer contains only the sizes and pointers to the items to be sent. When pvm_send is called, the items are copied directly out of the user's memory. This option decreases the number of times a message is copied at the expense of requiring that the user not modify the items between the time they are packed and the time they are sent. The PvmDataInPlace is also not implemented in PVM 3.2.

pvm_mkbuf is required if the user wishes to manage multiple message buffers and should be used in conjunction with pvm_freebuf. pvm_freebuf should be called for a send buffer after a message has been sent and is no longer needed.

Receive buffers are created automatically by the pvm_recv and pvm_nrecv routines and do not have to be freed unless they have been explicitly saved with pvm_setrbuf.

Typically multiple send and receive buffers are not needed, and the user can simply use the pvm_initsend routine to reset the default send buffer.

There are several cases where multiple buffers are useful. One example where multiple message buffers are needed involves libraries or graphical interfaces that use PVM and interact with a running PVM application but do not want to interfere with the application's own communication.

When multiple buffers are used, they generally are made and freed for each message that is packed.

Examples

C:

```
        bufid = pvm_mkbuf( PvmDataRaw );
          /* send the message */
        info = pvm_freebuf( bufid );
```

Fortran:

```
        CALL PVMFMKBUF(PVMDEFAULT, MBUF)
*        SEND MESSAGE HERE
        CALL PVMFFREEBUF( MBUF, INFO )
```

Errors

The following error condition can be returned by **pvm_mkbuf**.

Name	Possible Cause
PvmBadParam	giving an invalid encoding value.
PvmNoMem	Malloc has failed. There is not enough memory to create the buffer.

pvmfmstat()   pvm_mstat()

Returns the status of a host in the virtual machine.

Synopsis

```
C        int mstat = pvm_mstat( char *host )
Fortran  call pvmfmstat( host, mstat )
```

Parameters

host   –   character string containing the host name.
mstat –   integer returning machine status:

Value	Meaning
PvmOk	host is OK
PvmNoHost	host is not in virtual machine
PvmHostFail	host is unreachable (and thus possibly failed)

Discussion

The routine pvm_mstat returns the status mstat of the computer named host with respect to running PVM processes. This routine can be used to determine whether a particular host has failed and whether the virtual machine needs to be reconfigured.

Examples

C:

```
        mstat = pvm_mstat( "msr.ornl.gov" );
```

Fortran:

```
        CALL PVMFMSTAT( 'msr.ornl.gov', MSTAT )
```

Errors

The following error conditions can be returned by pvm_mstat.

Name	Possible Cause
PvmSysErr	pvmd not responding.
PvmNoHost	giving a host name not in the virtual machine.
PvmHostFail	host is unreachable (and thus possibly failed).

pvmfmytid()   pvm_mytid()

Returns the *tid* of the process.

Synopsis

C   int tid = pvm_mytid(void)
Fortran   call pvmfmytid(tid)

Parameters

tid – integer task identifier of the calling PVM process is returned.
        Values less than zero indicate an error.

Discussion

The routine enrolls this process into PVM on its first call and generates a unique `tid` if this process was not created by pvm_spawn. pvm_mytid returns the `tid` of the calling process and can be called multiple times in an application. Any PVM system call (not just pvm_mytid) will enroll a task in PVM if the task is not enrolled before the call.

The tid is a 32-bit positive integer created by the local pvmd. The 32 bits are divided into fields that encode various information about this process, such as its location in the virtual machine (i.e., local pvmd address), the CPU number in the case where the process is on a multiprocessor, and a process ID field. This information is used by PVM and is not expected to be used by applications.

If PVM has not been started before an application calls pvm_mytid, the returned `tid` will be < 0.

Examples

C:

        tid = pvm_mytid( );

Fortran:

        CALL PVMFMYTID(TID)

Errors

The following error condition can be returned by **pvm_mytid**.

Name	Possible cause
PvmSysErr	pvmd not responding.

pvmfnotify()   pvm_notify()

Requests notification of PVM event such as host failure.

Synopsis

C   int info = pvm_notify(int what, int msgtag,
                                       int cnt, int *tids)

Fortran   call pvmfnotify(what, msgtag, cnt, tids, info)

Parameters

what   –   integer identifier of what event should trigger the notification.
            Presently the options are:

Value	Meaning
PvmTaskExit	notify if task exits
PvmHostDelete	notify if host is deleted
PvmHostAdd	notify if host is added

msgtag –   integer message tag to be used in notification.

cnt   –   integer specifying the length of the tids array for PvmTaskExit
            and PvmHostDelete. For PvmHostAdd specifies the number of
            times to notify.

tids   –   integer array of length ntask that contains a list of task or
            pvmd tids to be notified. The array should be empty with the
            PvmHostAdd option.

info   –   integer status code returned by the routine. Values less than zero
            indicate an error.

Discussion

The routine pvm_notify requests PVM to notify the caller on detecting certain events.
In response to a notify request, some number of messages (see below) are sent by PVM
back to the calling task. The messages are tagged with the code (msgtag) supplied to
notify.

The tids array specifies who to monitor when using TaskExit or HostDelete; it contains
nothing when using HostAdd. If required, the routines pvm_config and pvm_tasks can
be used to obtain task and pvmd tids.

The notification messages have the following format:

PvmTaskExit One notify message for each tid requested. The message body contains a single tid of exited task.

PvmHostDelete One message for each tid requested. The message body contains a single pvmd-tid of exited pvmd.

PvmHostAdd Up to cnt notify messages are sent. The message body contains an integer count followed by a list of pvmd-tids of the new pvmds. The counter of PvmHostAdd messages remaining is updated by successive calls to pvm_notify. Specifying a cnt of -1 turns on PvmHostAdd messages until a future notify; a count of zero disables them.

Tids in the notify messages are packed as integers.

The calling task(s) are responsible for receiving the message with the specified msgtag and taking appropriate action. Future versions of PVM may expand the list of available notification events.

Note that the notify request is "consumed"; for example, a PvmHostAdd request generates a single reply message.

Examples

C:

```
info = pvm_notify( PvmHostAdd, 9999, 1, dummy )
```

Fortran:

```
CALL PVMFNOTIFY( PVMHOSTDELETE, 1111, NPROC, TIDS, INFO )
```

Errors

The following error conditions can be returned by **pvm_notify**.

Name	Possible Cause
PvmSysErr	pvmd not responding.
PvmBadParam	giving an invalid argument value.

pvmfnrecv()   pvm_nrecv()

Checks for nonblocking message with label `msgtag`.

Synopsis

C   int bufid = pvm_nrecv(int tid, int msgtag)

Fortran   call pvmfnrecv(tid, msgtag, bufid)

Parameters

tid   –   integer task identifier of sending process supplied by the user. (A
             -1 in this argument matches any tid (wildcard).)

msgtag   –   integer message tag supplied by the user. msgtag should be $>= 0$.
             (A -1 in this argument matches any message tag (wildcard).)

bufid   –   integer returning the value of the new active receive buffer iden-
             tifier. Values less than zero indicate an error.

Discussion

The routine pvm_nrecv checks to see whether a message with label `msgtag` has arrived
from `tid`. If a matching message has arrived, pvm_nrecv immediately places the message
in a new *active* receive buffer, which also clears the current receive buffer, if any, and
returns the buffer identifier in `bufid`.

If the requested message has not arrived, then pvm_nrecv immediately returns with a 0
in `bufid`. If some error occurs,c /which `bufid` will be < 0.

A -1 in `msgtag` or `tid` matches anything. This allows the user the following options. If
tid $= -1$ and msgtag is defined by the user, then pvm_nrecv will accept a message from
any process that has a matching msgtag. If msgtag $= -1$ and tid is defined by the user,
pvm_nrecv will accept any message that is sent from process tid. If tid $= -1$ and msgtag
$= -1$, then pvm_nrecv will accept any message from any process.

pvm_nrecv is non-blocking in the sense that the routine always returns immediately either
with the message or with the information that the message has not arrived at the local
pvmd yet. pvm_nrecv can be called multiple times to check whether a given message has
arrived yet. In addition, pvm_recv can be called for the same message if the application
runs out of work it could do before receiving the data.

If pvm_nrecv returns with the message, the data in the message can be unpacked into
the user's memory using the unpack routines.

The PVM model guarantees the following about message order. If task 1 sends message A to task 2, then task 1 sends message B to task 2, message A will arrive at task 2 before message B. Moreover, if both messages arrive before task 2 does a receive, then a wildcard receive will always return message A.

Examples
C:

```
          tid = pvm_parent();
          msgtag = 4 ;
          arrived = pvm_nrecv( tid, msgtag );
          if ( arrived > 0 )
            info = pvm_upkint( tid_array, 10, 1 );
          else
          /* go do other computing */
```

Fortran:

```
          CALL PVMFNRECV( -1, 4, ARRIVED )
          IF ( ARRIVED .GT. 0 ) THEN
             CALL PVMFUNPACK( INTEGER4, TIDS, 25, 1, INFO )
             CALL PVMFUNPACK( REAL8, MATRIX, 100, 100, INFO )
          ELSE
*            GO DO USEFUL WORK
          ENDIF
```

Errors

The following error conditions can be returned by **pvm_nrecv**.

Name	Possible Cause
PvmBadParam	giving an invalid tid value or msgtag.
PvmSysErr	pvmd not responding.

pvmfpack()   pvm_pk*()

Packs the active message buffer with arrays of prescribed data type.

Synopsis

C
```
int info = pvm_packf( const char *fmt, ... )
int info = pvm_pkbyte(  char    *xp, int nitem, int stride )
int info = pvm_pkcplx(  float   *cp, int nitem, int stride )
int info = pvm_pkdcplx( double  *zp, int nitem, int stride )
int info = pvm_pkdouble(double  *dp, int nitem, int stride )
int info = pvm_pkfloat( float   *fp, int nitem, int stride )
int info = pvm_pkint(   int     *ip, int nitem, int stride )
int info = pvm_pkuint( unsigned int *ip, int nitem, int stride )
int info = pvm_pkushort( unsigned short *ip, int nitem, int stride )
int info = pvm_pkulong( unsigned long *ip, int nitem, int stride )
int info = pvm_pklong(  long    *ip, int nitem, int stride )
int info = pvm_pkshort( short   *jp, int nitem, int stride )
int info = pvm_pkstr(   char    *sp )
```

Fortran
```
call pvmfpack( what, xp, nitem, stride, info )
```

Parameters

fmt   – printflike format expression specifying what to pack (see discussion).

nitem – the total number of *items* to be packed (not the number of bytes).

stride – the stride to be used when packing the items. For example, if stride= 2 in pvm_pkcplx, then every other complex number will be packed.

xp   – pointer to the beginning of a block of bytes. Can be any data type, but must match the corresponding unpack data type.

cp   – complex array at least nitem*stride items long.

zp   – double precision complex array at least nitem*stride items long.

dp   – double precision real array at least nitem*stride items long.

fp   – real array at least nitem*stride items long.

ip   – integer array at least nitem*stride items long.

jp   – integer*2 array at least nitem*stride items long.

sp   – pointer to a null terminated character string.

what   –   integer specifying the type of data being packed.

what options			
STRING	0	REAL4	4
BYTE1	1	COMPLEX8	5
INTEGER2	2	REAL8	6
INTEGER4	3	COMPLEX16	7

info   –   integer status code returned by the routine. Values less than zero indicate an error.

Discussion

Each of the pvm_pk* routines packs an array of the given data type into the active send buffer. The arguments for each of the routines are a pointer to the first item to be packed, nitem which is the total number of items to pack from this array, and stride which is the stride to use when packing.

An exception is pvm_pkstr() which by definition packs a NULL terminated character string and thus does not need nitem or stride arguments. The Fortran routine pvmf-pack(STRING, ...) expects nitem to be the number of characters in the string and stride to be 1.

If the packing is successful, info will be 0. If some error occurs, info will be < 0.

A single variable (not an array) can be packed by setting nitem= 1 and stride= 1. C structures have to be packed one data type at a time.

The routine pvm_packf() uses a printflike format expression to specify what and how to pack data into the send buffer. All variables are passed as addresses if count and stride are specified otherwise, variables are assumed to be values. A BNF-like description of the format syntax is:

```
format : null | init | format fmt
init : null | '%' '+'
fmt : '%' count stride modifiers fchar
fchar : 'c' | 'd' | 'f' | 'x' | 's'
count : null | [0-9]+ | '*'
stride : null | '.' ( [0-9]+ | '*' )
modifiers : null | modifiers mchar
mchar : 'h' | 'l' | 'u'
```

Formats:
   + means initsend - must match an int (how) in the param list.
   c pack/unpack bytes

```
d  integers
f  float
x  complex float
s  string
```

```
Modifiers:
  h  short (int)
  l  long  (int, float, complex float)
  u  unsigned (int)
```

`'*' count or stride must match an int in the param list.`

Future extensions to the `what` argument in pvmfpack will include 64 bit types when XDR encoding of these types is available. Meanwhile users should be aware that precision can be lost when passing data from a 64 bit machine like a Cray to a 32 bit machine like a SPARCstation. As a mnemonic the `what` argument name includes the number of bytes of precision to expect. By setting encoding to PVMRAW (see pvmfinitsend) data can be transferred between two 64 bit machines with full precision even if the PVM configuration is heterogeneous.

Messages should be unpacked exactly like they were packed to insure data integrity. Packing integers and unpacking them as floats will often fail because a type encoding will have occurred transferring the data between heterogeneous hosts. Packing 10 integers and 100 floats then trying to unpack only 3 integers and the 100 floats will also fail.

Examples

C:
```
        info = pvm_initsend( PvmDataDefault );
        info = pvm_pkstr( "initial data" );
        info = pvm_pkint( &size, 1, 1 );
        info = pvm_pkint( array, size, 1 );
        info = pvm_pkdouble( matrix, size*size, 1 );
        msgtag = 3 ;
        info = pvm_send( tid, msgtag );
```
Fortran:
```
        CALL PVMFINITSEND(PVMRAW, INFO)
        CALL PVMFPACK( INTEGER4, NSIZE, 1, 1, INFO )
        CALL PVMFPACK( STRING, 'row 5 of NXN matrix', 19, 1, INFO )
        CALL PVMFPACK( REAL8, A(5,1), NSIZE, NSIZE , INFO )
        CALL PVMFSEND( TID, MSGTAG, INFO )
```

Errors

The following error conditions can be returned by **pvm_pk***.

Name	Possible Cause
PvmNoMem	Malloc has failed. Message buffer size has exceeded the available memory on this host.
PvmNoBuf	There is no active send buffer to pack into. Try calling pvm_initsend before packing message.

pvmfparent()   pvm_parent()

Returns the tid of the process that spawned the calling process.

Synopsis

C	`int tid = pvm_parent( void )`
Fortran	`call pvmfparent( tid )`

Parameters

tid   –   integer returns the task identifier of the parent of the calling process. If the calling process was not created with pvm_spawn, then tid = PvmNoParent.

Discussion

The routine `pvm_parent` returns the `tid` of the process that spawned the calling process. If the calling process was not created with pvm_spawn, then `tid` is set to PvmNoParent.

Examples

C:

```
tid = pvm_parent();
```

Fortran:

```
CALL PVMFPARENT( TID )
```

Errors

The following error condition can be returned by **pvm_parent**.

Name	Possible Cause
PvmNoParent	The calling process was not created with pvm_spawn.

pvmfperror()   pvm_perror()

Prints the error status of the last PVM call.

Synopsis

C   int info = pvm_perror(char *msg)
Fortran   call pvmfperror(msg, info)

Parameters

msg   –   character string supplied by the user which will be prepended to
          the error message of the last PVM call.

info –   integer status code returned by the routine. Values less than zero
          indicate an error.

Discussion

The routine pvm_perror returns the error message of the last PVM call. The user can
use msg to add additional information to the error message, for example, its location.

All stdout and stderr messages are placed in the file /tmp/pvml.<uid> on the master
pvmd's host.

Examples

C:
```
        if ( pvm_send( tid, msgtag )
          pvm_perror();
```
Fortran:
```
            CALL PVMFSEND( TID, MSGTAG )
            IF( INFO .LT. 0 ) CALL PVMFPERROR( 'Step 6', INFO )
```

Errors

No error condition is returned by pvm_perror.

pvmfprecv()   pvm_precv()

Receives a message directly into a buffer.

Synopsis

C   int info = pvm_psend(int tid, int msgtag,
        char *buf, int len, int datatype)
        int atid, int atag, int alen)

Fortran call pvmfpsend(tid, msgtag, buf, len, datatype,
        atid, atag, alen, info)

Parameters

tid   –   integer task identifier of sending process (to match).
msgtag   –   integer message tag (to match) msgtag should be $>= 0$.
buf   –   pointer to a buffer to receive into.
len   –   length of buffer (in multiple of data type size).
datatype   –   type of data to which buf points (see below).
atid   –   returns actual TID of sender.
atag   –   returns actual message tag.
atid   –   returns actual message length.
info   –   integer status code returned by the routine. Values less than zero
               indicate an error.

Discussion

The routine pvm_recv blocks the process until a message with label msgtag has arrived
from tid. pvm_precv; it then places the contents of the message in the supplied buffer,
buf, up to a maximum length of len * (size of data type).

pvm_precv can receive messages sent by pvm_psend, pvm_send, pvm_mcast, or pvm_bcast.

A -1 in msgtag or tid matches anything. This allows the user the following options. If
tid $= -1$ and msgtag is defined by the user, pvm_recv will accept a message from any
process that has a matching msgtag. If msgtag $= -1$ and tid is defined by the user,
pvm_recv will accept any message that is sent from process tid. If tid $= -1$ and msgtag
$= -1$, pvm_recv will accept any message from any process.

In C the datatype parameter must be one of the following, depending on the type of data
to be sent:

datatype	Data Type
PVM_STR	string
PVM_BYTE	byte
PVM_SHORT	short
PVM_INT	int
PVM_FLOAT	real
PVM_CPLX	complex
PVM_DOUBLE	double
PVM_DCPLX	double complex
PVM_LONG	long integer
PVM_USHORT	unsigned short int
PVM_UINT	unsigned int
PVM_ULONG	unsigned long int

In Fortran the same data types specified for unpack should be used.

The PVM model guarantees the following about message order. If task 1 sends message A to task 2, then task 1 sends message B to task 2, message A will arrive at task 2 before message B. Moreover, if both messages arrive before task 2 does a receive, then a wildcard receive will always return message A.

pvm_recv is blocking, which means the routine waits until a message matching the user specified tid and msgtag values arrives at the local pvmd. If the message has already arrived, pvm_recv returns immediately with the message.

pvm_precv does not affect the state of the current receive message buffer (created by the other receive functions).

Examples

C:

```
        info = pvm_precv( tid, msgtag, array, cnt, PVM_FLOAT,
                          &src, &atag, &acnt );
```

Fortran:

```
        CALL PVMFPRECV( -1, 4, BUF, CNT, REAL4,
                        SRC, ATAG, ACNT, INFO )
```

Errors

The following error conditions can be returned by **pvm_send**.

Name	Possible Cause
PvmBadParam	giving an invalid tid or a msgtag.
PvmSysErr	pvmd not responding.

pvmfprobe()   pvm_probe()

Checks whether message has arrived.

Synopsis

C   int bufid = pvm_probe(int tid, int msgtag)
Fortran call pvmfprobe(tid, msgtag, bufid)

Parameters

tid   —   integer task identifier of sending process supplied by the user. (A
             -1 in this argument matches any tid (wildcard).)
msgtag   —   integer message tag supplied by the user. msgtag should be $>= 0$.
             (A -1 in this argument matches any message tag (wildcard).)
bufid   —   integer returning the value of the new active receive buffer iden-
             tifier. Values less than zero indicate an error.

Discussion

The routine pvm_probe checks to see if a message with label msgtag has arrived from tid.
If a matching message has arrived, pvm_probe returns a buffer identifier in bufid. This
bufid can be used in a pvm_bufinfo call to determine information about the message
such as its source and length.

If the requested message has not arrived, pvm_probe returns with a 0 in bufid. If some
error occurs, bufid will be < 0.

A -1 in msgtag or tid matches anything. This feature allows the user the following
options. If tid $= -1$ and msgtag is defined by the user, then pvm_probe will accept a
message from any process that has a matching msgtag. If msgtag $= -1$ and tid is defined
by the user, then pvm_probe will accept any message that is sent from process tid. If tid
$= -1$ and msgtag $= -1$, then pvm_probe will accept any message from any process.

pvm_probe can be called multiple times to check whether a given message has arrived
yet. After the message has arrived, pvm_recv must be called before the message can be
unpacked into the user's memory using the unpack routines.

Examples

   C:

```
         tid = pvm_parent();
         msgtag = 4 ;
         arrived = pvm_probe( tid, msgtag );
         if ( arrived > 0 )
           info = pvm_bufinfo( arrived, &len, &tag, &tid );
         else
         /* go do other computing */
```

   Fortran:

```
         CALL PVMFPROBE( -1, 4, ARRIVED )
         IF ( ARRIVED .GT. 0 ) THEN
            CALL PVMFBUFINFO( ARRIVED, LEN, TAG, TID, INFO )
         ELSE
   *        GO DO USEFUL WORK
         ENDIF
```

Errors

The following error conditions can be returned by **pvm_probe**.

Name	Possible Cause
PvmBadParam	giving an invalid tid value or msgtag.
PvmSysErr	pvmd not responding.

pvmfpsend()   pvm_psend()

Packs and sends data in one call.

Synopsis

C   int info = pvm_psend(int tid, int msgtag, char *buf,
                                  int len, int datatype)
Fortran   call pvmfpsend(tid, msgtag, buf, len, datatype, info)

Parameters

tid   —   integer task identifier of destination process.
msgtag   —   integer message tag supplied by the user. msgtag should be $>= 0$.
buf   —   pointer to a buffer to send.
len   —   length of buffer (in multiple of data type size).
datatype —   type of data to which buf points (see below).
info   —   integer status code returned by the routine. Values less than zero
              indicate an error.

Discussion

The routine pvm_psend takes a pointer to a buffer buf, its length len, and its data type datatype and sends this data directly to the PVM task identified.

pvm_psend data can be received by pvm_precv, pvm_recv, pvm_trecv, or pvm_nrecv.

msgtag is used to label the content of the message. If pvm_send is successful, info will be 0. If some error occurs, info will be < 0.

The pvm_psend routine is asynchronous. Computation on the sending processor resumes as soon as the message is safely on its way to the receiving processor. This approach is in contrast to synchronous communication, during which computation on the sending processor halts until the matching receive is executed by the receiving processor.

In C the datatype parameter must be one of the following, depending on the type of data to be sent:

datatype	Data Type
PVM_STR	string
PVM_BYTE	byte
PVM_SHORT	short
PVM_INT	int

```
PVM_FLOAT        real
PVM_CPLX         complex
PVM_DOUBLE       double
PVM_DCPLX        double complex
PVM_LONG         long integer
PVM_USHORT       unsigned short int
PVM_UINT         unsigned int
PVM_ULONG        unsigned long int
```

In Fortran the same data types specified for pack should be used.

The PVM model guarantees the following about message order. If task 1 sends message A to task 2, then task 1 sends message B to task 2; message A will arrive at task 2 before message B. Moreover, if both messages arrive before task 2 does a receive, then a wildcard receive will always return message A.

pvm_psend does not affect the state of the current outgoing message buffer (created by pvm_initsend and used by pvm_send).

Examples

  C:

```
        info = pvm_psend( tid, msgtag, array, 1000, PVM_FLOAT );
```

  Fortran:

```
        CALL PVMFPSEND( TID, MSGTAG, BUF, CNT, REAL4, INFO )
```

Errors

The following error conditions can be returned by **pvm_send**.

Name	Possible Cause
PvmBadParam	giving an invalid tid or a msgtag.
PvmSysErr	pvmd not responding.

pvmfpstat()   pvm_pstat()

Returns the status of the specified PVM process.

Synopsis
C   int status = pvm_pstat(tid)
Fortran call pvmfpstat(tid, status)

Parameters
tid   –   integer task identifier of the PVM process in question.

status –   integer returns the status of the PVM process identified by tid.
             Status is PvmOk if the task is running, PvmNoTask if not, and
             PvmBadParam if the tid is bad.

Discussion
The routine pvm_pstat returns the status of the process identified by tid. Also note
that pvm_notify() can be used to notify the caller that a task has failed.

Examples
C:

```
        tid = pvm_parent();
        status = pvm_pstat( tid );
```
Fortran:

```
          CALL PVMFPARENT( TID )
          CALL PVMFPSTAT( TID, STATUS )
```

Errors
The following error conditions can be returned by pvm_pstat.

Name	Possible Cause
PvmBadParam	bad parameter (most likely, an invalid tid value).
PvmSysErr	pvmd not responding.
PvmNoTask	task not running.

pvmfrecv()   pvm_recv()

Receives a message.

Synopsis

C   int bufid = pvm_recv(int tid, int msgtag)
Fortran call pvmfrecv(tid, msgtag, bufid)

Parameters

tid   –   integer task identifier of sending process supplied by the user. (A
            -1 in this argument matches any tid (wildcard).)
msgtag –   integer message tag supplied by the user. msgtag should be $>= 0$.
            It allows the user's program to distinguish between different kinds
            of messages . (A -1 in this argument matches any message tag
            (wildcard).)
bufid   –   integer returns the value of the new active receive buffer identifier.
            Values less than zero indicate an error.

Discussion

The routine pvm_recv blocks the process until a message with label msgtag has arrived
from tid. pvm_recv then places the message in a new *active* receive buffer, which also
clears the current receive buffer.

A -1 in msgtag or tid matches anything. This allows the user the following options. If
tid $= -1$ and msgtag is defined by the user, then pvm_recv will accept a message from
any process which has a matching msgtag. If msgtag $= -1$ and tid is defined by the
user, then pvm_recv will accept any message that is sent from process tid. If tid $= -1$
and msgtag $= -1$, then pvm_recv will accept any message from any process.

The PVM model guarantees the following about message order. If task 1 sends message
A to task 2, then task 1 sends message B to task 2, message A will arrive at task 2
before message B. Moreover, if both messages arrive before task 2 does a receive, then a
wildcard receive will always return message A.

If pvm_recv is successful, bufid will be the value of the new active receive buffer identifier.
If some error occurs, bufid will be < 0.

pvm_recv is blocking, which means the routine waits until a message matching the user
specified tid and msgtag values arrives at the local pvmd. If the message has already
arrived, then pvm_recv returns immediately with the message.

Once pvm_recv returns, the data in the message can be unpacked into the user's memory using the unpack routines.

Examples

C:

```
        tid = pvm_parent();
        msgtag = 4 ;
        bufid = pvm_recv( tid, msgtag );
        info = pvm_upkint( tid_array, 10, 1 );
        info = pvm_upkint( problem_size, 1, 1 );
        info = pvm_upkfloat( input_array, 100, 1 );
```

Fortran:

```
        CALL PVMFRECV( -1, 4, BUFID )
        CALL PVMFUNPACK( INTEGER4, TIDS, 25, 1, INFO )
        CALL PVMFUNPACK( REAL8, MATRIX, 100, 100, INFO )
```

Errors

The following error conditions can be returned by **pvm_recv**.

Name	Possible Cause
PvmBadParam	giving an invalid tid value, or msgtag < -1.
PvmSysErr	pvmd not responding.

pvm_recvf()

Redefines the comparison function used to accept messages.

Synopsis

C   `int (*old)() = pvm_recvf( int (*new)( int bufid,`
                                  `int tid, int tag ))`

Fortran   NOT AVAILABLE

Parameters

tid   –   integer task identifier of sending process supplied by the user.

tag   –   integer message tag supplied by the user.

bufid   –   integer message buffer identifier.

Discussion

The routine **pvm_recvf** defines the comparison function to be used by the pvm_recv and pvm_nrecv functions. It is available as a means to customize PVM message passing. pvm_recvf sets a user supplied comparison function to evaluate messages for receiving . The default comparison function evaluates the source and message tag associated with all incoming messages.

pvm_recvf is intended for sophisticated C programmers who understand the function of such routines (like signal) and who require a receive routine that can match on more complex message contexts than the default provides.

pvm_recvf returns 0 if the default matching function; otherwise, it returns the matching function. The matching function should return the following:

Value	Action Taken
< 0	return immediately with this error code
0	do not pick this message
1	pick this message, and do not scan the rest
> 1	pick this highest ranked message after scanning them all

Example: Implementing probe with recvf

```
#include "pvm3.h"

static int foundit = 0;

static int
foo_match(mid, tid, code)
        int mid;
        int tid;
        int code;
{
        int t, c, cc;

        if ((cc = pvm_bufinfo(mid, (int*)0, &c, &t)) < 0)
                return cc;
        if ((tid == -1 || tid == t)
        && (code == -1 || code == c))
                foundit = 1;
        return 0;
}
int
probe(src, code)
{
        int (*omatch)();
        int cc;

        omatch = pvm_recvf(foo_match);
        foundit = 0;
        if ((cc = pvm_nrecv(src, code)) < 0)
                return cc;
        pvm_recvf(omatch);
        return foundit;
}
```

Errors

No error condition is returned by pvm_recvf.

pvmfreduce()   pvm_reduce()

Performs a reduce operation over members of the specified group.

Synopsis

```
C       int info = pvm_reduce( void (*func)(),
                void *data, int count, int datatype,
                int msgtag, char *group, int root)
Fortran  call pvmfreduce( func, data, count, datatype,
                msgtag, group, root, info )
```

Parameters

func   – function that defines the operation performed on the global data.
            Predefined are PvmMax, PvmMin, PvmSum, and PvmProduct.
            Users can define their own function.
data   – -ointer to the starting address of an array of local values. On
            return, the data array on the root will be overwritten with the
            result of the reduce operation over the group.
count   – integer specifying the number of elements in data array.
datatype – integer specifying the type of the entries in the data array.
msgtag   – integer message tag supplied by the user. msgtag should be ≥ 0.
group   – character string group name of an existing group.
root   – integer instance number of group member who gets the result.
info   – integer status code returned by the routine. Values less than zero
            indicate an error.

Discussion

The routine pvm_reduce() performs global operations such as max, min, and sum over all the tasks in a group. All group members call pvm_reduce() with their local data, and the result of the reduction operation appears on the user-specified root task root. The root task is identified by its instance number in the group.

The pvm supplies the following predefined global functions that can be specified in func.

```
PvmMin
PvmMax
PvmSum
PvmProduct
```

PvmMax and PvmMin are implemented for datatypes byte, short, integer, long, float, double, complex, and double complex. For complex values the minimum (maximum) is that complex pair with the minimum (maximum) modulus. PvmSum and PvmProduct are implemented for datatypes short, integer, long, float, double, complex, and double complex.

C and Fortran defined `datatypes` are as follows:

```
        C Data Types    Fortran Data Types
        ----------------------------------

        PVM_BYTE        BYTE1
        PVM_SHORT       INT2
        PVM_INT         INT4
        PVM_FLOAT       REAL4
        PVM_CPLX        COMPLEX8
        PVM_DOUBLE      REAL8
        PVM_DCPLX       COMPLEX16
        PVM_LONG
```

A user-defined function may be used used in `func`, the synax is:

```
C    void func(int *datatype, void *x, void *y,
             int *num, int *info)


Fortran    call func(datatype, x, y, num, info)
```

func is the base function used for the reduction operation. Both x and y are arrays of type specified by datatype with num entries. The arguments datatype and info are as specified above. The arguments x and num correspond to data and count above. The argument y contains received values.

Note: pvm_reduce() does not block. if a task calls pvm_reduce and then leaves the group before the root has called pvm_reduce, an error may occur.

The current algorithm is very simple and robust. A future implementation may make more efficient use of the architecture to allow greater parallelism.

Examples

C:

```
info =  pvm_reduce(PvmMax, &myvals, 10, PVM_INT,
                        msgtag, "workers", roottid);
```

Fortran:

```
CALL PVMFREDUCE(PvmMax, MYVALS, COUNT, INT4,
                    MTAG, 'workers', ROOT, INFO)
```

Errors

The following error conditions can be returned by **pvm_reduce**.

Name	Possible Cause
PvmBadParam	giving an invalid argument value.
PvmNoInst	calling task is not in the group.
PvmSysErr	local pvmd is not responding.

pvm_reg_hoster()

Registers this task as responsible for adding new PVM hosts.

Synopsis

C   #include <pvmsdpro.h>
    int info = pvm_reg_hoster()

Parameters

info   –   integer status code returned by the routine.

Discussion

The routine pvm_reg_hoster registers the calling task as a PVM slave pvmd starter. When the master pvmd receives a DM_ADD message, instead of starting the new slave pvmd processes itself, it passes a message to the hoster, which does the dirty work and sends a message back to the pvmd.

Note: This function isn't for beginners. If one doesn't grok what it does, he probably doesn't need it.

For a more complete explanation of what's going on here, the user should refer to the PVM source code and/or user guide section on implementation; this is just a man page. That said...

When the master pvmd receives a DM_ADD message (request to add hosts to the virtual machine), it looks up the new host IP addresses, gets parameters from the host file if it was started with one, and sets default parameters. It then either attempts to start the processes (using *rsh* or *rexec()*) or, if a hoster has registered, sends it a SM_STHOST message.

The format of the SM_STHOST message is as follows:

```
int nhosts              number of hosts
{
        int tid             of host
        string options      from hostfile so= field
        string login        in form [username@]hostname.domain
        string command      to run on remote host
} [nhosts]
```

The hoster should attempt to run each command on each host and record the result. A command usually looks like

```
$PVM_ROOT/lib/pvmd -s -d8 -nhonk 1 80a9ca95:0f5a 4096 3 80a95c43:0000
```

and a reply from a slave pvmd like

```
ddpro<2312> arch<ALPHA> ip<80a95c43:0b3f> mtu<4096>
```

When finished, the hoster should send a **SM_STHOSTACK** message back to the address of the sender (the master pvmd). The format of the reply message is as follows:

```
{
        int tid        of host, must match request
        string status  result line from slave or error code
} []                   implied count
```
The TIDs in the reply must match those in the request. They may be in a different order, however.

The result string should contain the entire reply (a single line) from each new slave pvmd, or an error code if something went wrong. Legal error codes are the literal names of the pvm_errno codes, for example "PvmCantStart". The default PVM hoster can return PvmDSysErr or PvmCantStart, and the slave pvmd itself can return PvmDupHost.

The hoster task must use pvm_setopt(PvmResvTids, 1) to allow sending reserved messages. Messages must be packed using data format PvmDataFoo.

pvm_reg_rm()

Registers this task as PVM resource manager.

Synopsis

C   #include <pvmsdpro.h>
     int info = pvm_reg_rm(struct hostinfo **hip)
     struct hostinfo{
         int hi_tid;
         char *hi_name;
         char *hi_arch;
         int hi_speed;
     } hip;

Parameters

hostp –   pointer to an array of structures that contain information about
           each host, including its pvmd task ID, name, architecture, and
           relative speed.
info   –   integer status code returned by the routine. Values less than zero
           indicate an error.

Discussion

The routine pvm_reg_rm() registers the calling task as a PVM task and slave host scheduler. This means it intercepts certain libpvm calls from other tasks in order to have a say in scheduling policy. The scheduler will asynchronously receive messages from tasks containing requests for service, as well as messages from pvmds notifying it of system failures.

Note: this is not a trivial task. It cannot be called simply to turn off the default round-robin task assignment. Rather, it allows the user to write his own scheduler and hook it to PVM.

To understand what the following messages mean, the user should refer to the PVM source code and/or user guide section on implementation; There's just too much to say about them.

When one of the following libpvm functions is called in a task with resource manager set, the given message tag is sent to to scheduler.

Libpvm call	Sched. message	Normal message
pvm_addhosts()	SM_ADDHOST	TM_ADDHOST
pvm_config()	SM_CONFIG	TM_CONFIG
pvm_delhosts()	SM_DELHOST	TM_DELHOST
pvm_notify()	SM_NOTIFY	TM_NOTIFY
pvm_spawn()	SM_SPAWN	TM_SPAWN
pvm_tasks()	SM_TASK	TM_TASK
pvm_reg_sched()	SM_SCHED	TM_SCHED

The resource manager must in turn compose the following messages and send them to the pvmds:

Sched. Message	Normal Message
SM_EXEC	DM_EXEC
SM_EXECACK	DM_EXECACK
SM_ADD	DM_ADD
SM_ADDACK	DM_ADDACK
SM_HANDOFF	(none)

The following messages are sent asynchronously to the resource manager by the system:

Sched. Message	Meaning
SM_TASKX	notify of task exit/fail
SM_HOSTX	notify of host delete/fail

The resource manager task must use pvm_setopt(PvmResvTids, 1) to allow sending reserved messages. Messages must be packed using data format PvmDataFoo.

pvm_reg_tasker()

Registers this task as responsible for starting new PVM tasks.

Synopsis

C   #include <pvmsdpro.h>
     int info = pvm_reg_tasker()

Parameters

info   –   integer status code returned by the routine.

Discussion

The routine pvm_reg_tasker registers the calling task as a PVM task starter. When a tasker is registered with a pvmd, and the pvmd receives a DM_EXEC message, instead of fork()ing and exec()ing the task itself, it passes a message to the tasker, which does the dirty work and sends a message back to the pvmd.

Note: If this doesn't make sense, don't worry about it. This function is for folks who are writing stuff like debugger servers and so on. For a more complete explanation of what's going on here, the user should refer to the PVM source code and/or user guide section on implementation; this is only a man page.

When the pvmd receives a DM_EXEC message (request to exec new tasks), it searches *epath* (the PVM executable search path) for the file name. If it finds the file, it then either attempts to start the processes (using fork() and exec()) or, if a tasker has registered, sends it a SM_STTASK message.

The format of the SM_STTASK message is as follows:

int tid	of task
int flags	as passed to spawn()
string path	absolute path of the executable
int argc	number of arguments to process
string argv[argc]	argument strings
int nenv	number of environment variables to pass to task
string env[nenv]	environment strings

The tasker must attempt to start the process when it gets one of these messages. The tasker doesn't reply to the pvmd if the task is successfully started; the task will reconnect to the pvmd on its own (using the identifier in envar PVMEPID).

The tasker must send a SM_TASKX message to the pvmd when any task that it owns (has started) exits, or if it can't start a particular task. The format of the SM_TASKX message is as follows:

int tid	of task
int status	the Unix exit status (from wait())
int u_sec	user time used by the task, seconds
int u_usec	microseconds
int s_sec	system time used by the task, seconds
int s_usec	microseconds

The tasker task must use pvm_setopt(PvmResvTids, 1) to allow sending reserved messages. Messages must be packed using data format PvmDataFoo.

pvmfsend()   pvm_send()

Sends the data in the active message buffer.

Synopsis

C   int info = pvm_send(int tid, int msgtag)

Fortran call pvmfsend(tid, msgtag, info)

Parameters

tid   –   integer task identifier of destination process.

msgtag –   integer message tag supplied by the user. msgtag should be $>= 0$.

info   –   integer status code returned by the routine. Values less than zero
            indicate an error.

Discussion

The routine pvm_send sends a message stored in the active send buffer to the PVM process
identified by tid. msgtag is used to label the content of the message. If pvm_send is
successful, info will be 0. If some error occurs, info will be < 0.

The pvm_send routine is asynchronous. Computation on the sending processor resumes
as soon as the message is safely on its way to the receiving processor. This is in contrast
to synchronous communication, during which computation on the sending processor halts
until the matching receive is executed by the receiving processor.

pvm_send first checks to see whether the destination is on the same machine. If so and
this host is a multiprocessor, then the vendor's underlying message-passing routines are
used to move the data between processes.

Examples

C:

```
info = pvm_initsend( PvmDataDefault );
info = pvm_pkint( array, 10, 1 );
msgtag = 3 ;
info = pvm_send( tid, msgtag );
```

Fortran:

```
CALL PVMFINITSEND(PVMRAW, INFO)
CALL PVMFPACK( REAL8, DATA, 100, 1, INFO )
CALL PVMFSEND( TID, 3, INFO )
```

Errors

The following error conditions can be returned by **pvm_send**.

Name	Possible Cause
PvmBadParam	giving an invalid tid or a msgtag.
PvmSysErr	pvmd not responding.
PvmNoBuf	no active send buffer. Try calling pvm_initsend() before sending.

pvmfsendsig()   pvm_sendsig()

Sends a signal to another PVM process.

Synopsis
C   int info = pvm_sendsig(int tid, int signum)
Fortran call pvmfsendsig(tid, signum, info)

Parameters
tid   – integer task identifier of PVM process to receive the signal.
signum – integer signal number.
info   – integer status code returned by the routine. Values less than zero
          indicate an error.

Discussion
The routine pvm_sendsig sends the signal number signum to the PVM process identified
by tid. If pvm_sendsig is successful, info will be 0. If some error occurs, info will be
< 0.

pvm_sendsig should be used only by programmers with signal-handling experience. It
is very easy in a parallel environment for interrupts to cause nondeterministic behavior,
deadlocks, and even system crashes. For example, if an interrupt is caught while a process
is inside a Unix kernel call, then a graceful recovery may not be possible.

Examples
C:

```
        tid = pvm_parent();
        info = pvm_sendsig( tid, SIGKILL);
```
Fortran:

```
        CALL PVMFBUFINFO( BUFID, BYTES, TYPE, TID, INFO );
        CALL PVMFSENDSIG( TID, SIGNUM, INFO )
```

Errors
The following error conditions can be returned by pvm_sendsig.

Name	Possible Cause
PvmSysErr	pvmd not responding.
PvmBadParam	giving an invalid tid value.

pvmfsetopt()   pvm_setopt()

Sets various libpvm options

Synopsis

C   int oldval = pvm_setopt(int what, int val)
Fortran call pvmfsetrbuf(what, val, oldval)

Parameters

what   –   Integer defining what is being set. Options include:

Option Value		Meaning
PvmRoute	1	routing policy
PvmDebugMask	2	debugmask
PvmAutoErr	3	auto error reporting
PvmOutputTid	4	stdout device for children
PvmOutputCode	5	output msgtag
PvmTraceTid	6	trace device for children
PvmTraceCode	7	trace msgtag
PvmFragSize	8	message fragment size
PvmResvTids	9	allow messages to reserved tags and TIDs

val   –   Integer specifying new setting of option. Predefined route values
            are as follows:

Option Value		Meaning
PvmRoute	1	routing policy
PvmDontRoute	1	
PvmAllowDirect	2	
PvmRouteDirect	3	

oldval –   Integer returning the previous setting of the option.

Discussion

The routine pvm_setopt is a general-purpose function to allow the user to set options in
the PVM system. In PVM 3.2 pvm_setopt can be used to set several options, including

automatic error message printing, debugging level, and communication routing method for all subsequent PVM calls. Pvm_setopt returns the previous value of set in oldval.

PvmRoute: In the case of communication routing, pvm_setopt advises PVM on whether to set up direct task-to-task links PvmRouteDirect (using TCP) for all subsequent communication. Once a link is established, it remains until the application finishes. If a direct link can not be established because one of the two tasks has requested PvmDontRoute or because no resources are available, then the default route through the PVM daemons is used. On multiprocessors such as Intel Paragon this option is ignored because the communication between tasks on these machines always uses the native protocol for direct communication. pvm_setopt can be called multiple times to selectively establish direct links, but is typically set only once near the beginning of each task. PvmAllowDirect is the default route setting. This setting on task A allows other tasks to set up direct links to A. Once a direct link is established between tasks, both tasks will use it for sending messages.

PvmDebugMask: For this option val is the debugging level. When debugging is turned on, PVM will log detailed information about its operations and progress on its stderr stream. The default is no debug information.

PvmAutoErr: In the case of automatic error printing, any PVM routines that return an error condition will automatically print the associated error message. The argument val defines whether this reporting is to be turned on (1) or turned off (0) for subsequent calls. A value of (2) will cause the program to exit after printing the error message (not implemented in 3.2). The default is reporting turned on.

PvmOutputTid: For this option val is the stdout device for children. All the standard output from the calling task and any tasks it spawns will be redirected to the specified device. Val is the tid of a PVM task or pvmd. The default val of 0 redirects stdout to master host, which writes to the log file /tmp/pvml.<uid>

PvmOutputCode: Only meaningful on task with PvmOutputTid set to itself. This is the message tag value to be used in receiving messages containing standard output from other tasks.

PvmTraceTid: For this option val is the task responsible for writing out trace event for the calling task and all its children. Val is the tid of a PVM task or pvmd. The default val of 0 redirects trace to master host.

PvmTraceCode: Only meaningful on task with PvmTraceTid set to itself. This is the message tag value to be used in receiving messages containing trace output from other tasks.

PvmFragSize: For this option val specifies the message fragment size in bytes. The default value varies with host architecture.

PvmResvTids: A val of 1 enables the task to send messages with reserved tags and to non-task destinations. The default (0) results in a PvmBadParam error instead.

Examples

C:

```
oldval = pvm_setopt( PvmRoute, PvmRouteDirect );
```

Fortran:

```
CALL PVMFSETOPT( PVMAUTOERR, 1, OLDVAL )
```

Errors

The following error conditions can be returned by **pvm_setopt**.

Name	Possible Cause
PvmBadParam	giving an invalid arg.

pvmfsetrbuf()   pvm_setrbuf()

Switches the active receive buffer and saves the previous buffer.

Synopsis

C   `int oldbuf = pvm_setrbuf( int bufid )`

Fortran   `call pvmfsetrbuf( bufid, oldbuf )`

Parameters

bufid   –   integer specifying the message buffer identifier for the new active receive buffer.

oldbuf   –   integer returning the message buffer identifier for the previous active receive buffer.

Discussion

The routine pvm_setrbuf switches the active receive buffer to bufid and saves the previous active receive buffer oldbuf. If bufid is set to 0, the present active receive buffer is saved, and no active receive buffer exists.

A successful receive automatically creates a new active receive buffer. If a previous receive has not been unpacked and needs to be saved for later, then the previous bufid can be saved and reset later to the active buffer for unpacking.

The routine is required when managing multiple message buffers. For example, in switching back and forth between two buffers, one buffer could be used to send information to a graphical interface while a second buffer could be used send data to other tasks in the application.

Examples

C:

```
        rbuf1 = pvm_setrbuf( rbuf2 );
```

Fortran:

```
        CALL PVMFSETRBUF( NEWBUF, OLDBUF )
```

Errors

The following error conditions can be returned by pvm_setrbuf.

Name	Possible Cause
PvmBadParam	giving an invalid bufid.
PvmNoSuchBuf	switching to a nonexistent message buffer.

pvmfsetsbuf()   pvm_setsbuf()

Switches the active send buffer.

Synopsis

C   int oldbuf = pvm_setsbuf(int bufid)
Fortran call pvmfsetsbuf(bufid, oldbuf)

Parameters

bufid – integer the message buffer identifier for the new active send buffer.
          A value of 0 indicates the default receive buffer.

oldbuf – integer returning the message buffer identifier for the previous
          active send buffer.

Discussion

The routine pvm_setsbuf switches the active send buffer to bufid and saves the previous
active send buffer oldbuf. If bufid is set to 0, the present active send buffer is saved,
and no active send buffer exists.

The routine is required when managing multiple message buffers. For example, in switching back and forth between two buffers, one buffer could be used to send information to
a graphical interface while a second buffer could be used send data to other tasks in the
application.

Examples

C:
        sbuf1 = pvm_setsbuf(sbuf2);
Fortran:
        CALL PVMFSETSBUF(NEWBUF, OLDBUF)

Errors

The following error conditions can be returned by pvm_setsbuf.

Name	Possible Cause
PvmBadParam	giving an invalid bufid.
PvmNoSuchBuf	switching to a nonexistent message buffer.

pvmfspawn()   pvm_spawn()

Starts new PVM processes.

Synopsis

```
C   int numt = pvm_spawn(  char *task, char **argv,
                           int flag, char *where,
                           int ntask, int *tids )


Fortran  call pvmfspawn(  task, flag, where,
                          ntask, tids, numt )
```

Parameters

task   –   character string containing the executable file name of the PVM
           process to be started. The executable must already reside on the
           host on which it is to be started. The default location PVM looks
           at is `$HOME/pvm3/bin/$PVM_ARCH/filename` .

argv   –   pointer to an array of arguments to the executable with the end
           of the array specified by NULL. If the executable takes no argu-
           ments, then the second argument to pvm_spawn is NULL.

flag   –   integer specifying spawn options.
           In C `flag` should be the **sum** of the following:

Option value		Meaning
PvmTaskDefault	0	PVM can choose any machine to start task
PvmTaskHost	1	`where` specifies a particular host
PvmTaskArch	2	`where` specifies a type of architecture
PvmTaskDebug	4	start processes under debugger
PvmTaskTrace	8	processes will generate PVM trace data *
PvmMppFront	16	start process on MPP front-end
PvmHostCompl	32	use complement host set

where – character string specifying where to start the PVM process. Depending on
          the value of **flag**, **where** can be a host name such as "ibm1.epm.ornl.gov"
          or a PVM architecture class such as "SUN4". If **flag** is 0, **where** is ignored,
          and PVM will select the most appropriate host.

ntask – integer specifying the number of copies of the executable to start up.

tids   – integer array of length at least **ntask**. On return the array contains the
          tids of the PVM processes started by this pvm_spawn call. If there is a
          error starting a given task, then that location in the array will contain the
          associated error code.

numt   – integer returning the actual number of tasks started. Values less than
          zero indicate a system error. A positive value less than **ntask** indicates a
          partial failure. In this case the user should check the **tids** array for the
          error code(s).

Discussion

The routine pvm_spawn starts up **ntask** copies of the executable named **task**. On systems
that support environment, spawn passes selected variables in parent environment to children tasks. if set, the environment variable PVM_EXPORT is passed. if PVM_EXPORT
contains the names of other variables (separated by ':'), they are passed too. This is useful, for example, for the following:

```
setenv DISPLAY myworkstation:0.0
setenv MYSTERYVAR 13
setenv PVM_EXPORT DISPLAY:MYSTERYVAR
```

The hosts on which the PVM processes are started is set by the **flag** and **where** arguments. On return, the array **tids** contains the PVM task identifiers for each process
started.

If pvm_spawn starts one or more tasks, **numt** will be the actual number of tasks started.
If a system error occurs, **numt** will be < 0, If **numt** is less than **ntask**, some executables
have failed to start and the user should check the last **ntask** - **numt** locations in the **tids**
array that will contain the associated error codes (see below for meaning). The first
numt tids in the array are good, which can be useful for functions such as pvm_mcast().

When **flag** is set to 0 and **where** is set to NULL (or "*" in Fortran), a heuristic is used
to distribute the **ntask** processes across the virtual machine. Currently, the heuristic is
round-robin assignment starting with the next host in the table. Later PVM will use the

metrics of machine load and rated performance (sp=) to determine the most appropriate hosts.

If the PvmHostCompl flag is set, the resulting host set gets complemented. Also, the TaskHost hostname "." is taken as localhost. This allows spawning tasks on "." to get the localhost or to spawn $n-1$ things on TaskHost—HostCompl "." to get any but the localhost.

In the special case where a multiprocessor is specified by where, pvm_spawn will start all ntask copies on this single machine using the vendor's underlying routines.

If PvmTaskDebug is set, the pvmd will start the task(s) in a debugger. In this case, instead of executing pvm3/bin/ARCH/task args, pvmd will executes pvm3/lib/debugger pvm3/bin/ARCH/task args. The debugger is a shell script that the users can modify to their individual tastes. Currently, the script starts an xterm with dbx or a comparable debugger in it.

Examples

C:

```
numt = pvm_spawn( "host", 0, PvmTaskHost,
                  "sparky", 1, &tid[0] );
numt = pvm_spawn( "host", 0, (PvmTaskHost+PvmTaskDebug),
                  "sparky", 1, &tid[0] );
numt = pvm_spawn( "node", 0, PvmTaskArch,
                  "RIOS", 1, &tid[i] );
numt = pvm_spawn( "FEM1", args, 0, 0, 16, tids );
numt = pvm_spawn( "pde", 0, PvmTaskHost,
                  "paragon.ornl", 512, tids );
```

Fortran:

```
FLAG = PVMARCH + PVMDEBUG
CALL PVMFSPAWN( 'node', FLAG, 'SUN4', 1, TID(3), NUMT )
CALL PVMFSPAWN( 'FEM1', PVMDEFAULT, '*', 16, TIDS, NUMT )
CALL PVMFSPAWN( 'TBMD', PVMHOST, 'cm5.utk.edu', 32, TIDS, NUMT )
```

Errors

The following error conditions can be returned by pvm_spawn either in numt or in the tids array.

Name	Value	Possible Cause
PvmBadParam	−2	giving an invalid argument value.
PvmNoHost	−6	Specified host is not in the virtual machine.
PvmNoFile	−7	Specified executable cannot be found. The default location PVM looks in `~/pvm3/bin/ARCH` where ARCH is PVM architecture name.
PvmNoMem	−10	Malloc failed. Not enough memory on host.
PvmSysErr	−14	pvmd not responding.
PvmOutOfRes	−27	out of resources.

pvmftasks()   pvm_tasks()

Returns information about the tasks running on the virtual machine.

Synopsis

```
C         int info = pvm_tasks( int where, int *ntask,
                                struct pvmtaskinfo **taskp )
          struct pvmtaskinfo{
              int  ti_tid;
              int  ti_ptid;
              int  ti_host;
              int  ti_flag;
              char *ti_a_out;
              int  ti_pid;
          } taskp;
Fortran   call pvmftasks( where, ntask, tid, ptid,
                          dtid, flag, aout,info )
```

Parameters

where   – integer specifying what tasks to return information about. The options are the following:

    0   for all the tasks on the virtual machine

    pvmd tid   for all tasks on a given host

    tid   for a specific task

ntask   – integer returning the number of tasks being reported on.

taskp   – pointer to an array of structures which contain information about each task including its task ID, parent tid, pvmd task ID, status flag, the name of this task's executable file, and task (O/S dependent) process id. The status flag values are waiting for a message, waiting for the pvmd, and running.

tid   – integer returning task ID of one task

ptid   – integer returning parent task ID

dtid   – integer returning pvmd task ID of host task is on.

flag   –   integer returning status of task

aout   –   character string returning the name of spawned task. Manually
           started tasks return blank.

info   –   integer status code returned by the routine. Values less than zero
           indicate an error.

Discussion

The routine **pvm_tasks** returns information about tasks running on the virtual machine. The information returned is the same as that available from the console command **ps**. The C function returns information about the entire virtual machine in one call. The Fortran function returns information about one task per call and cycles through all the tasks. Thus, if where = 0, and pvmftasks is called ntask times, all tasks will be represented.

If pvm_tasks is successful, **info** will be 0. If some error occurs, **info** will be < 0.

Examples

C:

          info = pvm_tasks(0, &ntask, &taskp);

Fortran:

          CALL PVMFTASKS(DTID, NTASK, INFO)

Errors

The following error conditions can be returned by **pvm_tasks**.

Name	Possible Cause
PvmBadParam	invalid value for **where** argument.
PvmSysErr	pvmd not responding.
PvmNoHost	specified host not in virtual machine.

pvmftidtohost()   pvm_tidtohost()

Returns the host ID on which the specified task is running.

Synopsis

```
C        int dtid = pvm_tidtohost( int tid )
Fortran  call pvmftidtohost( tid, dtid )
```

Parameters

tid   – integer task identifier specified.

dtid – integer tid of the host's pvmd returned.

Discussion

The routine pvm_tidtohost returns the host ID **dtid** on which the specified task **tid** is running.

Examples

C:

```
        host = pvm_tidtohost( tid[0] );
```

Fortran:

```
        CALL PVMFTIDTOHOST(TID, HOSTID)
```

Errors

These error conditions can be returned by **pvm_tidtohost**.

Name	Possible cause
PvmBadParam	giving an invalid tid.

pvmftrecv()   pvm_trecv()

Receives with timeout.

Synopsis

```
C          int bufid = pvm_trecv( int tid, int msgtag,
                                     struct timeval *tmout )
Fortran  call pvmftrecv( tid, msgtag, sec, usec, bufid )
```

Parameters

tid   –   integer to match task identifier of sending process.
msgtag   –   integer to match message tag; should be ≥ 0.
tmout   –   time to wait before returning without a message.
sec, usec –   integers defining Time to wait before returning without a
                message.
bufid   –   integer returns the value of the new active receive buffer identifier.
                Values less than zero indicate an error.

Discussion

The routine pvm_trecv blocks the process until a message with label msgtag has arrived from tid. pvm_trecv, then places the message in a new *active* receive buffer, also clearing the current receive buffer. If no matching message arrives within the specified waiting time, pvm_trecv returns without a message.

A -1 in msgtag or tid matches anything. This allows the user the following options. If tid $= -1$ and msgtag is defined by the user, then pvm_recv will accept a message from any process that has a matching msgtag. If msgtag $= -1$ and tid is defined by the user, then pvm_recv will accept any message that is sent from process tid. If tid $= -1$ and msgtag $= -1$, then pvm_recv will accept any message from any process.

In C, the tmout fields tv_sec and tv_usec specify how long pvm_trecv will wait without returning a matching message. In Fortran, two separate parameters, sec and usec, are passed. With both set to zero, pvm_trecv behaves the same as pvm_nrecv(), which is to probe for messages and return immediately even if none are matched. In C, passing a null pointer in tmout makes pvm_trecv act like pvm_recv(); that is, it will wait indefinitely. In Fortran, setting sec to -1 has the same effect.

The PVM model guarantees the following about message order. If task 1 sends message A to task 2, then task 1 sends message B to task 2, message A will arrive at task 2 before message B. Moreover, if both messages arrive before task 2 does a receive, then a wildcard receive will always return message A.

If pvm_trecv is successful, bufid will be the value of the new active receive buffer identifier. If some error occurs, bufid will be < 0.

Once pvm_trecv returns, the data in the message can be unpacked into the user's memory using the unpack routines.

Examples
C:

```
struct timeval tmout;

tid = pvm_parent();
msgtag = 4 ;
if ((bufid = pvm_trecv( tid, msgtag, &tmout )) >0) {
  pvm_upkint( tid_array, 10, 1 );
  pvm_upkint( problem_size, 1, 1 );
  pvm_upkfloat( input_array, 100, 1 );
}
```

Fortran:

```
CALL PVMFRECV( -1, 4, 60, 0, BUFID )
IF (BUFID .GT. 0) THEN
CALL PVMFUNPACK( INTEGER4, TIDS, 25, 1, INFO )
CALL PVMFUNPACK( REAL8, MATRIX, 100, 100, INFO )
ENDIF
```

Errors

The following error conditions can be returned by pvm_trecv.

Name	Possible Cause
PvmBadParam	giving an invalid tid value, or msgtag < −1.
PvmSysErr	pvmd not responding.

pvmfunpack()   pvm_upk*()

Unpacks the active message buffer into arrays of prescribed data type.

Synopsis

C

```
int info = pvm_unpackf( const char *fmt, ... )
int info = pvm_upkbyte(  char   *xp, int nitem, int stride )
int info = pvm_upkcplx(  float  *cp, int nitem, int stride )
int info = pvm_upkdcplx( double *zp, int nitem, int stride )
int info = pvm_upkdouble(double *dp, int nitem, int stride )
int info = pvm_upkfloat( float  *fp, int nitem, int stride )
int info = pvm_upkint(   int    *ip, int nitem, int stride )
int info = pvm_upklong(  long   *ip, int nitem, int stride )
int info = pvm_upkshort( short  *jp, int nitem, int stride )
int info = pvm_upkstr(   char   *sp )
```

Fortran
```
call pvmfunpack( what, xp, nitem, stride, info )
```

Parameters

fmt   – printf-like format expression specifying what to pack (see discussion).

nitem   – the total number of *items* to be unpacked (not the number of bytes).

stride   – the stride to be used when packing the items. For example, if stride= 2 in pvm_upkcplx, then every other complex number will be unpacked.

xp   – pointer to the beginning of a block of bytes. Can be any data type, but must match the corresponding pack data type.

cp   – complex array at least nitem*stride items long.

zp   – double precision complex array at least nitem*stride items long.

dp   – double precision real array at least nitem*stride items long.

fp   – real array at least nitem*stride items long.

ip   – integer array at least nitem*stride items long.

jp   – integer*2 array at least nitem*stride items long.

sp   – pointer to a null terminated character string.

what   –   integer specifying the type of data being unpacked.

what options			
STRING	0	REAL4	4
BYTE1	1	COMPLEX8	5
INTEGER2	2	REAL8	6
INTEGER4	3	COMPLEX16	7

info   –   integer status code returned by the routine. Values less than zero indicate an error.

Discussion

Each of the pvm_upk* routines unpacks an array of the given data type from the active receive buffer. The arguments for each of the routines are a pointer to the array to be unpacked into, nitem which is the total number of items to unpack, and stride which is the stride to use when unpacking.

An exception is pvm_upkstr() which by definition unpacks a NULL terminated character string and thus does not need nitem or stride arguments. The Fortran routine pvm-funpack(STRING, ...) expects nitem to be the number of characters in the string and stride to be 1.

If the unpacking is successful, info will be 0. If some error occurs, info will be < 0.

A single variable (not an array) can be unpacked by setting nitem= 1 and stride= 1.

The routine pvm_unpackf() uses a printf-like format expression to specify what and how to unpack data from the receive buffer. All variables are passed as addresses. A BNF-like description of the format syntax is as follows:

```
format : null | init | format fmt
init : null | '%' '+'
fmt : '%' count stride modifiers fchar
fchar : 'c' | 'd' | 'f' | 'x' | 's'
count : null | [0-9]+ | '*'
stride : null | '.' ( [0-9]+ | '*' )
modifiers : null | modifiers mchar
mchar : 'h' | 'l' | 'u'
```

Formats:
```
 +  means initsend - must match an int (how) in the param list.
 c  pack/unpack bytes
 d  integer
 f  float
```

```
x   complex float
s   string
```

Modifiers:
```
h   short  (int)
l   long   (int, float, complex float)
u   unsigned (int)
```

`'*'` count or stride must match an int in the param list.

Future extensions to the what argument will include 64-bit types when XDR encoding of these types is available. Meanwhile, users should be aware that precision can be lost when passing data from a 64-bit machine like a Cray to a 32 bit machine like a SPARCstation. As a mnemonic the what argument name includes the number of bytes of precision to expect. By setting encoding to PVMRAW (see pvmfinitsend), data can be transferred between two 64-bit machines with full precision even if the PVM configuration is heterogeneous.

Messages should be unpacked exactly as they were packed to ensure data integrity. Packing integers and unpacking them as floats will often fail because a type encoding will have occurred transferring the data between heterogeneous hosts. Packing 10 integers and 100 floats, then trying to unpack only 3 integers and the 100 floats, will also fail.

Examples
   C:
```
          info = pvm_recv( tid, msgtag );
          info = pvm_upkstr( string );
          info = pvm_upkint( &size, 1, 1 );
          info = pvm_upkint( array, size, 1 );
          info = pvm_upkdouble( matrix, size*size, 1 );
```
   Fortran:
```
          CALL PVMFRECV( TID, MSGTAG );
          CALL PVMFUNPACK( INTEGER4, NSIZE, 1, 1, INFO )
          CALL PVMFUNPACK( STRING, STEPNAME, 8, 1, INFO )
          CALL PVMFUNPACK( REAL4, A(5,1), NSIZE, NSIZE , INFO )
```

Errors
The following error conditions can be returned by pvm_upk*.

Name	Possible Cause
PvmNoData	Reading beyond the end of the receive buffer. Most likely cause is trying to unpack more items than were originally packed into the buffer.
PvmBadMsg	The received message cannot be decoded. Most likely because the hosts are heterogeneous and the user specified an incompatible encoding. Try setting the encoding to PvmDataDefault (see pvm_mkbuf).
PvmNoBuf	There is no active receive buffer to unpack.

Bibliography

[1] R. Butler and E. Lusk. Monitors, messages, and clusters: The p4 parallel programming system. Technical Report Preprint MCS-P362-0493, Argonne National Laboratory, Argonne, IL, 1993.

[2] L.E. Cannon. A cellular computer to implement the kalman filter algorithm. Phd thesis, Montana State University, 1969.

[3] Nicholas Carriero and David Gelernter. LINDA in context. *Communications of the ACM*, 32(4):444–458, April 1989.

[4] David Cheriton. VMTP: Versatile Message Transaction Protocol. RFC 1045, Stanford University, February 1988.

[5] J. Wang et. al. LSBATCH: A Distributed Load Sharing Batch System. Csri technical report #286, University of Toronto, April 1993.

[6] J. Flower, A. Kolawa, and S. Bharadwaj. The Express way to distributed processing. *Supercomputing Review*, pages 54–55, May 1991.

[7] Message Passing Interface Forum. Mpi: A message-passing interface standard. Computer Science Dept. Technical Report CS-94-230, University of Tennessee, Knoxville, TN, April 1994. (To appear in the International Journal of Supercomputer Applications, Volume 8, Numbers 3/4, 1994).

[8] G. C. Fox, S. W. Otto, and A. J. G. Hey. Matrix algorithms on a hypercube I: Matrix multiplication. *Parallel Computing*, 4:17–31, 1987.

[9] David Gelernter and David Kaminsky. Supercomputing out of recycled garbage: Preliminary experience with Piranha. In *1992 International Conference on Supercomputing*, pages 417–427. ACM, ACM Press, July 1992.

[10] T. Green and J. Snyder. DQS, A Distributed Queuing System. Scri technical report #92-115, Florida State University, August 1992.

[11] M. Litzkow, M. Livny, and M. Mutka. Condor – A hunter of idle workstations. In *Proceedings of the Eighth Conference on Distributed Computing Systems*, San Jose, California, June 1988.

[12] John K. Ousterhout. *Tcl and the Tk Toolkit*. Addison-Wesley, 1994.

[13] J. Postel. Transmission control protocol. RFC 793, Information Sciences Institute, September 1981.

[14] J. Postel. User datagram protocol. RFC 768, Information Sciences Institute, September 1981.

[15] Daniel A. Reed, Robert D. Olson, Ruth A. Aydt, Tara M. Madhyastha, Thomas Birkett, David W. Jensen, Bobby A. A. Nazief, and Brian K. Totty. Scalable performance environments for parallel systems. In Quentin Stout and Michael Wolfe, editors, *The Sixth Distributed Memory Computing Conference*, pages 562–569. IEEE, IEEE Computer Society Press, April 1991.

[16] Sun Microsystems, Inc. XDR: External Data Representation Standard. RFC 1014, Sun Microsystems, Inc., June 1987.

[17] Louis Turcotte. A survey of software environments for exploiting networked computing resources. Draft report, Mississippi State University, Jackson, Mississippi, January 1993.

Index

ATM, 5

bottleneck, 125

C
  language binding, 12
C++
  language binding, 12
chat script, 107
comments, xvi
comp.parallel.pvm, xvi
console program, 124
control messages, 101
Cray Research's CS6400, 127
crowd computing, 33

daemon, 12
data parallelism, 12
debugging, 124, 157
  imalloc, 160
  log, 161
  mask, 159
  pvm_setopt(), 159
  runtime, 159
  system, 158
  tickle, 159
debugmask, 159
DEC's VMS, 140
distributed computing, 1
dynamic configuration, 50–51
dynamic process groups, 60–62

environment variables, 121
ethernet, 4
examples
  Cannon's algorithm, 36
  dot product, 68–73
  embarrassingly parallel, 34
  failure, 73–76
  fork join, 63–68
  heat equation, 83–89
  Mandelbrot, 34
  matrix multiply, 36, 76–78
  tree computations, 37
Express, 6, 7

fault detection, 106
fault tolerance, 113
FDDI, 4
file descriptor, 125
firewall machines, 107
Fortran, 111
  language binding, 13
functional parallelism, 12

Gantt chart, 138
getting options, 52–53
global max, 62
global sum, 62
Grand Challenge problems, 1
group of tasks, 14

heterogeneity, 2
HiPPI, 4
host pool, 11
host table, 102
host-node, 33
hoster, 109
hostfile, 23, 29
hostless, 129

IBM's OS/2, 140
inplace message, 126
Intel
  iPSC/860, 127, 129
  Paragon, 127, 128
Intel iPSC/860, 142
Intel NX operating system, 128

libfpvm3.a, 111
libgpvm3.a, 15
Linda, 6, 8
  Pirhana, 8
  tuple-space, 8

m4, 111
machine configuration, 102
manual startup, 107
massively parallel processors MPP, 1
master-slave, 33
memory limit, 125
message
  maximum size, 126
message buffers, 53–55
message passing, 1, 53
message routing, 117
MID, 98
MPI, 6–7
MPP, 129
MPSD, 41
multicast address, 121
multicasting, 120
multiple consoles, 28
multiprocessor systems, 126
multiprocessors, 142

netlib, 135
node-only, 33
non-Unix systems, 140